Take Care of
Your Elderly Relative

Take Care
of Your
Elderly Relative

J. A. Muir Gray, MB, ChB, DPH

Community Physician, Oxfordshire Area Health Authority, Oxford

Heather McKenzie, LLB

*Administrative Director of the National Council for the
Single Woman and Her Dependants, London*

published jointly by

London
GEORGE ALLEN & UNWIN
Boston   Sydney

and

BEACONSFIELD PUBLISHERS
Beaconsfield

First published in March 1980
Reprinted in June 1980
George Allen & Unwin (Publishers) Ltd
40 Museum Street, London WC1A 1LU

British Library Cataloguing in Publication Data

Gray, J A Muir
    Take care of your elderly relative.
    1. Aged – Home care – Great Britain
    I. Title   II. McKenzie, Heather
    649.8   HV1481.G52

ISBN 0–04–618015–X
ISBN 0–04–618016–8 Pbk

Set in 10½ on 12 point Times, and
printed and bound in Great Britain
by Billing and Sons Limited and Kemp Hall Bindery,
Guildford, London, Oxford, Worcester

To our parents

Acknowledgements

It is customary for authors to acknowledge those who have helped them in their preparation; for us this is impossible. So many people have helped us that it is not possible for us to thank each individually. All those colleagues in both voluntary and professional services who have worked with us on the problems which we have met in the course of our work have taught us more than they know. All those relatives, friends and neighbours of elderly people who thought we were helping them were, in fact, helping us, teaching us what suggestions were practicable and what were not, and exposing the difficulties which are often hidden from those who work in positions like ours: we wish to thank all supporters of elderly people and teachers of ourselves. Finally, we must pay tribute to all those elderly people we have met, directly or indirectly; they have taught us both about the problems which occur particularly in old age, and about their past – the biography of their generation, which composes the early chapters of the biography of our generation.

A number of individuals deserve special mention, however, because of the guidance they have given us at various stages in the development of our typescript. They are: Mr Duncan Adams, Miss Janet Allen, Miss Judy Baron, Mr Bill Bradshaw, Mrs Anne Faulkner, Mr Bob Freedland, Dr Jeffrey Garland, Major-General R. J. Gray, Mrs Barbara Hull, Mrs E. C. Kenny, Mrs Janice Lloyd, Miss Paddy McCartney, Miss Jill McKay, Mrs Janet Miller, Mrs Frances Morrell, Mr Richard Nettleton, Mr David Plank, Dr Brice Pitt, Mrs Sheila Rimmer, Dr Simon Smail, Dr Anthea Tinker, Miss Ruth Waddle, Miss Olive Wagstaff, Mrs Dorothy Walster, Mr J. M. Widdecombe, and Mrs Gill Wood. To Jo Wilkins and Priscilla Bunn we owe a considerable debt for their typing; to Brenda Marshall we are grateful for her meticulous sub-editing; and to John Churchill, our publisher, we must pay a special tribute. Conscientious, committed and careful, his advice and help throughout the gestation of this book have been invaluable.

In addition, the officials of the following organisations were also extremely helpful, although this does not imply that their employing organisations agree with the content of this book: Association of Environmental Health Officers, British Association of the Hard of Hearing, British Association of Occupational Therapists, British Deaf Association, British Gas, British Red Cross Society, British Rheumatism and Arthritis Association, Chest, Heart and Stroke Association, Colostomy Welfare Group, Conference for World Mission, British Council of Churches, Council for the Professions Supplementary to Medicine, Department of Energy, Department of the Environment, Department of Health and Social Security, Department of Prices and Consumer Protection, Domestic Coal Consumers' Council, Electricity Council, the staff of *In Touch*, Health Visitors' Association, Hearing Aid Council, National Association of Almshouses, Parkinson's Disease Society, Partially-sighted Society, Research Institute for Consumer Affairs, Royal National Institute for the Blind, Royal National Institute for the Deaf, Saint Dunstan's, Society of Chiropodists, Solid Fuel Advisory Service, Union of Speech Therapists. Heather McKenzie's views do not necessarily reflect those of the NCSWD.

Finally, we wish to thank our spouses, not only for their patient tolerance of our hours of anti-social scribbling but for their contributions. Norman's sound common sense and critical faculty was continually helpful, and Jackie's firm command of English, typing ability, and professional expertise with the problems of elderly people and their relatives was of central importance.

The strengths of this book we owe to other people, its weaknesses are our responsibility.

Muir Gray
Heather McKenzie

Foreword

by Dame Flora Robson, DBE

During the War I took over the care of two very ill relatives, whose own children were either in the Forces, or nursing. While playing a star part in the London theatre I came home to the country in Buckinghamshire late at night, washed clothes, cooked and helped by day, and gave them a warm home. There was no Health Council, only an overworked doctor without a partner, no social workers or kindly visitors, no benefits and no help.

I write this, not to ask for sympathy, but because it means that I have great concern and sympathy for those who care for the elderly. This wonderfully helpful book will give the carers the expert information that is so important for their task. It is a book that should be in every family home, as necessary as a dictionary or telephone directory. It will help the elderly and greatly support the carers.

Flora Robson

Contents

Chapter 1
How to Use this Book

THE PURPOSE OF THIS BOOK

Society has at last woken up to the plight of the many elderly people who are living in deprivation in the midst of plenty, for we are still a very rich society. Its slumbering conscience has been stirred by many factors, notably the activities of groups such as Age Concern, Help the Aged and the National Corporation for the Care of Old People. The publication of a government White Paper on the problems of older people in 1979 was a great leap forward. However, the problems of the supporters of elderly people – relatives, friends and neighbours – are still largely ignored; indeed it is not uncommon to hear professionals working with the elderly people claim that 'families don't care for old people nowadays' and that 'the community doesn't care'. This has not been our experience. In the course of our work we have come upon many cases of friends, neighbours, and, most of all, relatives, bearing such a burden that their own health has been broken in caring for their elders. Rather than refusing to care because they expect the welfare state to cope, we have known many families broken by deficiencies in the services provided by the welfare state. Married couples who have never had a night out together for years, and who are unable to entertain friends; single daughters looking after elderly parents alone and unsupported, in houses from which they may be forced to move when the elder dies; elderly husbands and wives, themselves disabled, caring at home for spouses so disabled that they are not considered fit enough for an old people's home.

This book is about a substantial minority of our elders who have physical, social, and mental problems, and is written for those people who are supporting and looking after them – sons and daughters, husbands and wives, relatives and friends. We hope, also, that it will prove useful to those professionals working with old people who are not already aware of all the possibilities for help which we describe.

We emphasise that the book is about coping. Some problems can be finally and completely solved, heating problems for example, but many of the problems of old age are not like that; many of the problems of physical and mental health, and of isolation, will continue as long as the elder lives. For such problems our purpose is to help supporters minimise and mitigate the burden of caring, and to help the elder cope with her own difficulties more easily. For this reason we include two chapters which are specifically about supporters' problems and consider the needs of supporters in each chapter. We firmly believe it is the right of elderly people to stay in the community if that is what they wish, but we believe equally strongly that it is the right of their supporters not to be broken by the burden of caring.

It is also appropriate to explain at this stage in the book the terms which we use to refer to elderly people. In certain parts of the text we use 'she', in others 'he', more often the former than the latter because there are more elderly women than elderly men. Sometimes the term chosen is determined by the nature of the problem being considered. For example 'he' is used in the section on prostate disease, but there is, in general, no reason why we have chosen one in preference to the other. We also use the term 'elder' frequently. Although this word has dropped out of fashion we believe it to be the best term for elderly people; in particular we prefer it to 'the elderly', or 'the old', because the use of an adjective in this way, the grouping together of all these people who happen to share a single characteristic, leads to misleading generalisations being made about them. To speak of 'the elderly', makes them sound like an alien group, as we speak of the 'Chinese' or the 'Russians'. Those who happen to be old are all individuals: each has unique needs. We have had to generalise in writing this book about the problems of our elders, but we hope that it will help both them and their supporters to cope in the manner best suited to each person's individual needs.

Old age is a good age, but not for everyone all the time. A minority of old people, usually those who are also physically and mentally disabled, are affected by problems, but many of them can be overcome.

Some of the illnesses which affect an old person's physical wellbeing are preventable and curable and are not inevitable consequences of ageing. Some of the factors which disturb an old person's mental and social wellbeing are not created by the process of ageing, but by the attitudes of a society which denies old people a just income or adequate services. No old person will suffer from all the problems described, but some will experience one or more of them.

We stress that this book is not for the majority of old people, except those (and there are many of them) who are helping other more disabled people as a relative, friend or member of one of the many invaluable voluntary societies. It is not a book to help people prepare for retirement. The Pre-Retirement Association (PRA) through its journal *Choice*, and through the courses run by the PRA and the Workers Educational Association, have that objective. It is not a book which tries to describe old age, for most old people lead full, rich and rewarding lives with only fleeting contact with problems. As Alex Comfort made clear in *A Good Age*, growing old is not necessarily a depressing march towards the problems described. However, hundreds of thousands of old people do experience these problems every year; some experience them year after year.

IT IS NOT EASY IN PRACTICE

Books like this are often annoying. The authors make it all seem so simple. Available services are outlined and the implication is that they are easy to contact, and give sympathetic assistance. In 'real life' this does not happen so easily. We know that we will make things sound very simple, although help can often be difficult to obtain. People promise to visit but fail to do so, or make one visit and say they will 'see what they can do', but nothing else is heard from them again. Services may be in short supply or non-existent. We feel that it would make the book too complicated and too long if we were to describe all the possible difficulties you might face, and offer instead some general guidelines to help you.

1) Except in emergencies – write, don't phone. Professionals may be annoyed by phone calls which interrupt interviews or meetings, but they usually set aside a time each day to read, and consider, their mail. If you write, be sure to keep a copy of your letter. Letters sent to professionals will be kept and often a file will be opened, which makes your request for help just that little bit more formal.

2) Don't get angry if the professional does not help you immediately. He may be under pressure not only from your request but from all the other calls on his time. If you are finding the old person's problem a strain on you tell the professional; ask him for his help, don't turn it into anger.

3) Find an ally. Social workers, health visitors and home help organisers can assist you not only by providing help for the old person, but by supporting you. They know how the system works, for example whether a doctor's letter might be helpful, the name of the person to approach in a certain office, what to do if your request is turned down.

The Citizens Advice Bureau, Housing Aid Centre, or the local Age Concern can also be effective advocates. Ex-servicemen and their families can find an ally in the British Legion.

4) Don't go to the top too soon. If you don't immediately receive the help you have asked for, it may not be wise immediately to approach the head of the department. If you write to the chief when the problem is only a misunderstanding, the person with whom you have been in touch may be annoyed by having a note from his boss when he never realised anything was wrong. It may be preferable to make an appointment with the professional concerned, if you have not met him, and try to resolve the difficulty. Don't be reticent about asking for an appointment. Of course, if you do not then get satisfaction, you have to complain to a higher authority.

5) Don't involve the politicians too soon. Local government or health authority officials often become impatient and annoyed if an MP or councillor is involved in a case before all the possible channels of complaints have been tried. If you are not satisfied with the reply you receive from the chief officer of a local authority department, approach the councillor for the ward in which the elder lives. If you are not satisfied with the answer you receive from the administrator of the health authority, contact the Community Health Council. If you are still not satisfied, write to the appropriate MP, but don't complain too soon (see page 31).

6) Don't give up. It is easy for us to say that, we know; at times you will be frustrated, tired and angry by the apparent insensitivity of those who are paid to help you and your elder, and the advice in this book may not seem to be of any help. However, we hope that will not occur very often. The time it takes to obtain help is often frustratingly long, but it is usually given to those who persevere.

MAKING DECISIONS

There are no general rules which apply to all old people. There is no rule that daughters rather than sons should care for their parents, although they often do because of the strength of the bond between mother and daughter. There is no rule that the youngest child should look after the parents, although older brothers and sisters often expect the youngest member of the family to care, especially if he or she is unmarried.

There is one rule which we would recommend: that honesty and openness be used on every occasion. We do not just believe that honesty is the *best* policy, but that honesty is the *only* policy. No matter how 'confused' an old person appears to be, consult with her on almost every decision. There are many cases reported in which an elder who was not consulted, because she was thought to be 'too confused', becomes more disturbed, believing that those she trusted were conspiring against her. Old people are usually able to face up to decisions, no matter how unpleasant. In fact to deny an elder the opportunity of involvement in decisions which affect her future is to deny her a basic human right. Nevertheless, it is not always advisable to tell an elder that you are going to consult a professional on her behalf. For example, if you thought that she had cancer you might wish to consult her GP to find out the truth. It would obviously be unwise to tell the elder that you were worried that she had cancer and raise her fears needlessly, but you should remember that she might have the same worry as you. It is generally right to tell an old person if you are going to meet other people to discuss her problems and, whenever possible, she should be involved in discussion and decision making. If it is not possible, then it is polite and considerate to ask her permission before speaking to others.

Remember that the tensions which are an essential part of any family's relationships sometimes make open discussion difficult; your respect for your parent and her attitude towards you can make full frankness impossible. In such instances an outsider can be very useful. A fresh look at the elder's problem and the ability to raise topics which family members cannot, both prove invaluable.

A health visitor, GP, minister, social worker, or any other trusted outsider can help by acting as chairman, and sometimes as referee, in family debates. If you ask for an outsider's help, tell the elder why he is coming to her house. There is nothing more awkward for a professional than to be introduced as 'a plumber' or 'someone who likes to speak to old folk', although this sometimes happens.

Although it may appear that decisions are the same whether there is one or two old people, an elderly couple is very different from a single old person. Two elders living together can manage very well, even though each of them is very disabled, because the abilities of one can compensate for the disabilities of the other. For example, if one has visual problems and the other is deaf, they can combine their faculties. However, there is more to it than that. It is not just that the abilities of the two are added together; there is a great psychological strength which comes from being a couple – the psychological strength of a couple is greater than the strengths of the two individuals added together. Outsiders almost always under-estimate the ability of an elderly couple to manage; even if they appear to fight like cat and dog, there is strength in being a couple which cannot be measured. In fact sometimes couples who appear to disagree continually are very supportive to one another; the two of them argue because they respect each other.

Any decision is also affected by your own situation, whether you are married or single, a friend, a neighbour or a relative (see chapter 11).

Two questions should always be asked before a decision is made. These are: 'Who is anxious?' and 'What is the real problem?'

WHO IS ANXIOUS?

The people who are anxious about an old person sometimes press urgently for a decision to be made. The elder's GP may be anxious that she should not be left alone because she is liable to fall; a social worker may feel anxious because the elderly person appears unwilling to heat her house adequately; staff in hospital may say 'She's not fit to live alone'; and all these anxieties can generate pressure on you. Other members of the family are also often anxious, and you yourself may be worried. However, the key factor is whether or not the old person is anxious. If the old person is anxious, decisions are easier to make than if she is not. It is not uncommon for all the professionals, friends and family members to be very anxious, but for the old person herself to appear quite unconcerned, which can make decisions very difficult. Many old people are aware that they are at risk of falling down, that their house is difficult to heat, or that they are isolated, but they prefer to live like that rather than to move house or to a home. This has to be respected, but respect for an elder does not mean that you should never disagree with her. If a doctor says she is at risk of hypothermia, it should be explained to the old person that she is at special risk due to her age, and that the housing conditions which she could cope with in her youth require to be changed if she wants to stay in them as long and as well as possible. There is no reason why you should not admit your anxieties, or that the amount of time you are having to devote to the elder is affecting your health.

The fact that an elder decides to continue her lifestyle unchanged, although she is aware that there are some risks to herself involved, is one thing. The fact that she is a risk to other people, most commonly her neighbours, is another. Elderly people more frequently set fire to themselves and their houses than young people. The sight of an elderly person struggling to fill a paraffin heater, or the knowledge that she is very forgetful but still tries to use a gas cooker, can be very alarming to a neighbour, who may put a great deal of pressure on the social worker or GP, saying that 'something should be done'. The neighbour may say that he is worried about the old person because he does not wish to appear selfish, but the real basis of anxiety should be recognised. Again, it is necessary to try to discuss the anxieties of other people with the old person who is the cause of them. If she wishes to exercise her right to live in the community, she has to accept that she still has obligations to other people in that community. Very often it is possible to take practical steps to remove the cause of the anxiety, for example by replacing a paraffin heater by an enclosed gas convector heater (see page 123).

Remember that an old person may become anxious about the anxieties of other people. She may come to believe that other people are talking about her, making plans to persuade her to move from her home to somewhere else, and of course she is often accurate in her perception of events. Anxieties which are not brought out for open discussion can build up, and everyone who is trying to help an old person should make his or her own anxiety clear.

WHAT IS THE REAL PROBLEM?

Although a problem is said to be serious and urgent, it is often expressed in vague terms; for example 'She shouldn't live in that house', or 'She shouldn't be left alone,' or 'She can't manage,' or 'She can't look after herself any longer'. Such sentences describe the reason why the speaker is anxious, but say very little about the actual problem. If someone says something like this to you then you should ask them exactly what they mean.

The correct response, when it is suggested that an old person can no longer be independent, is to reply with another question 'Why not?', and ask specific questions:

- Has the old person been given the most appropriate medical treatment? In many cases the GP and the consultant in geriatric medicine, together with nurses, physiotherapists and occupational therapists, can greatly increase the elder's independence, by their combined attack on underlying diseases such as immobility, instability or incontinence (see chapter 6).
- How much help is she getting at present? Although many of the services are stretched, they can often be persuaded to provide extra help if you make it clear that the elder's independent existence is at stake. Even a little extra help from a social worker, home help, or domiciliary nurse can make a big difference both to you and to her (see chapter 11).
- Are there any problems caused by her housing conditions, heating apparatus or low income which can be solved? (see chapter 8). Can isolation be lessened? (see chapter 5).

Some professionals may not be all that happy with your questioning, but co-operation is possible if you explain your anxieties and make it clear that you are not criticising them.

We hope that this book will help you ask these questions. However, in the end each decision is different and must be considered on its own grounds. One piece of general advice which we would give is not to make any decision, or help the elder make any decision, too quickly. Very many decisions are made too quickly; fewer decisions have been made too slowly.

Chapter 2
Understanding Ageing and Growing Old

AGEING

The Normal Process of Ageing

Ageing is a normal biological process which starts as the first phase, the phase of growth and development, comes to an end. Although the whole body ages, not all parts age at the same rate and there is great variation from person to person. For example, the skin of some white-haired people does not age as quickly as their hair. The process of ageing is gradual and there is no sudden acceleration of ageing at 60, 65 or at any other age, although certain changes which affect women at the time of the menopause can be considered to be an acceleration of ageing. There is no evidence to suggest that there is a male menopause.

To understand the current theories of ageing, for no one theory is universally accepted, it is necessary to explain the normal process of body maintenance. Every cell has its own spare parts service. Cells do not carry ready made spare parts, they stamp out exact replicas of worn out components where needed, but this process does not prevent cells from dying. The body replaces some types of cells continually. Skin and blood cells have a limited life span; all the blood cells die and are replaced every 120 days, three times per year. Other types of cell, for example liver and kidney cells, have a much longer life span. However, if any tissue is destroyed by infection or injury, the remaining cells can take over the lost function, either by making more cell components and becoming bigger cells, or by stamping out exact replicas for those lost. A third type of cell, brain and nerve cells, can neither divide nor grow bigger to take over the function of any cells lost.

It is not surprising that small errors occur in the process of making identical copies of cell components and whole cells, since millions of cells and components are made every day. Because the new cells and cell components are not exact replicas, the tissues neither function so efficiently nor do they heal and repair so quickly or completely. This is one way in which the body ages, but there is a twist to the tale. The immune system consists of white blood cells which normally attack and destroy foreign invaders, bacteria and viruses. The battles between invaders and white cells take place in lymph nodes, the small painful lumps which swell in your neck when you have a sore throat. White blood cells are a very powerful defence force. When the normal errors of ageing affect the immune system the altered white blood cells produced are not only less effective at dealing with invaders, but they actually attack the other body tissues.

Although much has been learned recently, gerontologists, who study ageing scientifically, still have many unanswered questions. Is ageing a common cause of death? Surprisingly, few people die of old age, most people die prematurely. All types of animal have different life spans. The human life span is on average about eighty years – as is that of the whale. However, very many people die before they reach the end of their possible life span, some illness or accident killing them 'prematurely' – before their life has reached full maturity, the end of their span.

What influences the rate of ageing? Both genetic and environmental factors are important. Some races live longer than others and, within each race, some individuals live longer. Genetic factors undoubtedly affect the rate of ageing and the length of possible life span, but it is not clear how great this effect is. Long-living children of parents who reached a great age may do so, not because of the genes they have *inherited* from their parents but because of the behaviour patterns, their habits of smoking, exercise and diet, which they *learned* from them. No-one whose parents died young should assume that they will inevitably die young also.

Can anything slow down the ageing process? The answer appears to be no. The prospect of eternal life is not so attractive as it first seems, although the search for the elixir of life has fascinated man since he first appreciated the finality of death. In some countries substances are sold which, it is claimed, slow down ageing and the process of degeneration, most commonly mixtures of vitamins and Ginseng, but there is no evidence that they are effective. Such advertisements are not allowed in Britain, but there is one elixir on sale in this country – whisky – the word is adapted from the Gaelic, *uisge beatha*, itself a translation of the Latin *aqua vitae*, meaning the water of life. However, there is no evidence that a glass of Glenfiddich or Macallan prolongs life, although it certainly makes it more pleasant for many of us.

The Ageing Mind – Facts and Myths

Physical ageing can be seen with the naked eye and under a microscope, but ageing of the mind is not so easily seen. Brain tissue certainly ages – from early adult life brain cells are steadily lost. It has always been assumed that the mind also ages, and that there was a certain pattern of changes in mood, behaviour and thinking which were typical of ageing. Three features were said to be particularly marked – decreasing intelligence, increasing rigidity of attitude and decreasing sexuality – but it is now realised that this has been greatly over-emphasised.

Decreasing intelligence
It is true that certain aspects of intelligence, such as the ability to retain new facts,

deteriorate with age. Because intelligence (IQ) tests concentrate on such aspects of intelligence, it has been claimed that IQ falls dramatically with age. However, there are many other aspects of intelligence than those measured, and some do not fall away so quickly with age; in fact some improve, especially the sense of proportion and judgement, which we call wisdom. As we grow older we are less able to acquire knowledge, but our wisdom allows us to make better use of that which is in store.

Increasing rigidity
Elderly people are often slower and more cautious in making decisions which involve change. However, research suggests that the difference between older and younger people is not so much that older people cannot change, but that they are less willing to take the risk that change usually involves. Older people do not appear to be so greedy, and are more often content with the grass on their side of the fence. Younger people make decisions more quickly and more often, not because they are better at changing, but because they are keener to try the grass on the other side. Another factor which must be considered is that the longer a person has been set in a habit the less likely it is that he will change. The unwillingness of some elders to change is not so much due to the age of their brain or mind, but simply because they have long established habits.

Decreasing sexuality
Ageing of the organs of reproduction decreases fertility in both men and women from the middle twenties, and female fertility comes to an end at the menopause. However, sexuality, the capacity to respond to other people physically, need not decline so quickly or completely as fertility. The frequency of sexual intercourse does decline with age, but this is often due to physical illness and disability rather than to mental ageing. Some couples do indeed have sexual intercourse less frequently as they age for psychological reasons, but this is sometimes brought about

by their belief that sex is wrong, or indecent for old people – a widely held belief which is very deep seated in our society. Young people are expected to show an interest in the opposite sex, but the same responses in an elder are met with disapproval and even the word 'dirty' may be used.

The ageing of the brain and dementia are distinct processes. Dementia is a disease, an abnormal process, which affects no more than a minority of old people. It is a myth that old age inevitably brings dementia, a myth which influences attitudes towards old age.

In fact the influence of society's attitudes is very important in preserving all the myths of ageing. If an industrialised society like ours expects elders to be less intelligent, more rigid, and less interested in sex, and the elders go along with these expectations, they come to believe the myths themselves.

GROWING OLD

In Society

Ageing is a biological process determined by our genes. Growing old is a social process determined by the attitudes, expectations and traditions of society.

In all societies, there are three main social stages through which each member passes between birth and death. First he is a child, then an adult and finally an elder. Such a pattern can be seen on all continents, in societies in every stage of development. In an industrial society the same three stages are equally clear cut, but there are two major differences from pre-industrial societies.

- The transition from one stage to another does not take place naturally, depending on the physical and mental abilities of the individual, but chronologically, depending on the number of their years. Children have to stay on at school till they are sixteen no matter how adult they may be, but they can leave at the same age no matter how childish. Similarly, adults become elders depending on their age and

the retirement policy of their employer – retirement age takes no account of the physical or mental capabilities of the individual.

- Elders in an industrial society are the group of lowest status. In pre-industrial society they often have the highest status, the older men decide where to hunt, whence to move and when to fight; the women control their extended families. The changes imposed by retirement are profound. One day a man is respected and important, an expert and an authority; the next he is retired. The Pre-Retirement Association and the Workers Educational Association do much to prepare people for retirement, as do many employers, but the blow is still very heavy for many men and women. It might seem that housewives have less to lose, but in fact they lose freedom. Until her husband retires a housewife has over half her waking hours to herself. These are lost, and for not a few couples the strains are considerable, particularly in the first year or so after retirement. The income of these households in which the head is retired is only 41 per cent of the average income of non-retired households, including unemployed people (1975 figures). Not only does this create practical problems for retired couples, but it indicates the value society places upon their contribution.

In spite of these difficulties, most people adapt to retirement successfully, moving easily, often eagerly, into other activities. Much more difficult is adaptation to bereavement (see page 196) and disability (see page 85).

In the Family

Elders as parents
To understand growing old it is important to remember not only the social changes which affect groups of people as they grow older, but also the psychological development of each of us as individuals.

It is customary to think of three stages of psychological development:

Childhood – a period of rapid psychological growth during which the developing personality acquires knowledge and skills, but uses the attitudes, values and opinions of his parents;

Adolescence – the period of conflict and rebellion against these parental attitudes and values as the young person draws up his own rules of conduct, proving to his own satisfaction that he is a person distinct from his father and mother;

Adulthood – the stable state, when the adult has both skills and a set of rules, and has become an independent person as well formed as his parents.

Useful though it is to think of these three phases, it is far too simple to imagine that we pass from one to another as though moving from a lower to a higher class on passing an examination. We are all capable of psychological growth and learning at every age – learning does not only occur in childhood. Rebelling against our parents is not only an adolescent phenomenon. As long as our parents are alive we are, if not in open conflict, at least in a state of armed neutrality, ready to take issue with them. It is a mistake to think that when we become adults in the eyes of the world we relate to our parents as one adult does to another. We are still both child and adolescent, and the parent is still the parent. For many people the influence of one or both parents remains a powerful one, long after childhood and adolescence are said to be past. Even after a parent is dead his or her influence can live on.

There are always tensions in families. Tensions between parents and children, and tensions between brothers and sisters are normal and are part and parcel of the affection each feels for the other. Only those who are indifferent to one another are free from tension and, fortunately, few people are completely indifferent to other members of their family. Such tensions often diminish as children grow older, but they may increase and be further complicated by the marriage of a child.

Elders as in-laws
The individual marrying into the family may feel that he is in continuing competition with his spouse's family. He may feel that too much time is spent 'at the in-laws'. There is also a feeling that any incompatibility or disagreement is due to the fact that the marital partner is still too attached to the values, attitudes and customs of his or her parents, the in-laws.

These tensions are present whether the in-laws are in their forties and the young couple in their twenties, or whether the in-laws are in their eighties and and the young couple in their sixties. The relationship is of the same nature but it may be aggravated if disability affects one of the older generation, causing her to make greater calls on her child.

There is no magic formula to resolve these tensions. As long as people care about one another there will be tension and anger associated with love and affection. The only advice which is applicable to everyone is that honesty is the best policy. A husband may not think it is worth while telling his parents-in-law exactly what he feels about them if they live five hundred miles away, and are seen only once or twice a year, but husband and wife should not keep resentment bottled up if it is continually present. When an elder requires continuous care and help, and therefore makes more demands on her child, husband and wife have to speak openly and honestly to one another. Children who are helping may feel guilty – that they are neglecting their spouse, that they are not helping the elder sufficiently, or that they are grudging that help because of the effect it is having on their marriage. Those feelings have to be brought into the open.

Elders as grandparents
Elderly people are not only parents and in-laws, they also are often grandparents. Practically all grandparents are very useful.

With the increasing number of one-parent families, more and more old people are looking after a grandchild while their child goes out to work, acting like the famous Russian *babushka* who can be seen in every Moscow park with one or two swaddled toddlers in tow. However, the psychological relationships between the elder and other family members create new tensions.

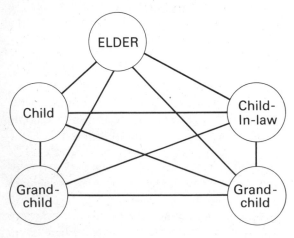

The diagram shows the complexity of the relationship network. The relationship with grandchildren is almost always good, but this may upset the balance of the family. Either the child or the child-in-law, or both, may be jealous of the quality of the grandparent's relationship with their children. Either, or both, may be angry if the elder 'spoils' the grandchildren, allowing them freedom which the parents deny them. On the other hand, the old person may upset her child and child-in-law by criticism that they are too free – 'I don't think that girls of that age should be allowed out till ten o'clock'. Sometimes the grandparent is felt both to spoil and to criticise, to give too much freedom in some things, for example giving chocolate before lunch, while complaining that the parents are giving the child too much

freedom in other aspects of life, and this can create tremendous tension.

These conflicts may be unintentional. A grandmother may be unaware of the standards and rules laid down by her married child. There is also the possibility that the elder wishes to differ, to continue the struggle between her and her child, using her grandchildren as a means of criticising her child, her child-in-law and their marriage.

The resolution of these problems can be very difficult. Honesty must once more be the watchword. Resentment and anger should be brought into the open and any misunderstandings cleared up. However, there may be tensions which cannot be resolved by the family members themselves without the help of an outsider, a marriage guidance counsellor, a social worker, a health visitor or the GP.

For most children, the death of a loved grandparent is the first experience of bereavement. It is common practice to exclude the bereaved child from the funeral or even knowledge of the death, for example by saying that 'Gran has gone away'. This can make the child feel insecure and unwilling to let his parents out of sight, believing that they too will never return if he lets them 'go away'. Children should be allowed the opportunity to mourn. Discussion with the child's health visitor can be helpful in deciding how the news should be broken and how to cope with the mourning.

Every family is different. No child reacts in the same way to his parents, but the pattern of relationships and tensions which we have described here can be seen in many families in our society. We present them in detail because we feel that individual problems, both emotional and practical, have to be seen in the light of these traditions and customs to be understood and solved.

Chapter 3
Helpers, Advisers and Supporters

However isolated and alone you feel with a problem you should be able to find help, advice and support. The professionals and organisations we describe try to work with the old person, rather than do things to or for her. Similarly, they don't try to do things instead of the elder's family, relatives and friends, except where special skill is required. They try to work with them, in partnership. You can make contact with them even if you are not sure you need help. It is often useful to discuss whether they think help would be appropriate before you really feel in need. A trouble shared may not always be halved, but it is almost always reduced and occasionally it vanishes.

VOLUNTARY HELP

Volunteers have much to offer elderly people and their supporters. Health and social services are now making much more use of volunteers, realising that they do not just perform tasks more cheaply but that they often do them better.

Volunteers usually prefer to be involved in tasks which have an end in sight, rather than those which seem interminable. For example, it is usually easier to find a volunteer to take an old person to the optician to have his vision tested, and to collect his glasses when the prescription has been made up, than to find a volunteer willing to take an old person to a day centre on the same day every week of the year, or to visit him at home week after week.

Volunteers generally prefer helping people who are physically disabled rather than those who are mentally infirm. If communication is difficult, the volunteer may feel uneasy and nervous unless she is well supported.

Volunteers do not, as a rule, like to touch those they help. Dressing and undressing, washing and bathing are tasks which are better left to the professionals, although some trained volunteers are willing and able to help with personal care.

In every part of the country there are many voluntary organisations. Churches, the Red Cross, St. John's, St. Andrew's, Fish and Good Neighbour Schemes, the British Legion, student groups, the WRVS and Age Concern are active everywhere, and there are always other groups of volunteers which spring up to meet local needs. To find a suitable volunteer for the task which requires to be done, it is best to approach the local Age Concern office or the Council for Voluntary Service (see page 13), who are aware of all the local organisations and the type of task which each is best suited to tackle. They may make the initial contact, or give you a name, address and phone number for you to make the link with the organiser.

Volunteers offer their services free but often appreciate help with the cost of the petrol. If they refuse to take money or say that they have incurred no expenses, donations to their organisation's funds will be greatly appreciated to help with postage and telephone bills. A present to a volunteer at Christmas is a direct expression of your gratitude, and a letter to the local paper praising the organisation's work rewards the organisers.

The Church

Churches offer many practical types of help to old people, but the greatest benefit to many is the spiritual comfort and support which the priest or minister and the congregation are able to offer. Old age is a time in which religion plays a more important part

11

in the lives of many people. The deaths of friends and contemporaries inevitably turns the mind to the question of after-life, and the leisure offered by retirement, together with the opportunity for contemplation offered by isolation, provide time to think about spiritual matters. Some elders who suffer trials and tribulations after a hard and honest life wonder about the meaning of their afflictions and, seeing no hope of physical relief, find comfort in a faith. It is essential to recognise these thoughts and feelings. Sometimes an old person who is said to be 'confused' is thinking about religious and mystical questions which have arisen in her mind. She does not need a tranquilliser, but the opportunity to speak to someone who is not afraid or embarrassed by the discussion of such topics.

Priests and ministers are now very busy people. They often have two or more parishes in their care and have less time for regular visiting. However, priests still visit at times of special need, for example following a bereavement or on the anniversary of the death of a loved one.

Church members are increasingly active in voluntary visiting and providing transport for housebound people, not only to church but to the optician and other essential services. The Church of England developed these good neighbour schemes, called Fish Schemes, which are now found in many areas, and care of elderly people is a part of the stewardship arrangements in every parish. Volunteers from a church usually help all the old people in the neighbourhood, but often spend more time with church members. Whether or not a housebound old person can reach church occasionally, volunteers who are prepared to sing hymns or read the Bible to her in her own home can make the life of an elder rich and rewarding, even though she is in pain and disabled.

The British Red Cross Society

The Red Cross, as it is usually called, organises First Aid and Nursing courses and publishes excellent manuals on these subjects, in association with the St. John Ambulance Association and Brigade, and the St. Andrew's Ambulance Association (in Scotland). These Nursing and First Aid Manuals are best used in conjunction with attendance at a course. The Red Cross also runs short courses of four sessions especially for relatives looking after elderly people, called 'Nursing for the Family'.

The Red Cross can lend aids for disabled people and for those who are ill. Bedpans, commodes and urinals can be borrowed and the local branch may be able to lend a wheelchair for a short period of time if an old person who is unable to walk long distances wishes to go to the theatre or cinema, or to go out in the fresh air in summer. In some areas the old people's clubs are organised by the Red Cross, and some of these clubs are now being developed into day centres. There is a Red Cross Housing Association which provides flats for elderly people with the services of a warden and the provision of a mid-day meal. The ability of the Red Cross to supply volunteers to visit, provide transport or otherwise help an old person, varies from one part of the country to another.

The Red Cross is in the phone book under 'British Red Cross Society'.

The St. John Ambulance Association and Brigade, and in Scotland, the St. Andrew's Ambulance Association

These organisations, usually called St. John and St. Andrew's, also run First Aid and Nursing courses. The members are usually seen at sports events and cinemas in readiness for emergencies, but they are increasingly involved in voluntary work with disabled people of all ages.

Women's Royal Voluntary Service

The WRVS is well known by the green uniforms of its members, although not all the helpers wear uniforms. The WRVS organises the meals-on-wheels services in many areas.

The WRVS also organises books-on-wheels in some parts of the country, and volunteers visit old people as good neighbours. Lunch clubs, day centres and old people's clubs are run by the WRVS, and it arranges holidays for some old people. It has both sheltered housing and nursing homes; although the number of places is limited, this service is very valuable. Some local WRVS offices are able to supply clothing or blankets for old people in need.

Former Employer's Welfare Services

A retired person can often be helped by approaching his former employer or, in the case of a widow, the employer of her deceased husband. In some cases the retired person will be known to, and perhaps visited by, someone from their place of previous employment or the company for which they worked. For example, the Civil Service Retirement Fellowship exists to help retired civil servants and their dependants, and maintains regular contact with many of them. Sometimes it happens that such an organisation loses touch with a former employee, usually because of a change of residence, and welcomes the opportunity to visit and restore their links if a former employee is facing financial or other difficulties. The *Charities Digest* (see page 139) maintains a list of the major national organisations, but the simplest approach is to phone or write directly to the former employer's personnel department. Ex-servicemen and their dependants can frequently be helped from funds kept specially for this purpose by their former regiment or other service unit. The Forces Help Society, 118–122 Brompton Road, London, SW3 1JE, has a full list of all the various funds' addresses but their local representative can be contacted through the Citizens Advice Bureau or the local branch of the British Legion.

Each city and county has a War Pensions Committee (composed of people who give their time voluntarily) which is recognised by the Department of Health and Social Security as an official body. It helps ex-servicemen and their dependants to appeal against decisions which they believe to be unjust; it links individuals with the Forces Help Society and is a general source of advice.

The Citizens Advice Bureau at the local branch of the British Legion will be able to provide the address and telephone number of the War Pensions Committee.

Charities

There is a wide range of charities which have resources to help elderly people. The principal national charities are listed in the *Charities Digest.* Some help only those people who are, or were, members of certain occupational groups, such as teachers, nurses or brewers; others are less restrictive. There are also local charities which usually help those who were born, or live within, a certain geographical area, such as a parish or town. The Citizens Advice Bureau or the local Age Concern Office know how these charities can be approached.

Remember that charities themselves need help if they are to help people in need.

Council for Voluntary Service

In some towns this is called the Council for Social Service. In rural areas the Rural Community Council performs a similar function. The main function is to link together all the voluntary organisations. The secretary of the Council knows about the whole range of voluntary services and can usually advise an enquirer which service to approach. The Council can also advise people who wish to work as volunteers which service might best suit their talents.

Frequently the Council produces a directory of local voluntary organisations.

Age Concern

This is the key local organisation. The secretary will be able to advise on income, housing or heating problems. She will be aware of the recreational and educational opportunities open to people over retirement age, and of the clubs, day centres, lunch clubs, voluntary visiting and transport schemes in the area. She may also know of local charities which can be approached for financial help. Another very useful function is advice to elderly people and their relatives on how to deal with those professionals and officials in the Health and Social Services, who are not as helpful as they might be.

If the secretary does not know the answer she will call on the advice of a service which does, for example the Community Health Council (see page 29) or the Citizens Advice Bureau.

Citizens Advice Bureau

The CAB is also able to answer many of the questions which we suggested could be asked of Age Concern. Usually the advisers of the CAB know less about the problems of old age, especially physical and mental disorder, than the workers in Age Concern. The CAB advisers, on the other hand, usually know more about legal matters, such as consumers' rights, tenants' rights and the law relating to Wills. The CAB can advise if Legal Aid is possible, and also how to obtain it. In some towns and cities Housing Aid Centres have opened, which advise only on housing matters. These Centres work closely with Citizens Advice Bureaux.

PROFESSIONAL HELP

The Social Services Department and Social Workers

Many old people are confused by the similarity of the names 'Department of Health and Social Security' and 'Social Services Department' (in Scotland 'Social Work Department'), but they have very different functions. The Department of Health and Social Security is based in London with local social security offices concerned with financial help, either National Insurance or Supplementary Benefits (see page 136). Social Services and Social Work Departments are local government services supervised by local councillors, which have four main responsibilities regarding elderly people:

1) The provision of services to help elderly people who wish to live at home.

Home help (see page 16).

Meals-on-wheels (see page 84).

Lunch clubs and day centres, and the transport to reach them (see page 55).

Aids to daily living and house alterations, which are arranged by a domiciliary occupational therapist (see page 86).

Telephone installation and the payment of rental (see page 56).

The supply and licensing of television sets and radios (see page 57).

A laundry service for soiled linen (see page 70).

These are only the major services. Under the Chronically Sick and Disabled Persons Act (1970), a Social Services Department can, in theory, pay for almost any aid or service which will help a handicapped elderly person live independently. In practice, however, Social Services Departments are limited in what they can provide, because the amount of money made available by the ratepayers is often insufficient to meet the demands made by the public on social services.

Each Social Services Department maintains a register of handicapped people, but it is not uncommon for a disabled person to refuse to allow his name to be put on the handicapped register. This does not matter, however, as it is not necessary for an elderly person to be registered to be eligible for any of these benefits. A handicapped person may be refused a benefit because he does not meet the criteria set by the Department, but he is eligible to be considered irrespective of whether his name is on the register of handicapped persons.

2) The provision of residential accommodation – old people's homes (see page 173) – and the supervision of private and voluntary old people's homes (see page 174).

3) The provision of information not only about its own services, but about all the housing, financial, legal and voluntary services which can assist an elder and his supporters.

4) The provision of social work support. Much of social workers' time is taken up with the functions outlined above. A social worker may be called upon to decide whether an individual is eligible to receive one of the domiciliary services, and social workers are always involved in the decision whether someone should enter a home. Many social workers do not enjoy this aspect of their work, feeling that the public does not give enough resources to Social Services Department and that they are placed in the position of rationing these services, of saying 'no' to more people than they are able to help. Social workers also provide information.

The skill of a social worker is distinct from her ability to provide the services of the Social Services Department. A doctor tries to deal with disorders which arise *in* an old person, but a social worker tries to deal with disorders which arise *around* an old person in her social environment.

A social worker is sometimes able to improve an elder's physical environment by arranging for the provision of benefits which are available from the Social Services Department, but the job of a social worker is not merely one of form filling. Social workers will help with this if necessary, but their skills are better used in helping an elder to decide whether he wants to fill out the form. Social workers are usually too busy to become involved when the only problem is a financial one, or is caused by unsuitable housing, unless there are other social problems. In such cases they might expect you to seek the help of Age Concern, the Citizens Advice Bureau or a Housing Aid Centre. If the service required by the elder is obtainable only from the Social Services Department, for example the payment of telephone installation and rental, a social worker will have to become involved. But her usefulness to the supporters of an elder is much greater where the elder's problem relates to his social environment – his friends and neighbours, the professionals who are trying to help him and, of course, his family.

A social worker's skill can be very helpful if a disabled old person is starting to become isolated and withdrawn from friends and neighbours, or if he starts to neglect himself and his home. A social worker would not necessarily be the person to consult in the first instance – a home help and her organiser might be able to lift his spirits and re-establish broken links and habits of self care. If depression or anxiety seems to be the cause, his health visitor and GP would be the appropriate source of help. But if it is considered that the elder might have to be admitted to an old people's home, it is necessary to call in a social worker. It is only a social worker who can decide whether the admission of an elder to a home is the most appropriate solution to his problems. Although the social worker may decide that admission is not the most appropriate step, she may wish to continue to take an interest in the case, helping the elder's family, home help and health visitor, to re-establish and support the elder in his community.

Many social workers feel that the best use of their skill is in work with families. There are often tensions in family relationships which create problems that can be resolved only by bringing these tensions out into the open. It is normal for members of a family to feel some anger and resentment towards one another periodically, but this often passes. However, if an elder becomes permanently disabled and makes demands on his children, resentment may build up. One child may feel angry at her brother and sister because they have left her to do all the caring. This anger can create resentment towards the elder, who feels both angry, because his children are not caring for him as he thinks they should, and guilty, realising he is the cause of family tension. It is this sort of situation that can often be helped by social work. You may decide to ask for social work help because you feel that an outsider's view is necessary, or the social worker may take the initiative herself if she feels that the reason an old person is being referred for admission to an old people's home is because of tensions in the family rather than the elder's disability.

It may be that you feel that there are no hidden tensions in your relationship with your elder or with other members of the family, or that discussion with a health visitor or GP is all that is necessary. However, if you feel that the elder's problems are causing or are caused by family problems, we recommend that you consider social work help, whatever your social background. If you do consult a social worker you have to be prepared to be honest, first of all with yourself, then with the social worker, and then with the elder and other members of the family.

You can consult a social worker directly, either by telephoning the Social Services Department or by writing to the director of the Social Services Department in your area, describing the problem as clearly as you can. Alternatively, you can just go along to the Department. It usually takes at least a week, except in emergencies, for the case to be allocated to a social worker, who will usually telephone or write to you to make an appointment. At the initial appointment the social worker will discuss with you whether she thinks she can be of help, and what sort of help would be best for the elder. You can, of course, consult a social worker without the elder's permission, but it is usually better to discuss it with him first.

In an emergency you can phone the Social Services Department and ask to speak to the social worker on duty. Outside normal office hours there is an *emergency* service; phone the number of the Social Services Department listed in the phone book under the local council, and you will be given the emergency number. Advice over the phone may be sufficient to sort out your problem.

Social workers have an extremely difficult and often nerve-wracking job. While a social worker is interviewing an old person or a relative she may still be very upset from her previous interview with a mother suspected of baby battering, or some other terrible problem. The social worker also needs support from those she is trying to help. An understanding of the difficulties faced by social workers and a willingness to be frank, honest and co-operative will help her use her skills wisely and well.

Home Help

Home helps do very much more than housework. They provide company and overcome isolation; they encourage the old person and raise her spirits. They keep an eye on the elder's wellbeing and alert other professionals if they are worried or see a deterioration. They may alert other helpers directly, for example by leaving a note for the district nurse, or indirectly through the home help organiser. Each organiser is responsible for all the home helps in a certain geographical area. The home help organiser, who works in the social services department, has to assess each application for home help. Her assessment must consider the elder's state of health, her physical and mental ability, her social problems and whether and why she is isolated. The organiser has to weigh up the difficulties with housework, shopping and food preparation, and must decide how much housing problems – such as the lack of a hot water supply – are contributory factors. To complete the picture she often has to consult other professionals such as the elder's GP, a social worker or a domiciliary occupational therapist. If the organiser decides that the old person should receive home help, she must work out how much help can be provided and assess how much the elder should pay.

The amount of home help that can be provided is determined by many factors. In some parts of the country it may be less help than the old person, or you, or the organiser, think is necessary, because there is sometimes insufficient money to employ enough home helps. Most home help is provided on weekdays, during working hours, but it is possible for Social Services Departments to provide help at weekends and in the evenings. As with so many other services, the organiser's ability to offer help depends not only on the number of staff at her disposal (taking into account those on holiday or sick), but the other demands made on them. In winter the home help service is often stretched and short staffed, because home helps or their children are themselves unwell.

Many home help services also have a good neighbour scheme. The good neighbour may be a volunteer or she may receive a modest sum of money to perform small tasks for the elder – for example, preparing lunch on Sunday – but she does not usually do the same type of work as a home help.

It is therefore impossible to say how much help you can reasonably expect. Some Social Services Departments are unwilling to admit someone to an old people's home, unless she is receiving at least daily, if not twice daily, home help visits, plus help at weekends, and is still not able to manage. This is a high standard of care which cannot be achieved in all parts of the country, but gives some idea of what is available.

Home help organisers
The organiser's task is very difficult. She has so many requests for help and so few staff that she has to make decisions which are bound to upset some people – organisers expect families to help wherever possible. If you apply for home help, and anyone can make direct application to a Social Services Department, tell the organiser not only about the elder's problems but about your own. Tell her if you have other claims on your time, such as a daughter with young children who needs your help. Tell her also, if you are

feeling resentful or angry towards your elder, or if caring seven days a week is really getting you down. It may be that the organiser will suggest meals-on-wheels to relieve you at lunch time, at least on one or two days a week. One problem which occasionally occurs is when the elder says she does not need a home help and prefers to rely on you. You have to be honest and tell the old person what you feel. The organiser, health visitor or social worker may be able to help you negotiate with the elder.

A home help is not meant to help the elder dress or undress, bathe or change her clothes if she is incontinent. However, they often do help out in emergency because they do not want to see the elder sitting in damp clothes until the district nurse can call. In some areas, specially selected home helps do give this type of personal care – they are sometimes called home care assistants – but personal care is primarily the task of the district nurse and the nursing auxiliary (see page 21). Home helps are also not meant to do any really heavy work, such as decorating or digging the garden, but you or the organiser may be able to find a volunteer for such work. The home help can collect the pension and help with budgeting.

Having decided how much help should be offered, the finances of the old person have to be assessed to see whether or not she should pay for the help. Supplementary pensioners receive help free of charge. The greater the financial resources of the elder, the higher the charge for help (up to a fixed maximum). The organiser or some other council officer has to enquire about the elder's financial affairs, asking questions which many elders find embarrassing. Organisers do not like this part of their work; they ask the questions because they have to. The financial questions asked and the method of assessment vary from one part of the country to another but re-assessments are usually made, either every six months or annually, to see if the need for help or the financial situation has changed. This process of financial assessment sometimes upsets the elder so much that they refuse to have anything further to do with the home help service. No matter how skilfully and sensitively the interview is carried out it may frighten the elder, so don't assume that your elder was ill-used if she complains about the questions which were asked. If she refuses to have home help because of this, then it can be difficult to persuade her to consider applying again, but it may help if you can be with her at the assessment.

It is sometimes possible to employ private help more cheaply than social services help, but if you live some distance from the old person and are not able to select and supervise her help personally, the safest course is to apply for home help. Home helps are carefully selected and supervised. Remember that you can assist the home help service by informing them immediately if the old person is admitted to hospital. This can save the home help a wasted journey, and the time can often be given to someone else. If you have any complaint to make, speak or write to the home help organiser. If you have any compliment or praise for an individual home help or the service, write to the top – to the Director of Social Services for the area. The merits of the home help service receive too little praise.

Staff in Old People's Homes

There are two types of staff involved directly with the residents: the care assistants who help the residents to help themselves, and the officers in charge of the home who have to arrange all aspects of the life of the home, including the organisation of the care assistants' work. The officers, who are sometimes called 'matron' or 'warden', also help individual residents. There are also domestic staff who clean the home and do the housework but do not help the residents with their personal care. It is not uncommon for relatives to feel that the staff are not doing enough for their old person, but before a complaint is made two points should be remembered. The first is that the staff are usually very busy and are often working

under strain, especially in winter when some of the staff may be off sick. In many homes the residents have become much more disabled in the last decade, without any adequate addition to the number of staff to cope with the increasing amount of disability. The second point is that it is not always in the best interests of the old person for the care assistants to do everything for her. Muscles which are not exercised grow weak and joints which are not moved stiffen up. The staff who decline to push an old person to the dining room in a wheelchair may have been told to do this by her GP, who wishes to encourage the elder to walk to prevent her disability increasing.

Staff in residential homes have a difficult and demanding life, and welcome any support which can be offered by relatives and friends of the residents. Many homes now have a League of Friends which raises funds for the residents, and support for the staff through the League can help them considerably.

General Practitioners

One of the most important people in the life of an old person is his doctor. A good GP does not only make an accurate diagnosis and treat with care but, by his links with the other services, he can greatly aid an elder and lighten the burden of his supporters, because it is only he who can refer a person to hospital.

Many GPs now work in group practices in new health centres, although it should not be assumed that those who work in such premises are necessarily better doctors than those who practise from old premises, or on their own. Most GPs now work in a primary care team composed of a number of GPs – two, three or four usually – a health visitor and a district nurse. The team often has links with a social worker and domiciliary occupational therapist.

The pattern of general practice is changing and GPs no longer pay so many home visits. In the past, the GP often visited all the old people on his list regularly, but the increase in the number of old people has been so great that this is no longer possible. Doctors now expect people whom twenty years ago they would have visited at home to come to the surgery, but will visit elderly people if their illness prevents them from going to the surgery or health centre.

If an old person cannot reach the health centre because of chronic disability, it is sometimes possible to find a voluntary driver to take him to the surgery, but if he is ill the GP should be asked to visit. The ambulance service is not allowed to convey people to a surgery or health centre. If you think that a home visit is necessary, try to phone the health centre before ten o'clock in the morning, to allow the doctor to arrange his day's visits to make the best use of his time. The receptionist at the health centre who answers the phone may ask if it is possible for the elder to come, or be brought, to see the doctor. If this is impossible, in your opinion, say so. If you are unable to reach agreement with the receptionist ask if you can speak to the doctor, but do not expect to speak to him immediately; few GPs like to be interrupted during a consultation with a patient by a phone call. Leave a phone number and ask if he can call you back.

Doctors cannot work all the time, and all the doctors in a primary care team take their turn of evening and night duty. If the team is small or the GP works on his own, a deputy is sometimes employed to cover nights and weekends. As a result the doctor who comes is sometimes unknown, and naturally knows less about the elder than her own GP. Criticism about the use of deputies has appeared in the press but much of it is unjustified. The GP is responsible for the actions of his deputy; the deputies are usually, therefore, well trained and competent hospital doctors, or other experienced GPs. The deputy may need to be told more about the elder's medical background than would his own GP, but the gaps in his knowledge can be easily filled.

GPs do not only prefer to see patients in their consulting rooms for their own convenience – they are often better able to perform a thorough examination with all their equipment to hand. An increasing number of practices now run an appointments system. Urgent problems can usually be seen the same day, but those which are less pressing may have to wait for a day or two. Sometimes there is a disagreement between the person asking for an appointment, the elder or relative, and the receptionist who is planning the doctor's timetable. If you really think the problem requires an appointment urgently, but the receptionist says that it is impossible to arrange one that same day, ask to speak to the GP so that he can make the decision.

Honesty is the only basis on which a relationship with a GP can be satisfactory. You must be frank and open with him. If, for example, you are feeling tired and would like some relief from caring, tell him so. Don't try to make it appear that you wish help for the old person's sake. It is, of course, for the sake of the elder, because you can then give her stronger and better support. But don't try to enlist the GP's help by saying the old person is unwell when it is you who need help. The GP may refer an old person to a consultant in geriatric medicine, or any other appropriate hospital specialist, for a 'second opinion'. The consultant in hospital can order many more tests than the GP. He can call on the advice of a social worker and physiotherapist, whereas the GP usually cannot, and the GP realises that it is often these other services which an elder requires.

People often complain about general practice. They say 'it is not what it was'. It is not, but the world in which the GP works has changed and so must he. Some of the formal complaints which elderly people and their relatives make about individual general practitioners also arise from misunderstandings. Before making a formal complaint to the Family Practitioner Committee of the Area Health Authority, ask for an interview with the GP and try to resolve the dispute yourself. (In Scotland, GP services are organised by the Primary Care Division of the Area Health Board.)

The GP is in partnership not only with other doctors but with his patients and their relatives. Try to remember the strain under which he is working. He has many problems on his mind and needs the help and co-operation of his patients and their supporters, whether they are relatives, neighbours, friends or other professionals, if he is to help an old person to the best of his ability.

Sometimes an old person thinks that his GP is unsatisfactory and wishes to change to another. He is entitled to do so, as is the GP entitled to discontinue treating any patient at seven days' notice. To leave a GP's list of patients, all that is required is for him to sign 'Part B' of the elder's medical card and return it to the patient, who can then take it to another GP. It is wise not to leave one GP's list before another GP has been found willing to accept the old person as a patient. If the old person does not wish to approach the GP directly, he can write to the Family Practitioner Committee of the Area Health Authority in which he lives and ask for them to arrange the transfer.

Choosing a general practitioner
Anyone who wishes to change his GP, or who has to find a new doctor after moving to a new dwelling, can find the names of all the GPs in the 'Medical List' which is kept in all Crown or major Post Offices, at the offices of the Family Practitioner Committee and in the larger public libraries. The 'Medical List' provides the following information about each GP:
● Name, address and telephone number.
● Whether he is in a group practice or works on his own in a 'single-handed' practice.
● His consulting hours and whether or not he runs an appointment system.

The List does not include the doctor's degrees and qualifications, but this is unimportant not only because there are no special letters after a doctor's name to show expertise in work with elderly people, but because those doctors with more qualifications are not necessarily better doctors. The final selection of a GP depends upon the convenience of his surgery, the reputation he has with your friends and acquaintances, and his willingness to accept the elder as his patient. This is very important. Those GPs who are courteous, competent and caring are most popular, and therefore their list of patients is usually as long as they can cope with, whereas those GPs whose reputations are not so good are more likely to be able to accept new patients. If no GP is willing to accept new patients, the Family Practitioner Committee should be approached.

If an old person moves within the same neighbourhood, his GP will usually continue to care for him. However, if the old person moves out of the district in which the GP's patients are concentrated, even by a few miles, his doctor is within his rights to ask him to find another GP. If the elder is admitted to an old people's home in the area, it is his right to keep on the list of the same GP, even if another GP is the home's doctor.

To register with a new GP all that is necessary is to hand in the medical card to the surgery. If the old person has lost his card, a replacement can be obtained from the Family Practitioner Committee. The letter asking for a new card should contain the following information:
● Surname.
● Any previous surnames.
● Full Christian names.
● Date of birth.
● Present address of elder.
● Name and address of the elder's previous GP.
● National Registration Number, if the elder had one prior to 1948.
The patient can register with a GP while a new card is being obtained. The new GP will be sent the elder's notes, but this can take some time – a month or more is not unusual.

Any GP can be called out in a real emergency if an old person is staying with you, but it is much more sensible to make a temporary registration with your own GP, if he is willing. Temporary registration lasts for three months and during that period the GP can treat the old person as if he were one of his permanent patients.

District Nurses (Domiciliary Nurses)

The district nurse, sometimes called the domiciliary nurse or home nurse, offers both practical and psychological help. In the district nursing service there are both qualified nurses, and nursing auxiliaries who visit an elderly person alone but whose work is supervised by the qualified district nurses. In most parts of the country nurses work in primary care teams, but they are also members of domiciliary nursing teams. These may consist of ten or twenty nurses, each of whom is attached to different primary care teams. This allows a seven day service to be provided, but means that the same nurse does not always visit the elder.

The qualified nurses perform the more highly skilled tasks, for example treating varicose ulcers and giving insulin injections. The nursing auxiliaries give general care, helping with dressing and undressing, bathing and washing. There is also an evening service for people who need help to get to bed and for those who require a pain killing injection before they can sleep. Nurses may also supervise any medication and are the best advisers on leg ulcers (varicose ulcers).

For patients dying of cancer the Marie Curie Fund can pay for a nurse to stay at night, and in some areas there is a night sitting service for other conditions. The district nurse will know whether a night sitter can be provided.

How much home nursing is it reasonable to expect? That depends on a number of factors. The service is very much busier in winter than in summer; more people require help but no more nurses are employed, and nurses themselves, of course, may be ill during winter. Also, there is less help available at weekends than during the week. However, if an elder is very disabled and has no family to help, the nursing service may be able to pay two visits daily, although the old person may have to adjust her time of rising and going to bed to fit in with the nurse's schedule.

If your elder lives with or very near you, the nurse will work with you. Many children find it embarrassing or unpleasant to bathe their parents or deal with incontinence, and it can greatly relieve the strain for a nurse to come in to lighten such tasks by direct help and the provision of incontinence pads. In acute illness the expert advice and practical help of a skilled nurse is very valuable.

The elder's GP may ask the nurse to call, but she can be phoned directly either at the health centre or at the office of the nursing team – look under 'Nurses' in the white pages of the phone book if you wish to ask for advice.

Remember that nurses are not only there to make the elder more comfortable physically. They are very experienced in the problems of elders and their supporters, and are willing and very able to discuss the emotional and personal problems which inevitably occur.

Private nursing

Nurses can be hired from nursing agencies – look under 'Nursing' in the Yellow Pages – but this service is very expensive and is not always covered by private insurance. Discuss the problem with the district nurse, or the nursing officer in charge of the nursing team, before you decide to use private nursing. It may be that the problem can be solved in another way.

Health Visitors

Health Visitors are fully qualified nurses who have trained for an extra year. The additional year of study, which is usually taken after the qualified nurse has worked in hospital for several years, is devoted to the psychology of human development, the study of society and the public services, and preventive medicine. Most health visitors are members of primary care teams, one health visitor working with a group of general practitioners. Each health visitor is also a member of a team of health visitors, so that her work can be covered if she is off sick or on holiday.

The health visitor does not usually perform any physical nursing, for example she does not bathe the elder. This is the job of the district nurse, although in an emergency the health visitor would help. In some rural areas the jobs of health visitor and district nurse are sometimes combined, the one nurse doing both jobs.

The health visitor has three main skills to offer:

- She is trained in preventive medicine, can recognise the early signs of illness and alert the GP if she thinks that an old person's physical and mental condition is changing.
- She can help you and the elder resolve anxieties and tensions by discussion and counselling, and is a useful outsider to help you see all sides of difficult decisions.
- She knows what services are available – social security, housing, social and voluntary services – and how to apply for them.

This is especially useful if you live some distance away because the health visitor can act as your agent if an old person requires help with a housing, income or any other social problem. Obviously this aspect of her work is similar to some of the tasks done by social workers and there is, in fact, a considerable overlap between the two professions. However, if the elder wants one of the services offered by the Social Services Department, for example a place in an old people's home, the health visitor has to ask a social worker to consider the application.

The elder's GP may ask the health visitor to call, but you can seek the help of a health visitor directly. Phone the GP's surgery and ask to speak to the health visitor. If the health visitor is not based at the surgery the receptionist will tell you where she can be contacted. It is best to phone health visitors between 9 a.m. and 10 a.m. because most make it a practice to be in the office between those hours.

In some parts of the country there are geriatric liaison health visitors working with consultants in geriatric medicine, who are responsible for ensuring that hospital and community services work smoothly together, especially at the time of hospital discharge. If there is no such liaison health visitor, the medical social worker in the hospital will be responsible for all the discharge arrangements.

Consultants in Geriatric Medicine

There are five main rungs on the hospital ladder and the consultant in geriatric medicine, sometimes called a consultant geriatrician, is on the top rung and is responsible for the medical care given to patients in his unit.

Consultant

Senior Registrar

Registrar

Senior House Officer

House Officer

All the patients seen by a consultant in geriatric medicine or members of his team are over the age of 65, but not all people who are over the age of 65 who have been referred to hospital are seen by a consultant in geriatric medicine. If an old person requires any kind of operation, she will be seen by a consultant surgeon, who treats people of all ages. If she is admitted as an emergency for a condition which does not require operative treatment, it may be to the wards of a consultant in general medicine, who treats the same diseases as consultants in geriatric medicine – for example thyroid disease, high blood pressure, or diabetes. However, a doctor who specialises in geriatric medicine develops a special interest and skill in the management of the diseases which occur most commonly in old age – incontinence, instability, immobility – and in the rehabilitation of old people who have become disabled, so the consultant in general medicine may call him in if he feels the elder requires such specialised knowledge. Sometimes old people are admitted directly to the care of a consultant in geriatric medicine.

A GP can obtain a second opinion on the diagnosis or treatment of an elder's problems by referring her to an out-patient clinic, or by asking the consultant to make a 'domiciliary visit' by calling to see the elder at home.

The consultant in geriatric medicine works in a team consisting of less senior doctors, a physiotherapist, an occupational therapist, a social worker and the nurses who work on the ward. He may refer the elder to another consultant – perhaps a cardiologist if he thinks a cardiac pacemaker might be beneficial or an ophthalmologist if there is cataract. The junior doctors who are members of his team perform much of the medical care for patients either at out-patients or in the wards, but the consultant is the leader of the medical team. You will usually see one of the junior doctors, but if you wish to see the consultant, either phone his secretary to make an appointment or ask the Ward Sister.

Occupational Therapists

Even after the best medical treatment and physiotherapy, some disability may remain to handicap the elder in her everyday life, in getting about the house or outside, or looking after herself. Although many people still think that occupational therapists teach basket-work and other types of hobbies to disabled people, this is only partly true. Some occupational therapists do not do any of this work and, for most, it is only a small part of their job. Their main task is to help the newly disabled person learn how to accept her reduced capabilities and adapt successfully to an unchanged environment. It is also commonly thought that this is achieved by the provision of mechanical aids, but this is not so. The main emphasis is on teaching the individual how to adapt, to help her learn new ways of dressing and undressing, washing and housework, and to encourage her in the belief that she can still perform these tasks. As with physiotherapy, much of the benefit of occupational therapy comes from the confidence which the therapist can foster and inspire. If, after she has thought about and learned new techniques from the occupational therapist, the elder is still handicapped, the therapist, or 'OT' as she is often called, may consider providing an aid or, if the elder's ability to move about is affected, adapting her dwelling or suggesting that a wheelchair would be helpful.

Because doctors know that certain diseases almost always leave some disability, and many diseases are very disabling during the healing phase even though recovery is eventually complete, they often involve occupational therapists in the management of disease right from the start of treatment.

Most OTs work in hospital, not only with consultants in geriatric medicine, but linked with consultants in many different specialties, for example orthopaedics and rheumatology. Like the physiotherapist, the OT may ask to see you, to show you how she is helping the elder learn to adapt to her disability and become independent, and how you could encourage her to persevere on her own. If you are worried about the elder's ability to dress or undress, to wash or bathe herself, to prepare and cook food, or care for herself in any way, you should ask the Ward Sister if you could discuss this with the OT.

Old people also see and work with OTs at day hospital, and you can seek the advice of an OT if your elder attends one (see page 96). The hospital-based occupational therapist often pays home visits before the patient is discharged from hospital. She may ask to meet you at the elder's home to discuss any alterations and adaptations which she might think necessary. At the time of discharge however, the hospital therapist usually refers the case to a domiciliary occupational therapist who is based in the community.

Very many disabled people are looked after by their GP. He can consult and call on the services of a domiciliary OT, who has had exactly the same training as the hospital OT. You can also contact the domiciliary OT directly. Ask the elder's health visitor how this can be done, or phone the Social Services Department of the area in which the old person lives.

The OT can advise on ways in which the elder could become less dependent. Independence comes not only from aids, wheelchairs and house alterations, however, but from attitudes. The attitude of the elder is obviously important, but so is that of her supporters. One of the most difficult situations you may have to face is to resist helping the disabled elder who is struggling to perform some task. If she is confident of success then it is comparatively easy. However, if she is frustrated and tearful at the prospect of yet another failure, you will often feel a great urge to do it for her. It may also be quicker, cleaner and more convenient to do it yourself. Additional pressure may be put on you by the presence of other people who do not see that it is to the advantage of the elder to struggle and overcome her handicaps herself. They may regard you as insensitive or callous.

The occupational therapist is the ideal person with whom to discuss such feelings, both alone and together with the elder. OTs are usually experienced in helping disabled people and their supporters through periods of sorrow, frustration, pity, anger and resentment. None of these emotions is uncommon in the supporters of disabled people.

Physiotherapists

Diseases have both direct and indirect effects. The direct effects occur at the site of the disease, for example in arthritis the joints are affected and in a stroke the brain is damaged. However, the loss of function or disability which results from disease is due just as much to its indirect effects. In arthritis the painful joints are kept still and this leads not only to the joints stiffening up but also to those muscles which are put out of action becoming weak. Following a stroke, the weakness and paralysis of the muscles leads to stiffness of joints and muscle contracture. These are some of the indirect effects of disease. Doctors treat the direct effects of disease by drugs and surgical operations, but they rely on physiotherapists to treat the indirect effects to prevent, or at least lessen, the disability that can so easily result.

It is often thought that physiotherapists treat patients with the use of electrical and other apparatus. They certainly make some use of apparatus, but their main skill is to teach and encourage the patient to work for his own recovery. They restore the patient's confidence in himself and encourage him to go just that little bit further each day. It is customary for physiotherapists to assess the individual's disability, physical potential for recovery, and motivation over a period, perhaps as long as a month or two. After this period they may still continue treatment themselves, or decide that the patient will continue to progress at home with the encouragement of family and other supporters.

Most physiotherapists work in hospital. This is one advantage of hospital referral, because GPs cannot ask for the opinion of a physiotherapist so easily as a consultant in geriatric medicine. In some parts of the country there is a domiciliary physiotherapy service which the GP can approach directly. This service is at present uncommon, but it is developing in many areas. The fact that most physiotherapists work in hospital does not mean that they do not pay home visits. Physiotherapists often visit a patient's home before discharge, usually with the old person, to prepare for the return home. If your elderly friend or relative is in hospital, the physiotherapist may ask to see you while you are visiting her. You can ask the Ward Sister if you may speak to the physiotherapist if you are worried about the elderly person's mobility, for example her ability to climb stairs safely.

Physiotherapy can be obtained privately. If a physiotherapist with the letters MCSP or MCsP or SRP after his name is chosen from the Yellow Pages of the phone book you can be assured that he is competent and responsible. Private physiotherapists can be approached directly but they often request a letter from the general practitioner before commencing treatment. Ask the advice of a National Health Service physiotherapist before incurring the expense of private physiotherapy.

Nurses

Although doctors are very important, they have only limited contact with elderly people while they are in hospital. The key members of staff are the nurses. Working on any ward are nurses who are fully trained and nurses who are still in training.

The uniforms of these different grades vary from one hospital to another so you should ask who's who in the ward when the elder is admitted, as there are also domestic staff who serve meals and make the beds.

People often equate nursing with such physical tasks as washing, dressing, lifting, but nursing is much more than this. Nurses also help a patient deal with the psychological effects of illness; what the patient fears might happen, her depressions and anxieties. Nurses see the patient as a person and when disease alters a person's body or mind, or both, the nurse tries to help her come to terms with the change. Nurses are aware that illness affects not only the patient but her

supporters – it makes their future uncertain and may increase their burden. The nurse is the person whom you will find most easily on the ward and she is often the person you will find most easy to talk to. She will arrange for you to see the doctor, social worker, occupational therapist or physiotherapist if it should be appropriate. She will know how to contact the hospital chaplain, how to deal with social security, arrange for hairdressing and how to solve a whole host of practical problems. Nurses are concerned not only with illness and its treatment, but with people and their problems.

The Psychiatrist and the Psychiatric Team

A general practitioner is able to manage most mental disabilities, but he may ask a consultant psychiatrist for a second opinion if:

- He is unsure what is wrong. The psychiatrist, who has more time and can call on the skills of other professionals, can help him come to a diagnosis.
- He wants advice on treatment. The psychiatrist, with his greater experience of the effect of drugs on old people, can give his opinion on management.
- He thinks that hospital admission would help the elder or his supporters.

In some hospitals one or two consultant psychiatrists specialise in the mental problems of old people. The title of such a specialist varies, he may be called a consultant

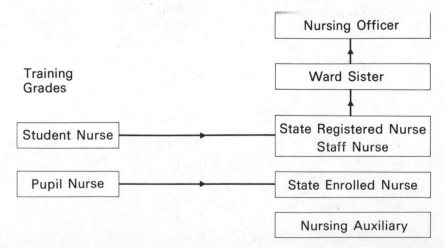

25

psychogeriatrician or a consultant in mental illness of old age, or some similar title. If there is no consultant psychogeriatrician the elder will be seen by one of the consultant psychiatrists who, although he will not have as much experience as the consultant working all the time with old people, is trained to manage the mental problems of old age. Even when there is a consultant psychogeriatrician, an old person may see another psychiatrist, especially in an emergency.

Many psychogeriatricians work in a team, together with a psychologist, a psychiatric community nurse and a social worker, and you may have direct contact with any or all of these team members. The psychiatrist's primary task is often to review the elder's physical condition. Physical illness causes mental symptoms so frequently that it may always be sought at the start of any investigation of mental disorder (see page 104). The psychologist assesses the mental condition of the elder, trying to decide how many of the symptoms are due to brain failure and how many to environmental factors, such as isolation and deafness. The psychiatric community nurse and the social worker try to ascertain whether or not the pattern of the old person's social relationships have changed, how these relationships affect the elder, and how they are affected by his mental disorder. The psychiatric community nurse is also able to supervise and advise on drugs and other problems, for example restlessness at night, incontinence or wandering. However, the team is very rarely as strong as this. Psychogeriatricians and psychiatric community nurses often work closely together but by no means all psychogeriatricians can call on the services of a psychologist. Some have to work alone, and perform all these skills without help.

Psychogeriatricians sometimes see patients at out-patient clinics, like other hospital doctors, but they prefer to see an elder in his own home. If the GP has requested a domiciliary visit and you would like to be present, phone the psychogeriatrician's secretary and ask when he is going to call.

She may not be able to give you an exact time, but should be able to say whether it is in the morning or afternoon. It may be decided that the elder should either attend day hospital or be admitted to hospital for assessment. While he is in hospital you can ask the psychogeriatrician's secretary for an appointment if you wish to see him, but you may be invited by the team to discuss with them what can be arranged to help both the elder and yourself.

Be honest with all members of the team and the hospital nursing staff. If you feel you need a break, if only for a night, say so. Remember that they too are under pressure and although they only work eight hours a day, many of them take their worries, and yours, home with them. Psychogeriatricians are under tremendous pressure. Psychogeriatrics is an unfashionable specialty and receives very little of the NHS resources. The team is often under simultaneous pressures from other hospital doctors, GPs, social workers and members of the public, and would often like to help much more than it can.

Psychiatrists don't have magic cures for mental illness. In many cases they don't even prescribe drugs and there is often little special treatment offered in hospital other than toleration and kindness. They can cure some physical illnesses which cause mental disorder, but their main contribution to disorders of the mind or brain is not in anything they do *to* the elder, but in making an accurate assessment of the elder's social situation. And, *with the help of* the elder and his supporters, reintegrating him more happily with family, neighbours and friends.

Environmental Health Officers

Formerly known as a public health inspector, the environmental health officer is able to do a great deal to help elderly people. Environmental problems such as noise, smells or air pollution can cause great distress but the EHO is often able to solve or alleviate them. If infestation with mice, rats, cockroaches or any other pest occurs, help should be sought from the Environmental Health Department at the district council offices. It is not always realised that environmental health officers have great skill in dealing with housing problems, including difficulties arising from the disrepair of rented houses, and know all about the grants available for house improvement (see page 158). They are used to meeting elderly people, and to helping tenants who are frightened of their landlord, so the environmental health officer can be relied on not only to give skilled help, but for a sympathetic approach. Phone the Town Hall if you cannot find the telephone number under 'Environmental Health' in the phone book.

Chiropractors and Osteopaths

These are often thought to be the same as 'bone-setters'. They are not. Chiropractic and osteopathy are branches of medicine although they are not available on the National Health Service. Unlike bone-setters, who have often just picked up their skills, osteopaths and chiropractors have a long training and know much more about the body than its bones.

The spine is composed of bones (the vertebrae), muscles, joints, ligaments and soft connecting tissue. Disorders of the spinal column, the tube of vertebrae, can cause pain in the other tissues. Impulses from these tissues pass inwards to the spinal cord, which runs through the spinal column, and pass outwards again to affect muscles and other tissues in the body. Sometimes there is direct pressure on the nerves as they pass out from the spinal column, causing pain and muscle spasm along the course of the nerve. Chiropractic and osteopathy deal with the underlying spinal disorder but they do not believe that it is the cause of all diseases. This is one of their strengths. Trained osteopaths and chiropractors recognise conditions which are better treated by doctors of medicine and refer the patient to his own GP in such cases. Their training includes the same basic sub-

jects as medical education, and they acquire the skill to diagnose the warning signs of serious disease.

The main condition which they treat is backache. Backache may be acute or it may be present for long periods of time. It may be low down in the spine (lumbago) or mainly in the neck. Lumbago is sometimes accompanied by pain down the leg (sciatica). Pain in the neck sometimes occurs with headaches or pain in the shoulder and arms. For any of these types of pain an osteopath or chiropractor can be consulted, both of whom can cure many people whom doctors are unable to help. They also treat many conditions which they regard as due to disordered nerve function, for example, migraine.

Although there has been hostility towards osteopaths and chiropractors on the part of doctors, some recognise their skill and suggest that patients with back problems seek their help.

If a doctor says that there is nothing more he can do for an old person's backache, you should ask him if he can recommend an osteopath or chiropractor.

If you would like to consult an osteopath or chiropractor you must decide which to choose, then select one who is well trained and properly qualified. In some parts of the country the first choice is easy because there is only one of the two in practice locally. If there is either an osteopath or a chiropractor with the qualifications listed below working near your elder choose him or her with confidence. If the old person lives in a city in which there are both qualified osteopaths and chiropractors the decision is much more difficult. Having spoken to many satisfied patients we do not feel we can recommend one in preference to the other. If you have the personal recommendation of a friend or doctor you can choose on this basis, otherwise you must consult the Yellow Pages of the phone book where they are listed under 'Chiropractors' and 'Osteopaths'. Unfortunately there is no control over the use of these titles. Anyone can call himself an osteopath or a chiropractor without having had any training, so they must be carefully chosen as follows.

Chiropractors

The letters DC after the name of a chiropractor stand for doctor of chiropractic. However, anyone can call himself a doctor of chiropractic irrespective of whether he has had any training. It is wise to choose a chiropractor who is a member of the British Chiropractor's Association because they only admit fully trained chiropractors. If there is no qualified chiropractor locally, the address of the nearest one can be found by writing to

The British Chiropractors Association,
5 First Avenue,
Chelmsford,
Essex.

Osteopaths

Recommended osteopaths are those with the qualifications MRO or MBNOA. MRO stands for Members of the Register of Osteopaths. Some members are specialist osteopaths, other members are doctors who have studied osteopathy after their medical qualification, and they have the initials LLCO – Licentiate of the London College of Osteopathy – after their names. There is no great advantage in choosing a doctor as an osteopath. Both are equally well trained in the practice of osteopathy. If there are no Members of the Register of Osteopaths listed in the Yellow Pages you can write or phone the Registrar at

The General Council and Register of Osteopaths Ltd,
16 Buckingham Gate,
London, SW1E 6LB.
01–828 0601

He will tell you the name and address of the nearest Members on the Register.

MBNOA stands for Member of the British Naturopathic and Osteopathic Association. Members may also include DO – Diploma in Osteopathy – and ND – Diploma in Naturopathy – after their names.

Naturopathy treats disorders of body function, for example stomach trouble, asthma and hay fever, by natural types of therapy, sunlight, exercise, a sensible diet of natural foodstuffs and breathing exercises. It may be combined with osteopathy, but the two types of treatment are usually given independently for different types of complaint. If there is no osteopath listed as MBNOA the name and address of the nearest Member of the Association can be obtained by writing or phoning

The British Naturopathic and Osteopathy Association,
6 Netherhall Gardens,
London, NW3.
01–435 7830

The letters MSO – Member of the Society of Osteopathy – sometimes follow the name of an osteopath. Those who are eligible are members of the Register of Osteopaths – MRO, Members of the British Naturopathic and Osteopathic Association – MBNOA, and those who have trained at the European College of Osteopathy in Maidstone. The name of the MSO who practises nearest the old person can be obtained from

The Secretary,
The Society of Osteopaths,
27 Leadenhall Street,
London, EC3A 1AB.

We do not recommend any one type of osteopath more strongly than the other. Those we have recommended are all well trained, qualified by examination and, like doctors, insured to cover any liability.

It is difficult for the osteopath or chiropractor to give you an accurate estimate of length and cost of a course of treatment until he has seen the results of tests and the response to the first treatment. Some cases respond after a few treatments, but others do not. Neither private health insurance nor Social Security cover the cost of osteopathy or chiropractic.

COMPLAINTS, SUGGESTIONS AND THANKS – YOUR RIGHTS AND OPPORTUNITIES

We will describe how you can express your dissatisfaction about certain specific services, but it is appropriate to discuss complaints in more general terms.

If the service given to you or an old person is less than perfect or is not the best, you have to accept that no-one is perfect and not everyone can be the best. The staff can offer you their skills only within the limits of the service, and many services are having to fight hard to maintain their standards. However, it is your right to expect that staff will offer you the best service they can. If you feel that the service falls short of that, then it is your right to express your dissatisfaction.

It is your right to be treated with reasonable skill and care in the NHS. If an old person is not so treated and damage results, the professional treating him may be considered to have been negligent. The definition of reasonable skill and care is not easy. 'Reasonable' must be considered in the light of the experience, training and qualifications of the doctor, nurse or other professional. You cannot expect a GP to have as much skill in the treatment of heart disease as a heart specialist, but you can expect reasonable skill. If you feel that there has been negligence in your treatment then you should consult a solicitor. You may wish to ask the advice of the Community Health Council or Citizens Advice Bureau before doing so. If you think the cost of legal fees is more than you can afford, ask at the Citizens Advice Bureau because you may be eligible for Legal Aid (see page 40).

Although complaints cannot bring back what is lost and make good damage done, it is your right to expect someone to account for the negligent act or a service which falls below what is possible for the staff to achieve. If a person is disciplined for an act which caused someone to suffer, that may give you some satisfaction, but complaints should be regarded as much more important

than that. If you point out what went wrong in your case, it may be that those running the service will change it and your suggestion will improve the service and save other people from suffering in the same way. You should not only make suggestions when something goes wrong. If you see ways in which the service could be improved or money saved, write to the administrator of your local Health Authority and make your suggestion.

Remember that many professionals are working under severe strain. Do not complain to someone's superior or to your MP until you have tried to sort the disagreement out with the person concerned. Many disagreements arise from misunderstandings, not from negligence. However, if you do decide to complain, do not be put off until you are satisfied.

Don't write only about things which are wrong. People working in the NHS hear little from the public except complaints. If you were pleased with your care, either medical or nursing, or even the way the food was cooked and presented don't just say thank you to the staff you see – write to the top, to the nursing officer or the administrator or the director of social services, and tell them how grateful you are, and write to the newspapers. They will pass the compliment down to the staff who get a double reward – your gratitude and the knowledge that a satisfied customer has told their boss how well they work.

The Community Health Council

In each Health Authority there exists a Community Health Council – 'CHC' – to represent the interests of the consumer. There is a great variation in the way these councils work. In some parts of the country the council takes up complaints from individual consumers. Other councils are not so keen to act as advocate, except when the complaint has been through the proper channels but is answered unsatisfactorily. In such cases the council might write to the Health Authority asking them to reconsider, or they might advise referral of the case to the Ombudsman.

Whatever their attitude to individual complaints, all Community Health Councils are very interested in the quality of service provided. In future it is likely that services will not grow so quickly as they did in the past, indeed some may be cut. As well as protesting to the Health Authority directly you should write to the secretary of the CHC if you are concerned about the standard of service. If the authority proposes to close your local hospital, or cancel the health centre planned for your area, write to the CHC. If an elderly relative cannot be admitted to hospital, is discharged too soon or is told she has to wait two years for chiropody treatment, you can write to the Community Health Council. Even if the issue seems to be too big for your opinion to matter, for example the opening of a hospital costing millions of pounds, write to the CHC if you feel strongly about it. Your views are never useless. The main problem of Community Health Councils and Health Authorities is not that they get too many opinions and suggestions from the public, but too few.

In Scotland the Local Health Council performs the same function as the Community Health Council in relation to the Area Health Boards.

The Patients Association

This is a national organisation which exists to fight for patients' rights. It reflects the patients' interest, taking up cases referred by Community Health Councils, by patients themselves or their relatives.

If you do not find the Community Health Council helpful, you can ask the advice of the Patients Association on how to complain or whether an unsatisfactory reply to your complaint should be taken further. You can approach the Patients Association directly at

11 Dartmouth Street,
London, SW1.

The Patients Association depends on the subscriptions of individuals to finance its work, as the grant it receives from the Department of Health does not cover all expenses. If you care for the National Health Service and the rights of patients you should consider joining.

MIND

The complaints procedure for services for mentally disturbed old people are the same as for other services, but there is one other important source of advice: MIND (The National Association for Mental Health), 22 Harley Street, London, W1N 2ED, 01–637 0741, (Northern Office, 155/157 Woodhouse Lane, Leeds, LS2 3EF, 0532 23926; Welsh Office, 7 St. Mary Street, Cardiff, CF1 2AT.) MIND is able to answer questions and give advice on all the services we have described, either by letter or phone.

The Councillor

The Councillor can be very helpful and you can be helpful to him by giving the consumer's viewpoint, but you should not approach him too soon. If you try to enlist a councillor's support or make a complaint to him before the local government officials have had an adequate opportunity to deal with the case they may be very annoyed, as they have every right to be. If, however, you have explored every avenue and are still not satisfied that your elder is receiving service of a reasonable quality, you can ask the councillor's advice.

The name and address of the councillor for the elder's ward can be found in the library or at the Citizens Advice Bureau. In metropolitan areas, for example London, Birmingham or Leeds, the councillors are responsible for both housing and social services. However, in rural counties, such as Devon, Leicestershire or Kent, county councillors are responsible for social services and district councillors for housing.

Remember that councillors hear many

complaints but little praise. When thanking people for the service they have provided, write a note to the councillor. It will please him and be passed on to the officials who have helped, who will thus be doubly thanked.

The MP

There is a fairly comprehensive system for dealing with complaints, but if you have explored all the avenues we have described and are still not satisfied, write to your MP. It is a waste of time writing to your MP unless and until you have approached officials and councillors unsuccessfully. He will just send your letter on to the appropriate person, to whom you should have written in the first place. You will have gained nothing and lost time. However, your MP is there for a final appeal.

MPs are often accused of being uninformed, but their knowledge depends upon what people tell them. They are interested to hear your views and opinions either on national issues, for example the level of pensions, or on local problems. Your MP is your representative, but he cannot represent your views if he does not know them.

The Health Services Commissioner (the Ombudsman)

The Health Services Commissioner is appointed to investigate complaints *except* those:
- Concerning GP services.
- Which are solely complaints about clinical decisions.
- Which have not been fully investigated by the Health Authority in which the cause for the complaint arose.

He is someone to whom an appeal can be made if you are not satisfied with the way your complaint has been answered locally. You can write to the Health Services Commissioner (Ombudsman) directly without the help of your MP. The advice of your local Community Health Council or the Patients Association will be very helpful if you are considering writing to the Health Services Commissioner at

Church House,
Great Smith Street,
London, SW1P 3BW, or

Queens Court,
Plymouth Road,
Cardiff, CF1 4DA.

The Commissioner for Local Administration (the Ombudsman)

If you feel that an old person has suffered because of maladministration by a local authority, and cannot find a satisfactory explanation after complaining to the appropriate office and seeking the advice of the elder's councillor, you can approach the Ombudsman for local authority services, the Commissioner for Local Administration as he is called. There are a number of Ombudsmen, one for Wales, one for Scotland and three covering different regions of England. If you feel that there has been maladministration in a housing, social services or any other local authority department, and think that you would like to take the case further, ask at the library or the Citizens Advice Bureau for details of the Ombudsman, his address, the type of grievance he will consider and the manner in which he can be approached.

Chapter 4
Some Answers on Legal Questions

It is valuable to have a knowledge of: the function of the coroner and operation of the Court of Protection; the legal implications of a will being made or not being made; what probate is; to what extent the consumer is protected; the law on unfair dismissal; insurance; where to go to get legal help; and who qualifies and what legal procedure is involved in buying a house. What is said below is not exhaustive and is intended only as a guide. Our motive is to prompt you to consult a solicitor about any legal problems you have.

THE CORONER

The coroner is a qualified lawyer or doctor who is appointed by the County or County Borough Council; however, he is responsible only to the Crown.

A death has to be reported to the coroner if the doctor had not attended the deceased at all during his last illness. And even if the doctor had been treating the deceased yet had not seen him for the last fourteen days, the death has to be reported to the coroner unless the doctor has seen the body. (In Northern Ireland there is a twenty-eight day period within which the doctor should have seen the patient.)

Usually, the doctor or the police are the persons who report a death to the coroner. The registrar of births and deaths will do so if the cause or circumstances of the death warrant it.

Not all deaths reported to the coroner end up with a post mortem being performed. In the case of the coroner concluding that there is no need for further investigation, he sends a formal notice of his decision to the registrar of the district and the body again becomes the responsibility of the family.

If the coroner reasonably suspects that the death was violent or unnatural, or if it was surrounded by suspicious circumstances, he should hold an inquest.

Inquests are formal proceedings. A coroner's court is a court of law. Witnesses are on oath and the coroner can admit any evidence.

The coroner questions the witness. With the coroner's permission, the witness can then be examined by anyone present who has a legal interest in the case.

There should not be any expense to the family arising from the inquest unless a solicitor's services are needed.

At the completion of an inquest the coroner will send a certificate after the inquest to the registrar of births and deaths of the district where the death took place.

THE COURT OF PROTECTION

This Court exists to protect the property of a person who is incapable of managing her own affairs because of mental disorder.

Under Part 8 of the Mental Health Act 1959 the Court may supervise nearly all aspects of a patient's affairs. However, jurisdiction can only be exercised after the Court of Protection has considered the medical evidence of the patient's mental capacity and has concluded that on the evidence the patient is no longer capable of managing her own affairs. The medical evidence must, of course, come from a qualified doctor.

One's closest relatives may make application to the Court for the appointment of a Receiver. Where the patient's affairs are complex, a professional (such as a solicitor) may apply for appointment. Where no-one is willing to act, the Official Receiver may be appointed Receiver.

When an application has been made to the Court of Protection, there is a statutory requirement that notice should be sent to the patient, telling her of the application, the name and address of the applicant and, additionally, informing her of the date the application is to be heard, so that she can, if she wants to, contest the assertion of her mental incapacity and object to the appointment of a Receiver.

Applications to the Court of Protection may be made by any person, either by instructing a solicitor to carry through the application or with the assistance of the Personal Application Branch of the Court. Any fees incurred are normally refundable out of the patient's assets.

The address of the Court of Protection is:

The Chief Clerk,
Court of Protection,
25 Store Street,
London, WC1E 7BP.

It should be noted that the compulsory admission of a patient to a mental hospital does not automatically take away her ability to manage her affairs.

Where someone first becomes ill, she may execute a power of attorney in favour of a relative, but where she is incapable of managing her affairs, it is the duty of her solicitor, where asked to prepare a Power of Attorney, to ensure that she can fully understand what she is doing.

As far as property management is concerned, it is a matter of general policy that a Receiver has to have special authority before he can sell a patient's house. It is advisable for a Receiver to continue to pay rent out of capital rather than to terminate a tenancy. In approved cases, supplementary benefit can be obtained out of which rent can be met.

Any Receiver appointed by the Court is required to give security (a bond through an insurance company) to cover the amount of cash that may be in the Receiver's hands at any one time. Every year he must also submit an account of dealings with the patient's property to the Court.

Where a Receiver has not acted properly or wishes to retire, the Court of Protection may appoint another Receiver.

Some relatives who are appointed Receivers are unscrupulous, and may refuse to release monies for the patient's general needs while she is in hospital. Professionals can apply to the Court of Protection for an order requiring the Receiver to meet the patient's needs as required.

Where a patient recovers and produces substantiating medical evidence of recovery, she may apply for a discharge of the Receiver.

CONSUMER PROTECTION

General

The most important information or directive that we can give you about any contract is that you must not sign it until you have read and understood every clause in it.

A simple contract does not have to be written, except in certain special cases prescribed by Statute. These include, among others, hire-purchase agreements which must be supported by a memorandum in writing, loans under the Moneylenders Act and bills of sale.

The terms of a contract must be certain. (This means that they should not be vague or ill-defined.) The acceptance of its terms must be absolute and must correspond with the terms of the offer.

In contracts for the sale of goods there are certain implied conditions: that the seller has the right to sell (or, in an agreement to sell, that he will have the right to sell the goods at the time the property is to pass); a warranty that the goods are free from any charge or encumbrance not disclosed or known to the buyer before the contract is made; where there is a sale by description there is an implied warranty that the goods shall correspond with the description; and if the sale is by sample and description it is not enough that the goods correspond with the sample , if they do not also correspond with the description. The goods must also be of saleable quality (called 'merchantable quality' by lawyers).

Exclusion Clauses

The Unfair Contract Terms Act 1977 protects one from any 'exclusion clauses' used by the firms that provide services. The Act makes any clause ineffective which a firm may put in its forms or notices to try to exclude or limit its liability for death or injury caused by its negligence. Additionally, any clause about 'not accepting responsibility for other loss or damage caused through negligence' will only be effective if the firm can prove in Court that the clause is 'reasonable'.

The Act also covers the sort of dispute which could arise if a firm tries to use its contract as a defence if it is complained that they haven't provided the standard of service promised.

The Act provides added protection when goods are bought; for example, it makes it impossible for a guarantee to limit a manufacturer's liability for any damage, loss, death or injury arising from a defect in the goods, caused by negligence.

WILLS

General

A will must be in writing, signed at the foot or end by the testator (the person making the will) in the presence of two witnesses present at the same time. The witnesses must then sign in the presence of the testator.

No will may be altered in any way and still be valid unless the alteration is signed and witnessed in the same way as the original will.

The sample will form shown here is intended for guidance only. Note that a will (or codicil) may be revoked by another will or codicil, or by destruction, or by marriage,

and that revocation may be conditional (for instance upon the happening of some event). For a will to be revoked by destruction it must be burned, torn or otherwise destroyed by the testator, or by some person in his presence and by his instruction, and with the intention of revoking it.

A legacy or bequest lapses if the beneficiary (the person named in the will to take) dies before the testator. The property that would have gone to her passes under any general or residuary gift in the will.

Intestacy (Where no will has been made)

If a person dies and leaves no effective will, then all property (which does not already consist of money) is held on trust for sale. Out of the sum produced from the sale, the personal representative must pay all funeral and administration of estate expenses, debts and other liabilities. Then the rest of the money must go to the persons who are said to be beneficially entitled.

Widows and widowers have equal rights which vary according to the categories of other surviving members of the intestate's family.

If the intestate leaves no children and no parent, brother or sister or child of a brother or sister, the widow or widower takes whatever is left after the other expenses and debts have been met.

If the intestate dies leaving children, the widow or widower takes the following interests:

a) The furniture, horses, cars, plate, books, jewellery, wines and

b) £25,000 absolutely free of death duties.

c) A life interest (for as long as she or he lives) in half the left over property.

A widow or widower has the first claim to administer the estate. Letters of Administration will generally have to be taken out unless the estate is very small. (A solicitor or the neighbourhood law centre can advise on procedure.)

Sample Will

This is a typical will. Other basic will forms can be obtained from Oyez Publishing Ltd., Norwich House, 14/15 Norwich Street, London, EC4A 1AB.

THIS IS THE LAST WILL of me (name) of (address) whereby I REVOKE all former wills or codicils heretofore made by me

1. I APPOINT (name) of (address) and (name) of (address) to be Executors hereof.
2. I DESIRE that my body (instructions for burial/cremation) ...
3. I GIVE the following legacies:

4. I GIVE DEVISE AND BEQUEATH the residue of my estate to:

5. LASTLY I DECLARE that any Executor being a Solicitor may act and be paid for any business or act done by him or his firm in connection with the administration of my estate though not of a professional nature.

IN WITNESS whereof I have hereunto set my hand this day of One Thousand Nine Hundred and

SIGNED by the said in the presence of us who in her presence and in that of each other have hereunto subscribed our names as witnesses:

The will may of course be adapted to meet one's individual wishes.

Children's rights
The children ((issue) who may be illegitimate or adopted) of an intestate have the following rights. Subject to the rights of the surviving spouse (husband or wife of the deceased) the property is held on what are called special statutory trusts for all the children of the intestate who are living at his death, in equal shares, but qualified as follows:
- A surviving child of a deceased child (who would be the intestate's grandchild) would take the deceased child's share.
- The child will get his interest (the legal term is that the interest will vest) when he is eighteen or marries.
- The child must bring into account any money or property which by way of advancement or at his marriage, the intestate had paid him or settled for his benefit, if he wants to share in the distribution of the estate.

Other rules apply in cases of partial intestacy.

Provisos
There are provisos to the above rules. Despite

the terms of the will or the effect of the intestacy rules, some persons may apply to the Court for financial provision to be made for them under a 1975 Act. These persons include a husband or wife, a child (including an illegitimate and adopted child) and anyone who was being maintained by the deceased. The Court may order reasonable provision for maintenance to be made out of the net estate. Application must be made to the Court not later than six months after the grant of probate or Letters of Administration. However, the Court has discretion to permit a later application if it thinks fit.

The maintenance may take the form of a payment of a lump sum or periodic payments.

The Court must consider the real needs of the applicant and the needs of the beneficiaries, the deceased's responsibility towards the applicant and the beneficiaries, the size of the estate and any particular disability of the applicant or the beneficiaries and, finally, the conduct of the applicant.

PROBATE

The two executors named in a will are responsible for administering the estate of the deceased. This means that they must gather the assets, pay the taxes and debts, and distribute the remainder (called the residue) of the estate according to the terms of the will. Usually the executors apply for a grant of probate.

Some assets can be handed over to the executors only on production of probate. It is obtained from the Probate Registry (which is listed under Probate in the phone book) or, where the net value of the estate is below £2000, from the County Court, and is the responsibility of the executors who may either apply for probate themselves or employ a solicitor. It can take a year to wind up an estate. It will take longer if a will is contested.

Proving a will or obtaining Letters of Administration in the cases of intestacy is not expensive, and it may not be necessary to use the services of a solicitor. The Probate Office staff are generally helpful and will explain procedure. The deceased person's property may not be sold or given away until probate has been granted or Letters of Administration have been granted. The personal representative must inform the bank of the death and it will stop payment on all bankers orders and cheques.

The main grounds for contesting any will are that it was not properly executed, that it lacks the testator's knowledge and approval, that he was not of sound mind or that the will was obtained by grave or undue influence.

CAPITAL TRANSFER TAX

This tax acts as a gift tax and estate duty. It has a wider application than estate duty because it applies to gifts a person has made during his lifetime, as well as to possessions left on his death. Everything he owns can count as taxable gifts where they're given away. When a person dies he is then considered to give away everything he then owns. There are tax-free gifts – those which are tax-free whenever they are made, those which are tax-free only if made on death, and those which are tax-free only if made in life.

Tax-free Gifts

Gifts tax-free in life and on death include:
- Gifts made between spouses.
- The first £100,000 of gifts to charities and to political parties.
- Gifts made to specified national institutions (such as the National Trust).
- Treasury-approved gifts such as historic buildings, works of art.

Gifts tax-free on death only
- Reasonable funeral expenses.
- Generally, lump sums paid to a person's dependants from his employer's pension scheme on his death.

Gifts tax-free in life only include:
- Gifts made out of income which represent part of usual spending. The proviso to this gift being tax free is that the donor, despite making the gift, can keep up his usual standard of living out of his income.
- Gifts of up to £100 each to any number of people in each tax year.
- Gifts to maintain any of one's own or one's wife's elderly (65 or over) or infirm relatives, or to maintain a widower, separated or divorced mother or mother-in-law.
- Gifts of up to £5000 if one is the parent of the bride or groom, £2500 if one is a grandparent or great-grandparent of a bride or groom, or £1000 if one is any other person.
- Up to £2000 worth of gifts during any tax year which are not otherwise tax-free. When one does not use the whole tax-free quota in one tax year, what remains can be carried over to the next tax year.

How much tax is due

The tax due depends on whether the gift is made during one's life or on one's death, or within three years of death.

Gifts made during a person's life
Tax is calculated on the amount by which the donor (the giver) loses as a result of making the gift.

Gifts made on death
The value of any taxable gifts made at a person's death is added to the running total (which includes any tax he had paid up to his death) and tax is charged on them at the prescribed rate.

For totals between £25,000 and £310,000, tax is charged at a higher rate for gifts made on death (or within three years of death) than for gifts made at least three years prior to death.

What happens where the donor dies within three years of making a taxable gift?

The donee (the person who receives the gift) may have to pay some extra tax – the difference between the tax due on the gift using column A of Table 4.1 and the tax due, using column B. If the rates of tax change between the date of the gift and the date of death, the extra tax will be based on the differential between the tax due using column A at the old rates and the tax using column B at the new rates (see Table 4.1).

There are situations in which the above rules do not apply and professional advice should be sought; the main categories are if a farm, woodland or business is owned, where trusts and settlements are involved, or a husband or wife lives abroad.

When does the tax have to be paid?

Gifts during the donor's life
With gifts made between October 1 and April 5, the tax is due six months after the end of the month in which the gift is made. Where a gift is made after April 5 but before October 1, the tax is due on April 30 of the next year. If the tax is remitted late, interest is charged at a rate of nine per cent from the due date.

It is the donor's duty to tell the tax people about any taxable gifts he makes. He should supply the information on form C5 obtainable from the Capital Taxes Offices:

England and Wales: Lynwood Road, Thames Ditton, Surrey, KT7 0EB.

Northern Ireland: Law Courts Buildings, Chichester Street, Belfast, BT1 3NU.

Scotland: 16 Picardy Place, Edinburgh, EH1 3HB.

Gifts made on death
Tax on these is due six months from the end of the month in which the donor died. In the event that the value of the estate isn't proven during that time, the tax will be calculated on an estimated value and later adjusted when the true figure is known. If tax is remitted late, interest is charged at a rate of six per cent a year from the due date.

Table 4.1 *Rates of capital transfer tax*

Tax on gifts made during one's life, calculated on grossed-up value of gifts, and tax on possessions left on death

running total of taxable gifts (including any tax paid by one so far) [1]	total tax due for gifts made during life [2]	on each £ over	up to	A rate of tax for gifts made during life [2]	B rate of tax for gifts on death
Under £25,000	nil	£0	£25,000	nil	nil
£25,000	nil	£25,000	£30,000	5%	10%
£30,000	£250	£30,000	£35,000	7½%	15%
£35,000	£625	£35,000	£40,000	10%	20%
£40,000	£1,125	£40,000	£50,000	12½%	25%
£50,000	£2,375	£50,000	£60,000	15%	30%
£60,000	£3,875	£60,000	£70,000	17½%	35%
£70,000	£5,625	£70,000	£90,000	20%	40%
£90,000	£9,625	£90,000	£110,000	22½%	45%
£110,000	£14,125	£110,000	£130,000	27½%	50%
£130,000	£19,625	£130,000	£160,000	35%	55%
£160,000	£30,125	£160,000	£210,000	42½%	60%
£210,000	£51,375	£210,000	£260,000	50%	60%
£260,000	£76,375	£260,000	£310,000	55%	60%
£310,000	£103,875	£310,000	£510,000	60%	60%
£510,000	£223,875	£510,000	£1,010,000	65%	65%
£1,010,000	£548,875	£1,010,000	£2,010,000	70%	70%
Over £2,010,000	£1,248,875	£2,010,000		75%	75%

[1] Including value of possessions left on death (but *not* any tax due on them), if tax on death is being worked out
[2] Provided gift is made at least three years before death; for gifts made within three years of death, use column B to work out tax due

(Reproduced by courtesy of the Consumers' Association.)

Tax by instalments
There are circumstances in which tax can be paid by instalments – over eight years.

How Capital Transfer Tax can be saved

- If a running total of the taxable gifts made is kept, it is possible to work out how much tax will be payable on any new gift.
- Advantage should be taken of the £100 tax-free gifts.
- Husband and wife can divide their possessions – each is allowed £25,000 worth of taxable gifts before any tax is payable.
- Check that one's will does save Capital Transfer Tax.
- A beneficiary under a will can get together with the other beneficiaries and if in accord, can change the will within two years of the death (making a deed of family arrangement).
- A husband and wife will pay less tax in the end if they leave their possessions to their children rather than to each other.
- On a life insurance policy, on one's life in favour of another. The proceeds are not taxable.
- Tax can usually be saved by making gifts

at least three years before death, so one needs a long term policy regarding gifts.

UNFAIR DISMISSAL

In the case of an old person requiring long periods of home care, many persons responsible for that care need to take a lot of time off work. Some employers are very tolerant and allow for reasonable periods of absence to take care of a disabled or infirm person. However, some firms are not so considerate.

The following gives some basic information on the law on unfair dismissal. Before an employee is entitled to make a complaint of unfair dismissal, he or she must have worked for an employer for six months and for at least sixteen hours a week. If an employer employs no more than three persons, including the complainant, the employer is excluded from having to comply with the law as it stands.

Unfair dismissal can occur under three heads: where one is sacked from one's job; where one was employed for a fixed period and the contract was not renewed; and where an employee has handed in notice because the employer had changed the terms of the contract without first consulting him or her.

There are three months from the date the notice to quit expired, or from the date one left the job (if earlier), in which to make a complaint to the tribunal.

THE LEGAL PROCEDURE INVOLVED IN BUYING A HOUSE

See page 163.

INSURANCE

Insurance for One's Possessions

For the best policy one should 'shop around'. Insurance policies must periodically be reviewed. The replacement value of all per-

sonal effects or goods and chattels should be worked out and insured accordingly. A house should be insured to cover the full rebuilding costs, taking inflationary trends into account.

Insurance for Personal Injuries

There are home owners' policies which cover injuries to persons on one's premises. When travelling, insurance should be taken out against personal injury.

Private Insurance for Illness

Cover for the expenses of illness, generally for those who prefer private medical treatment, can be provided through at least three large providential associations. Each association has different schemes to meet different circumstances. These societies are:

British United Provident Association
Provident House
Essex Street
London WC2R 3AX. 01–353 9451

The Provident Association for Medical Care
Eynsham House, Tunbridge Wells
Kent TN1 2PL. 0892–26255

The Western Provident Association
Culver House
Culver Street
Bristol BS1 3JE. 0272–23495

Life Insurance

These policies are available under:
Term Insurance – which will cover a person against death within a pre-selected period, and gives no money back where the insured survives longer than that period.
Endowment Insurance – this is where the company chosen pays out at the end of the pre-selected term or on earlier death.
Whole Life Assurance – is where the sum assured is paid when one dies. The family will benefit under this scheme (assuming that they are the beneficiaries).

The money a policy pays out at maturity is generally tax-free (see page 154).

The main disadvantage of an insurance policy is that the insured cannot draw out her money in case of emergency; she must wait until the policy matures or is payable, for any benefit to accrue. Therefore, not all savings should be put into life insurance. It is prudent to place some money in a building society or a Post Office account, where it is readily accessible.

LEGAL ADVICE AND LEGAL AID

Some persons let others infringe their legal rights because they are afraid of the legal machinery and the cost. There is now a system called 'fixed fee interviews', through which some solicitors will give anyone on a reasonable income an initial half hour interview for £5, inclusive of VAT. Therefore, where it is necessary to consult a solicitor, it should first be ascertained which solicitors will give such an interview and choose one from among them.

Where persons are in receipt of a supplementary pension, or their income (this means disposable income) and savings (disposable capital) are small, it is possible to get free or low-cost legal advice and Legal Aid. The CAB or Law Centre staff will know which solicitor to consult.

Among the many cases upon which one would be well advised to consult a solicitor are: drawing up a will; where there is a dispute between a landlord and tenant; and where a case has to be prepared for a tribunal. The scheme under which this advice may be given freely or cheaply is known as the 'Green Form' scheme.

The procedure used to determine whether or not you would qualify under the scheme is to:
• Add up all savings (including money in the building society, Post Office and bank, plus any other investments and add to it the equity you own in your house, less £6000. If you are married, all savings belonging to your husband or wife must be included in the total.
• When you have your total, subtract certain amounts (check with the solicitor what these are) for any dependants you support.
• The remainder is called 'disposable capital', and if it is less than £340 a first condition for qualification has been met.
• The next step is to check your disposable income. A second condition will have been satisfied if your income is at the general level of supplementary benefit or supplementary pension.

Where both conditions are satisfied, you will qualify. Note that if your income is higher than that stated above you may still qualify for free legal help, or at any rate for help at a lower level.

In the case of Legal Aid, to support legal representation the solicitor will send off an application to the Law Society. The DHSS will check income and savings and inform the Law Society whether or not you qualify. The Law Society will then decide whether or not the case you wish to bring or defend should be supported by public funds. If it decides that it should, you will be told how much you have to pay. If you don't have anything to pay, you will be given a Legal Aid certificate.

It is important to note that you may have to pay some contribution from your savings and from your income to get Legal Aid.

Where to Go for Other Legal Help
Citizens Advice Bureaux – legal advice is available from some CABs from 'honorary legal advisers'. These are local solicitors who work on a rota system to give advice at the CAB. Solicitors who work in this way are allowed to transfer cases to their own offices as necessary, when the person seeking advice will become responsible for the solicitors charges (these are recoverable by Legal Aid). Any interview with a solicitor at a CAB, however, is absolutely free. You usually have to make an appointment to see a lawyer, unless times are stated on a notice about

legal sessions, when you can just go along and wait your turn.

Legal Advice Centres – this kind of centre is usually run by volunteer lawyers and is only open at certain times during the week. Those needing advice should phone first to make an appointment. Bear in mind that the advice given at these centres normally deals with legal advice and the writing of certain letters, and they do not normally take on Court actions.

Law Centres – these are for those living in the vicinity of the centre, as a general rule, and advice given there is free of charge. Court actions can be dealt with, with or without Legal Aid and the centres are open during normal office hours, and some evenings.

LEGAL FEES INSURANCE

Did you know that you can take out an insurance policy for a premium of £15 a year, to cover any legal fees you may incur either by bringing an action or by defending an action? The following insurance company offers the policy:

DAS Legal Expenses Co. Ltd,
116 Finchley Road, London, NW3. 01–435 8431
1268 London Road, London, SW16. 01–679 1744

LEGAL AID OFFICES

Reproduced by courtesy of the Legal Aid Headquarters, Chancery Lane, London.

Legal Aid Offices

Normally you should telephone one of these offices rather than send an applicant personally.

BIRMINGHAM
Podium, Centre City House,
(Smallbrook Queensway),
5 Hill Street,
Birmingham, B5 4UD.
021–632 6541

BRIGHTON
9–12 Middle Street,
Brighton, BN1 1AS.
0273 27003

BRISTOL
98 Pembroke Road,
Bristol, BS8 3EH.
0272 38784

CAMBRIDGE
Leda House,
Station Road,
Cambridge, CB1 2RF.
0223 66511

CARDIFF
Arlbee House,
Greyfriars Road,
Cardiff, CF1 3JP.
0222 388971

CHESTER
North West House,
City Road,
Chester, CH1 3AL.
0244 23591

COLCHESTER
Fairfax House,
North Station Road,
Colchester, CO1 1QJ.
0206 5003

GILLINGHAM
55 Green Street,
Gillingham, Kent.
0634 53781

KINGSTON-UPON-THAMES
59 High Street,
Kingston-upon-Thames, KT1 1LX
01–546 7244

LEEDS
City House,
New Station Street,
Leeds, LS1 4JS.
0532 42851

LIVERPOOL
Moor House,
James Street,
Liverpool, L2 7SA.
051–236 8371

LONDON
29/37 Red Lion Street,
London, WC1R 4PP.
01–405 6991

MANCHESTER
Pall Mall Court,
67 King Street,
Manchester, M60 9AX.
061–832 7112

NEWCASTLE-UPON-TYNE
18 Newgate Shopping Centre,
Newcastle-upon-Tyne, NE1 5RU.
0632 23461

NOTTINGHAM
5 Friar Lane,
Nottingham, NG1 6BW.
0602 42341

PLYMOUTH
Mayflower House,
178 Armada Way,
Plymouth, Devon, PL1 1LE.
0752 63076

PRESTON
Unicentre,
Lords Walk,
Preston, PR1 3LB.
0772 55042

READING
Crown House,
10 Crown Street,
Reading, RG1 2SJ.
0734 53086

SOUTHAMPTON
Brunswick House,
8/13 Brunswick Place,
Southampton, SO9 3JF.
0703 27537

STOKE-ON-TRENT
Norwich Union House,
40 Trinity Street, Hanley,
Stoke-on-Trent, ST1 5LS.
0782 23734

Chapter 5
Isolation

ISOLATION ADVICE

It is important to find the cause, or causes, if an elderly person becomes isolated and the health visitor (see page 21) or social worker (see page 14) are the best people to approach initially. If there are other professionals who are trusted by the elder they may be able to throw a light on any psychological reasons why the elder has become isolated; the district nurse (see page 21) and the home help (see page 16) are two people who usually know the elderly person they visit very well. The health visitor and social worker may help you organise ways of overcoming the isolation but you will have to do much of this yourself, calling on the whole range of voluntary services (see page 11).

The *Directory for the Disabled*[1] is an excellent book, listing many activities and hobbies for house and people and ideas for helping them reintegrate with normal leisure activities. The domiciliary occupational therapist (see page 23) is able to advise on sport, such as swimming, and leisure opportunities for isolated disabled people in the elder's locality.

THE PREVENTION OF ISOLATION

Isolation can obviously be prevented by the speedy and efficient treatment of the physical disorders which can lead to it, but it is also possible to prevent isolation by tackling the social factors which cause a person to become isolated. Retirement inevitably means a reduction in the number of social engagements, but it also offers more time and opportunity for the development of new interests. The death of friends is undoubtedly depressing but new friendships can be made in old age. New friendships cannot replace those lost, for each friendship is unique, but they can prevent isolation.

The number of hobbies and leisure activities open to elderly people is uncountable. Even in small towns, new societies and special interest groups spring up continually. Although many activities are for able bodied people, there has been a tremendous increase in the activities open to people who are disabled. Much of this increase has been due to the initiative of young disabled people, but the opportunities they have created are also open to disabled older people. In addition to hobbies, sporting opportunities are more open than they have ever been before. The local Age Concern office will know of the leisure activities for old people. The domiciliary occupational therapist is also aware of the sport and leisure facilities for disabled people, and the public library should have a list of all local clubs and societies.

Although we have emphasised that many of the 'differences' between old and young people exist only in the minds and attitudes of both old and young, and we have described the social gap between old and young as being largely artificial, our elders are a different generation. They have all shared experiences which we have not, and these experiences have left them with memories and attitudes which are different from our own. It can be very supportive for a person who is losing contact with workmates or losing friends through death, to join in

[1] *Directory for the Disabled*, compiled by Ann Darnborough and Derek Kinrade, Woodhead Faulkner, in association with the Multiple Sclerosis Society of Great Britain and Northern Ireland.

activities with other people of her own generation. This is a big step to take, requiring the elder to admit her age. Many old people say that activities run by and for old people are 'not for me, I'm not that old', although they would like to participate. This is an attitude which has to be admitted before it can be discussed, and it has to be discussed before it can be modified. Old people's clubs have a 'tea and bingo' image, and it is true that some clubs often still follow this pattern, to the enjoyment of their members. An increasing number of clubs, however, are moving away from this pattern to become much livelier, organising trips and holidays, aiming to achieve social and political change, and generally trying to harness the skills of retired people and reinforce their self-confidence. Saga Holidays now organise holidays for people over retirement age, providing them with a chance to meet and form friendships with other people of the same age. (Saga Holidays, 119 Sandgate Road, Folkestone, Kent.)

A growing number of educational opportunities open up each year, from those run by community centres and colleges of further education, to the Open University. Some courses are offered at cheaper rates to retired people. The public library should have the details of all the further educational opportunities. The *Directory for the Disabled* has a useful list of all the educational, leisure, holiday and sport facilities, and many of these are suitable for disabled elderly people as well as young people

People who are retired have more time to help others. Children, disabled people and other deprived groups all benefit from closer involvement with old people. The job which will suit an elder best depends on her or his inclination and the local needs. In every large town and county there is a Council for Social Service, or a Council for Voluntary Service which places volunteers in a job to suit them (see page 13).

With all these opportunities, and the chance to offer more help to their families, it seems surprising that people should become

isolated, even if they become disabled, but some do. It is important to take action early to prevent isolation. Pre-retirement courses help some people think of such opportunities, but not all workers are fortunate enough to receive preparation for retirement. Some people say that even preparation for retirement is too late, that the prevention of isolation should start with an outgoing interested approach to life in the early years of adulthood. It is true that those people who have always been keen to learn new skills, and explore new possibilities as children and young adults, appear to adapt better to change and avoid isolation. We believe that it is also true that virtually every old person is capable of learning and changing more than he or she believes and that, no matter what their background may be, new interests can be started, new friendships formed and isolation prevented much more frequently than is thought possible.

THE EFFECTS OF ISOLATION

In our opinion isolation is one of the greatest problems affecting old people. Isolation causes not only great distress, but can lead to physical and mental illness. Unfortunately it often goes unrecognised; bad housing can be seen; poverty can be imagined; cold can be felt; but no one who has not been isolated can appreciate its effects. There are a number of factors which make old people more likely to be isolated than younger members of society. Retirement results in a loss of contacts with colleagues; the decrease in income means that the old person is limited in the amount of entertaining they can afford; and the mobility of many old people is reduced, as they can no longer afford to run a car and have to depend on shrinking public transport services; many become immobilised by disease (see page 59) and some begin to think that they are uninteresting to younger people.

To judge whether or not an individual old person is isolated is sometimes difficult. We have been able to give you a room temperature as a standard against which the warmth of the elder's environment can be measured, but we cannot give any standard for isolation. There is no standard number of weekly social contacts below which an old person is isolated, nor is there any number which is satisfactory. The social environment of an old person has to be judged in the light of her past, not set against any average figure. If an old person was born and raised in a large family, had a large family herself and was always meeting and enjoying herself with other people, she may be isolated even though she still has many social engagements, if they are fewer in number than before. In contrast, an old person who 'kept myself to myself' or was 'never much of a one for company' may have very many fewer social engagements, but not be so isolated.

We use the term 'social engagement' in preference to 'social contact' because it is not only the number of people whom the elder meets which is important, but the quality of each meeting. Someone who receives one visit a day from her daughter, who spends an hour talking and listening to her sympathetically, is usually less isolated than if she was receiving four brief visits from people she did not know very well. To prevent isolation it is not enough just to contact other people, it is necessary to engage with other personalities and minds.

It is almost inevitable that a disabled person will have fewer social engagements than she had before she became disabled. The effect of isolation depends on her ability to adapt to her changed circumstances. If they change quickly, for example due to a stroke, it is more difficult to adapt than if she becomes isolated gradually, because of slowly progressing arthritis. Also some people are more adaptable than others and no two people respond in the same way to the same challenge.

The effect of isolation is felt by the old person herself as loneliness. The relationship with loneliness is complicated and can be most simply presented in a table.

	Not isolated	Isolated
Not lonely	A	C
Lonely	B	D

Most of us are in Group A, neither isolated nor lonely, although almost everyone feels lonely sometimes even when surrounded by family and friends, and moves temporarily into Group B. Some unfortunate people of all ages are in Group B all the time and a few elderly people feel lonely even when they have plenty of company, the cause lying more in their personality than in their social environment. Some isolated old people are not lonely, Group C, others are, Group D. It might seem simple to differentiate between these two groups, to decide whether or not an isolated old person felt lonely by asking them, but this is not so.

It is natural to wish only for those things which are within the bounds of possibility, it is too disheartening to wish for the moon all the time. We all live like this, setting our sights realistically, but some elders are even more modest in their hopes and desires. Many old people have been disappointed so often in life – by the War to end all Wars which didn't, by the Homes Fit for Heroes which weren't there, by the General Strike which didn't succeed and by all the other disappointments of their generation – that they no longer have much faith in promises. Many people have asked them what they wanted and made promises but let them down. It is not uncommon for an elder to doubt whether the person who asks if she is lonely will do anything about it, even if she were to admit it. Therefore she does not admit her loneliness to the enquirer, because it makes it easier for her not to admit her loneliness to herself. You may have to judge the effect of isolation on the old person yourself. Anyone can be lonely, no matter how slowly she becomes isolated or how she lived before, but it may take her some time to admit it, even to a son or daughter.

In recent years there has been an upsurge of interest in isolation and a great deal of research has been carried out. The reason for this interest is that isolation is now used as a means of brain-washing prisoners, and is therefore of relevance to 'intelligence services'. Research findings show that after only forty-eight hours in isolation even healthy young men can forget where they are, lose track of time, become depressed and anxious and think people are persecuting them. Elderly people who are housebound are often alone for longer than this, week after week, year after year. An old person who lives far from her family can be alone for seventy hours from Friday lunch-time, when the home help leaves, until Monday morning when she returns. It is not surprising that many old people show these symptoms of isolation, which are sometimes diagnosed as being due to dementia (degeneration of the brain) which produces similar symptoms (see page 106). People who are suffering from dementia often become isolated because they are less interesting to talk to and less rewarding to visit than they were before. The effects of isolation on a person with dementia are even more severe than they are on a person whose brain is functioning normally.

If the isolation lasts for a long time, the effects can be even more damaging. We all remember who we are because other people keep reminding us. They write to us, call us by our name, expect us to turn up in certain places to perform certain tasks, and it is this stimulation and support which keeps our personalities intact. An old person who sees and engages with very few people each day loses this stimulation. Just as bones and muscles waste with disuse, so may the personality waste in isolation.

Nurses who visit isolated old people frequently find that, even if an old person recovers from the illness which was the reason for the initial visit, it is very difficult to stop visiting. The nurse often finds that the old person becomes more disabled when she realises that the nurse is not going to continue her regular visits, and home helps find the same. Old people sometimes burst into tears when they are told that they are 'better', and need no longer return to the out-patient clinic which they have attended regularly and come to regard as a social centre. It has even been known for an elderly hospital patient to rub her leg ulcer against a bedside locker, secretly and without the knowledge of the staff, to prolong her stay in hospital rather than be discharged home to isolation. Isolation can have such terrible effects as these, and an elder can quite unknowingly remain disabled so that their professional helpers, friends and family keep coming to see her. We emphasise that this is usually an unconscious process, the elder does not realise what isolation is doing to her, and what she is doing to prevent isolation.

Isolation can also cause nutritional problems (see page 76).

THE CAUSES OF ISOLATION

It is sometimes said about an old person that she is isolated 'because she wants to be'. This judgement is based on how few wishes she has expressed for more company, but we hope we have described how the stated wishes of an isolated old person can give a false picture of her true feelings. There are, however, some people who become isolated because of their personalities. Not all people are equally interesting or rewarding to talk *to.* Self-centred individuals find plenty of people to talk *at* when they are at work, or able to go out to pubs and parties, but when they are retired and immobilised by disease their situation is very different. They find that other people have never been keen on their company, and now that it is not forced on them they do not seek it out. Occasionally an old person becomes so bound up in her own worries that she becomes unrewarding to visit, although she was previously interesting to talk with, so that she becomes isolated and this gives her another cause for complaint.

People rarely become isolated for psychological reasons; the cause of isolation is usually practical.

The common causes of isolation are:

Incontinence and fear of incontinence (see page 65).

Instability – falling and fear of falling (see page 71).

Immobility (see page 59).

Communication Problems

We are not going to try to tell you how to converse with your father or mother. However, very many people make assumptions about elderly people and talk *to* them rather than conversing *with* them. Other people, including even some who are highly trained, sometimes speak to an elder in a way that is upsetting. You may feel that you wish to correct someone who is making one of the mistakes discussed below, although this can be difficult, but you can very often prevent such problems. For example, if a consultant in geriatric medicine is asked to see your parent or relative, he will find it helpful if you tell him that she is blind, but can hear very clearly. Introduce her by the name you would like him to use when he addresses her. It is important for these mistakes to be prevented whenever possible and picked up quickly if they do occur, because the elder can feel very bitter and resentful if she is addressed like a child or shouted at, and she may refuse any service which is offered to her as a result.

Not all old people are deaf
It is common for people, even those who are used to meeting elderly people, to raise their voices and shout at them. This can both frighten and upset them, but can be prevented if the fact that the elder can hear well is made clear to the person meeting her. However, some elders are hard of hearing and allowance must also be made for this.

Someone who is blind, or disabled in any other way, is not necessarily hard of hearing
Some people tend to shout at people who are visually handicapped or are obviously disabled, and this can be very disturbing. Remember, however, that everyone uses the information given by the face, lips and movements of speakers to understand what they are saying, and those who have lost these visual signals are handicapped. It is often useful to hold the hand of someone who is blind or partially sighted, while speaking to her. This at least allows her to locate the position of the speaker's arm and, by deduction, his body and head, thus permitting the blind person to turn her face or her good ear in the direction of the voice.

In conversation, as in other matters, treat an old person as you would an adult of any age
When an old person makes a mistake, the person with whom she is conversing sometimes lets it pass and does not correct it. We all make mistakes, many of them every day, but most of us manage to remain independent and achieve our objectives in spite of them. This is possible not because we notice and correct our own mistakes, but because others point them out to us, so that we can recognise and correct them. Elderly people who make mistakes are not corrected so frequently. For example, an elder who makes a mistake about the day of the week may not be corrected, the person to whom she is speaking thinking that it is kinder and more considerate not to tell an old person she is wrong, although he would immediately correct his wife or any other young person who made the same mistake. The elder, therefore, is allowed to remain in error. This happens all the time. Some staff in institutions answer 'Yes, yes' or 'oh really' to whatever an elder says and hurry on with their work. It is much quicker to do this, but it is a mark of disrespect to the elder and not a kindness. It can have serious consequences. An elder who is never corrected strays further and further from reality.

This tendency of *hearing* elderly people

talking without *listening* to what they are saying becomes most pronounced when it is said that the elder is 'demented' or 'confused'. Dementia and confusion do occur, and an old person may indeed say things that do not appear to be relevant, but they should be listened to with care and every effort should be made to correct mistakes, otherwise the symptoms will inevitably become worse. If someone persists in repeating something, it can be tiring and depressing to have to keep making the same correction, apparently without effect. In such a situation a determined effort has to be made to change the subject in the old person's mind (see page 112).

One distressing mistake is when an elderly person loses her pension book or some other valuable and says someone has stolen it – perhaps even accusing you, the home help or the district nurse. This can be very upsetting, especially if the home help then threatens to leave. Again, it is necessary to argue with the old person if you think she has lost it, to say that there is nothing wrong in losing things and to help her look for the lost article.

Elderly people do not have a second childhood and should not be spoken to like children

It is true that they often speak of the 'old days' and remember events of long ago better than those which happened in the last week or month. This is not because they go back into the past, but because they remember recent events less clearly. There are a number of reasons for this. The brain retains impressions less effectively as it ages, and childhood memories have been remembered more often than recent memories, therefore the brain remembers them more accurately because it has had more practice. Also, recent events to housebound people are often less memorable than the exciting events of their youth. For these reasons an old person may recall his youth better than his recent past, but he is not in a second childhood.

People are sometimes familiar with old people, calling them 'gran' or 'my duck'. Some do not mind this but, for others, this familiarity is offensive and they would much prefer to be called by their title – Mr, Mrs or Miss – and surname. Even worse is to call them a 'lovely baby' or a 'naughty little boy' and you may have to correct someone who speaks like this. This can be difficult, for the person is often doing it kindly and as a sign of affection. Remember that babies are incontinent and people treated as babies may become incontinent also.

Never allow the elderly person to be discussed in the third person in her presence

No matter how confused or unwell the elder might appear, try to draw her into the conversation. If this is impossible or appears to be so, and the doctor wishes to discuss something with you, ask if you can leave the elder's presence. People sometimes appear unconscious, but are able to hear and understand.

Finally, we would emphasise that an old person is almost always capable of a higher intellectual level of conversation than is demanded of her. It does her no harm to be stretched in discussion and, in fact, it can do a great deal of good. Make use of the storehouse of memories about her past, which is our past also. An old person's memories of the First World War, or the General Strike, or just about her childhood and times gone by, are as good as any history textbook or biography. In fact they are an essential complement to the more formal historical records. This is now widely recognised, and in many parts of the country there are 'oral history groups' whose members tape-record the memories of elders. If an old person can remember her past and enjoys doing so, ask the local museum if there is such a group. Encourage the elder to write her autobiography, which might be of interest to a local school as well as being of great interest to herself and her family.

Some old people have special difficulty with communication due to brain disease, which requires an understanding of the process of communication on the part of the helpers.

Human communication has a number of steps:

1) Understanding that certain collections of sounds and printed marks are words.
2) Remembering what the words heard and read mean.
3) Remembering the meaning of the grammar in which the words are set.
4) Thinking of an appropriate response.
5) Remembering the rules of grammar.
6) Remembering the appropriate words.
7) Forming the words either as speech or writing.

The first three steps are sometimes called the receptive stage and the last four the expressive stage of communication. These steps are carried out in separate areas of the brain which are connected by nerve pathways, in the same way as telephone exchanges are connected by cables. If these areas or the connecting nerves are damaged, the ability to communicate is affected. The diseases which most commonly affect the brain's ability to communicate are dementia (see page 104), stroke (see page 61) and Parkinson's disease (see page 62). Drugs can also affect the ability to communicate. The individual areas or any combination may be affected or, in the most severe cases, all these areas are affected. More simply it can be said that disorders of communication are either mainly receptive or mainly expressive, or a mixture of both types.

The consequences of an inability to communicate are not only depression and isolation, but also frustration and anger, especially if the disorder is mainly expressive. If an elder cannot understand what is being said to her she may be upset, or she may not even be able to think about being upset. (Remember that someone who has difficulty communicating with others may have the same difficulty communicating with herself.) On the other hand an elder who can understand what is being said to her, and can think of an appropriate response, will almost certainly become frustrated when she cannot translate her response into words and sentences. The frustration may be replaced by depression, if the elder gives up attempting to communicate his responses after a number of failures.

There are a number of common types of error. The elder may repeat the single word required as an answer, for example saying 'Yes, yes, yes, yes'. She may answer a question with exactly the same answer she gave to the previous question. She may be unable to remember one word or may substitute a wrong word for the one she wishes. The harder she tries the more upset she becomes.

Speech problems require expert assessment. If the elder has been admitted to hospital, or is attending day hospital, she may have been seen by a speech therapist. You can ask the Sister if she has been assessed. If so, you can arrange an interview with the speech therapist, who usually asks to see an elder's family and supporters as soon as she has assessed her problem. She may suggest cards with pictures and key phrases on them, which allow the elder to point to what she wants. The most important aid a speech therapist can give, however, is her advice to you. People who have had their power of communication affected can be greatly helped by the right approach and the correct sort of practice.

The basic principles of communication are simple:

- Speak slowly and clearly and allow the affected person to speak slowly too. Don't interrupt if you think you can see what she is trying to say – offering a wrong word can upset a train of thought.
- Remember that badly fitting false teeth, visual and hearing problems, can aggravate communication difficulties.
- Never forget that the elder's intelligence may be less damaged than their ability to communicate, so that even if she sounds as though she is thinking simply she may not be, and will be upset if people speak to her like a child.
- Try to be sensitive to the emotional upsets which are inevitable results of problems in

communication. Be sensitive but try not to get too upset yourself. The day to day support of a health visitor, district nurse, social worker or home help can be of great assistance.

- The powers of recovery are almost always underestimated by members of the public. Encourage the elder to practise and practise and practise. Listening to the radio, reading aloud, Scrabble, singing and many other opportunities should be made and taken.

A speech therapist will advise you on how these principles apply to your elder's particular problem and she will provide emotional support. In some fortunate areas volunteers run day clubs and organise home visiting for people who have a communication problem, to support and advise their families.

Hearing Problems

It is very common for hearing to start to deteriorate when people are in their sixties, but in only a small proportion does the hearing loss progress to cause extreme difficulty. If hearing loss is suspected at any age help should be sought. This is not always easy to suggest. Hearing loss may first become evident by difficulty in hearing the telephone or the door bell, listening to the radio or television, or in participating in conversation.

Deafness is often treated unsympathetically in our society; people are much less tolerant of someone who is deaf than someone who has failing vision. Because deafness creates social problems, people are sometimes apprehensive of it, and an old person may be reluctant to admit that his hearing is failing because of the fear of rejection or ridicule.

The GP is the first source of help. Some people form wax in the ears quickly and the GP may suggest that either he or the district nurse should syringe the ears regularly. If no reason for deafness can be found, the GP may refer the person to the Ear, Nose and

Throat Department where either surgery or a hearing aid may be suggested. No one should have a hearing loss dismissed as being 'just due to old age'.

Although there are increasing opportunities to operate on part of the hearing mechanism of the ear, hearing aids and lip-reading are the most useful sources of help for most affected people.

Someone who is hard of hearing will be helped if you make sure that he can always see your face clearly in a good light while you are speaking. Keep hands and cigarettes away from the mouth. If his hearing is better in one ear, ask how he would like you to sit to suit him best. Do not speak louder than is necessary as this often distorts both the voice and the speaker's face, and can also frighten or embarrass a deaf person. It is sometimes more helpful to speak slower rather than louder. Lip-reading classes are very useful for people with a hearing loss. The local education authority or voluntary organisations may run lip-reading classes. Some of them make a small charge and details of the classes can usually be obtained from the Town Hall or local authority Social Services Department, the British Association of the Hard of Hearing or the local Centre for the Deaf, which may be listed under 'Deaf' in the phone book.

If the hearing loss is noticeable and communication stressful, the elder should consider obtaining a hearing aid. The National Health Service provides either body-worn aids with the receiver box worn on the chest, or aids which fit behind the ear, but these are not suitable for every type of deafness. The audiologist at the Ear, Nose and Throat Department, or hearing aid technician, will advise on the most suitable aid for any particular patient. Not everyone will be able to benefit from a National Health Service hearing aid and some may have to buy a hearing aid privately. Listed under 'Hearing Aid Suppliers and Dispensers' in the yellow pages are a number of firms offering different aids, but some of these are no better than the National Health Service aids. The

Hearing Aid Council, under which all private dispensers must by law be registered, will provide a list of firms in any locality. The Department of Prices and Consumer Protection will give advice in respect of complaints about commercial hearing aid dispensers. When consulting a dispenser, the potential customer may wish to take along a friend who has normal hearing, and should insist on a trial period with the aid before purchasing. It should be borne in mind that a representative may call if one answers newspaper advertisements for hearing aids. If only because commercial hearing aids are generally expensive, it is essential to seek medical advice and to see if a National Health Service hearing aid can help before purchasing a commercial model.

It is not uncommon to find difficulties initially in learning to use a hearing aid but, after a time, it will become an invaluable source of help. Batteries and leads wear out and require replacing. People with a National Health Service aid can obtain batteries and leads from their local hearing aid centre, who usually offer a postal service. Hearing aid technicians will check the aid to ensure that it is properly adjusted and this should be done regularly. Batteries, leads and servicing of the National Health Service aids are provided free of charge. However, if it is a privately purchased aid, charges will be made for servicing, batteries and any other repairs or replacements, unless the repair is necessary because of faulty manufacture.

People can learn from other people who are hard of hearing, and many find it a great help to meet others at a hard of hearing club, a centre for the deaf or at a lip-reading class. Hearing aids do not restore full function, and everyone who is given a hearing aid will benefit from learning to lip-read.

There are practical aids and means of help. Telephones can be amplified and there are door and telephone bells which can flash as well as ring, adaptations to the radio and television to increase volume, and many others. The Royal National Institute for the Deaf has a technical department which can provide information leaflets on request, and the local Social Services Department may be able to arrange for an aid to be supplied.

Some Social Services Departments have a specialist social worker for the deaf. She can give advice on aids and whether they can be supplied by the department under the Chronically Sick and Disabled Persons Act. The social worker can also provide advice to any deaf or hard of hearing person and his family. She may be able to provide an interpreting service, that is, sign language or lip-reading for important interviews which the deaf person has to attend. Sometimes interpreting services are provided by voluntary organisations. If there are any difficulties in making contact with social workers with the deaf, write for futher information either to the National Council for Social Workers with the Deaf or to the Royal National Institute for the Deaf. The British Deaf Association and the British Association of the Hard of Hearing can inform you about local societies, clubs and other services.

Useful Addresses

Hearing Aid Council,
40A Ludgate Hill,
London, EC4A 7DE.

Royal National Institute for the Deaf,
105 Gower Street,
London, WC1E 6AH.

National Council for Social Workers with the Deaf,
Alban Deaf Association,
1 Old Bedford Road,
Luton, Beds.

British Deaf Association,
38 Victoria Place,
Carlisle, CA1 1EX.

British Association of the Hard of Hearing,
General Secretary,
16 Park Street,
Windsor,
Berks, SL4 1LU.

Visual Problems

If an old person's vision starts to fail, the first step is to make an appointment with the GP. He will probably look into the eyes with an ophthalmoscope to exclude any serious underlying eye disease, and then refer his patient to an ophthalmic optician or ophthalmic medical practitioner.

Opticians are listed under two headings in the yellow pages – Ophthalmic Opticians and Dispensing Opticians. Ophthalmic opticians are qualified to examine the eyes and test the ability to focus clearly, a procedure called refraction. Ophthalmic opticians can also supply the appropriate lenses depending on the results of their examination, and they are trained in the recognition of eye diseases. These they must refer back to the GP for him to refer to the hospital doctor specialising in eye diseases, who is called an ophthalmologist. In emergencies the optician may refer the patient directly to hospital, having informed the GP by telephone to avoid any delay. If an optician finds a disease that the GP has missed, this does not imply that the GP has been negligent. An optician sees very many eyes in comparison with a GP, and may be more practised in the recognition of conditions which require referral.

Dispensing opticians are not qualified to perform refraction. They can only dispense the lenses prescribed and insert them into frames. Usually dispensing opticians work in combination with a doctor who has specialised in eye diseases, called an ophthalmic medical practitioner. He refracts and writes a prescription for the glasses, which the dispensing optician then makes up. The dispensing optician makes all the arrangements for refraction, so it is as simple to consult him as an ophthalmic optician.

The National Health Service allows everyone to have at least one free examination every year. If more are clinically necessary these are, of course, also free. *It is wise for an old person to have his eyes checked at least every two years, whether or not he wears, or thinks he needs, glasses.*

Certain eye diseases occur in old age which have little effect on vision in the early stages, but can have serious and sometimes permanent effects if not detected and treated early. Of course, if vision fails before the two year period has passed since the last examination, another appointment should be made.

Anyone with a sudden loss of vision, blurring or flashing lights, whether it affects one or both eyes, should be taken to the local eye hospital to be seen by the doctor on emergency duty.

The National Health Service does not pay opticians for home visits, but this is not the reason they prefer to see old people in their consulting room! They require the apparatus in their consulting room for full examination and really accurate refraction. It is often possible to find a volunteer to take an old person to the optician if you cannot take him yourself (see page 11). The ambulance service cannot take people to the optician.

Old people who are receiving supplementary pension, and those whose incomes are just a little above this level, are entitled to free spectacles or glasses at a reduced rate, depending on which type of frame is chosen. If the old person thinks he is eligible he should ask the optician for Form F1, the claim form, which should be completed and sent to the Social Security Office. There are a good range of NHS frames, and it is important to ensure that the optician shows all the frames which are available on the NHS. A wide range of frames and lenses can be bought privately. It is possible to have NHS lenses fitted to some private frames, provided that the lens shape and size conform to NHS requirements, in which case the standard NHS lens charge is made. Remember that if an old person does not like any of the frames offered he can ask for the prescription, and look in another optician's stock for frames he prefers.

Frames are expensive. If you are told new lenses are needed, but the old person is satisfied with the frames, the optician can be asked to put the new lenses in the old frames.

There are now many types of lenses available. Lenses are now made in toughened and laminated glass, which break less easily but are heavier than ordinary glass. Plastic lenses can be prescribed on the NHS only for bifocals. Plastic lenses are lighter than glass and don't shatter, but they do scratch easily.

Complaints about optical services provided as part of the National Health Service should be made to the Family Practitioner Committee, which is part of the responsibility of the Area Health Authority, under which its address and telephone number are listed in the white pages of the telephone book. Complaints about private practice should be addressed to:

The Association of Optical Practitioners,
233 Blackfriars Road,
London, SE1 8NW
01-261 9661

Blindness and partial sight
Some people are still unable to read, watch television or walk about with confidence, even after the prescription of glasses and the best treatment possible. People who are blind or partially sighted need extra help. The first step is referral to an ophthalmologist, which can only be arranged by the GP.

The ophthalmologist will ensure that the cause of the visual failure is appropriately treated. Cataract, clouding of the lens of the eye, is a common, treatable cause of visual failure in old age. The clouded lens in cataract can be removed by a simple operation, but it is often sufficient in the early stages of the disease for the old person to have his visual powers accurately assessed, and the correct strength glasses prescribed, to allow him to be independent. Glaucoma is an increase in the pressure in the eyeball. It can be treated and the progress of the disease can be halted by means of tablets and eyedrops. It is particularly important for the old person with glaucoma to take the therapy correctly, but reminders to do so are often necessary (see page 91). Macular degeneration is the third common cause of visual failure.

Treatment has less to offer in this disease, but the old person can often be comforted by the ophthalmologist, because it very rarely leads to complete blindness.

Not only does an ophthalmologist assess whether any further treatment is possible, but he can certify that the person is 'Blind' or 'Partially Sighted'. This certification is sent to the Social Services Department who then place the name they have been sent on either the Blind Register or the Partially Sighted Register. Registration as 'partially sighted' has very few advantages but being on the Blind Register has many, of which the main one is the visit of a social worker. The hospital social worker may be the first contact the person has with the social services. She will ensure that the social worker in the area Social Services Office nearest to the person's home is aware of any particular difficulties created by blindness. The local social worker may help by discussing the difficulties and ways of overcoming them, as she is the link to many practical means of help.

Teachers, rehabilitation officers or technical staff for blind people (the name differs from place to place) help with practical problems, by teaching the blind person how to dress, how to ensure they don't put on odd coloured socks or how to apply make up. They also help with communication, for example by teaching the blind person how to use a tape recorder and introducing him to talking books. The British Talking Book Service provides a wide range of books recorded on special cassettes. The annual subscription is paid either by members of the library or by the local authority Social Services Department or library service. No additional charge is made for the loan of the special play-back machine, which is provided by the library. The cassettes are transmitted free of postal charges.

Under the Chronically Sick and Disabled Persons Act Social Services Departments can pay for telephones for blind people, but in some parts of the country their financial resources are so stretched that they cannot help every applicant. The Telephones for the Blind Fund may be able to help if the Social Services Department cannot.

The social worker or a specialist mobility officer can help with mobility. They can discuss whether a white stick or guide dog would be appropriate, and can arrange training in their use either locally or at a residential social rehabilitation centre.

A number of opportunities are open to registered blind people to help their financial problems. For example they are entitled to a higher level of social security. An Attendance Allowance (see page 140) can be paid to blind people as can an Invalid Care Allowance (see page 142) to their relatives. Blindness by itself is not sufficient reason for the payment of these allowances, but it is an important factor if there are other disabilities. Blind people also have a higher personal income tax allowance.

Spectacles alone may not be sufficient for someone who is partially sighted. He may need one of the new vision aids which are available, such as hand magnifiers, stand magnifiers or telescopes. These can be obtained through the NHS or privately, but as they are expensive it is wise to obtain an expert opinion before spending much money. The Department of Health issues a clearly written leaflet 'Your Sight and the National Health Service' (Leaflet NHS 6).

Emotional problems

Failing vision is just as much an emotional problem as it is physical, and it is common for an old person whose vision starts to fail to suspect and fear that this is the first sign of blindness. Even though blind people are treated with sympathy in our society, the thought of being blind is often terrifying. Only a very small proportion of old people with visual problems go blind, and some of those who are registered as blind retain enough vision to move around the house. However, if the old person does not accept the word of his GP or optician that he is not going blind, it is reasonable to ask his GP if he can be referred to hospital, to be seen by a consultant ophthalmologist who can reassure him. Ophthalmologists know that the emotional consequences of visual failure can be very upsetting. They are sensitive to patients' fears and are keen to reassure them whenever possible.

Even after an old person has been well treated, correctly refracted, and has had the right type of spectacles or aids provided, he often requires considerable emotional and psychological support. It is often difficult to adjust to an aid, or to the changes in vision which always follow a cataract removal. The elder may become depressed, this depression either being directly expressed or resulting in apathy and indifference. If an old person 'gives up' and no longer tries to use the visual powers with which he is left, or the aids he has been given, he may be suffering from depression, and the advice of the elder's GP should be sought (see page 98).

Someone who is unable to see clearly is also more likely to be anxious. He needs more warning when someone approaches him, and cannot see when other people wish to talk to him. All old people need physical contact and comfort, but those who are blind or have poor vision need it even more to comfort them and to inform them where those they are speaking to are sitting.

They are also at greater risk in traffic. It is particularly important that they are given the advice which should be given to every elder: always use crossings, always wear light-coloured clothing, never take a chance.

Useful Addresses

British Telephones for the Blind Fund,
Mynhurst Leigh,
Near Reigate,
Surrey.

British Wireless for the Blind Fund,
226 Great Portland Street,
London, W1N 6AA.

In Touch,
BBC Publications,
PO Box 234,
London, SW1.

A quarterly bulletin is published, available free if four large stamped addressed envelopes are sent to this address, which summarises the information broadcast each week on the excellent radio programme 'In-Touch'.

Partially Sighted Society,
40 Wordsworth Road,
Hove,
Sussex.

Royal National Institute for the Blind,
226 Great Portland Street,
London, W1N 6AA.
A source of information on all problems, including the donation of eyes to help other people.

St. Dunstan's, – for men and women blinded on war service.
191 Old Marylebone Road,
London, NW1 5QN.

The *Directory of Agencies for the Blind*, available in most public libraries, gives details of these and other agencies.

OVERCOMING ISOLATION

The first step in overcoming isolation is to cure or reduce any underlying cause, but even the most skilled medical treatment will not restore to everyone the ability to lead a normal social life. Some old people will always be unable to go out, entertain or communicate as well as they could when they were younger, and a special effort should be made to reduce their isolation.

There are three means by which the effects of isolation can be prevented.

Going Out More Often

Going out has two benefits: not only does the old person see, meet and engage with more people but the change of scenery is itself beneficial. The first objective is to try to restore the elder's previous social links. If she was a regular church attender, ask the minister if a church member could ensure she is taken to and from the service every Sunday, or at least once a month. Remember that people who have been housebound for months or years can become very nervous of going out and meeting people. If an old person appears to be reluctant it is often useful to ask the GP, health visitor or any professional whom she trusts to discuss her fears with her, and try to give her the necessary confidence to face the world again. Remember also that she may feel that her clothes are no longer suitable, so her wardrobe may have to be reviewed and new clothes bought before she has sufficient confidence to go back to church or any other social situation, where she was known when she was younger and less dependant. An old man may benefit greatly by being taken back to the pub at which he was formerly a regular. It may be possible for a regular to collect and return your elder once a week or more often, either in the evening or mid-day – pubs are friendly places at lunch-time. Ask the landlord if he knows of anyone who could help; he may be able to arrange a rota of drivers. If the pub is not too far away a taxi ride is a good investment if it is impossible to arrange voluntary transport.

If it proves impossible to reconnect the broken links, either a day centre or day hospital attendance can be very helpful. Most day centres, whether they are run by Social Services Departments or voluntary organisations, welcome anyone who can reach the centre independently and does not require physical help when there. If, however, transport has to be provided and help needed when at the centre, for example with going to the toilet, it may be necessary to wait before the centre can offer her a place. If a social worker visiting the elder realises how great a problem isolation is, she may suggest visiting a day centre. If there is no social worker visiting, either the old person or you can write directly to the Social Services Department and ask for a place at a day centre, and transport to and from it. If the elder's GP feels that isolation is a significant factor, ask him to write a letter to include with your own or the elder's letter of application. He may think it preferable to refer her to a consultant in geriatric medicine to see whether he thinks she would benefit from attending a day hospital. Like day centres, day hospitals relieve isolation but they also offer medical treatment, as there are always doctors and physiotherapists on the staff.

More Visitors at Home

Neither the health nor social services employ people whose only job is to visit lonely people. Many professionals – especially home helps, social workers, district nurses and health visitors – do, of course, visit isolated people. They do not visit primarily to relieve the elder's isolation. Each goes to perform her special task, for example the home help to help with problems in the home, the social worker to tackle social problems. The company they give to an isolated person is incidental to their special task and they cannot visit regularly solely to relieve isolation, even though they appreciate how serious the problem is.

Regular visiting to relieve isolation is something for relatives, friends and volunteers to do, although volunteers are sometimes less willing to undertake regular home visiting than they are to perform tasks which do not require such a long-term commitment. Some schools, polytechnics, universities and churches do run volunteer visiting schemes, so it is always worthwhile asking the local Age Concern office if such a scheme is in operation. Even where such schemes operate it can be difficult to find a volunteer willing to visit an old person who is self-centred or otherwise unrewarding, week after week. Whether or not you can find a volunteer to help, the main burden of visiting falls on the elder's family. For families there is one piece of advice which seems strange at first sight – the more often you visit an old person the easier it becomes. The more frequently she is visited the less will be the effects of isolation and the more pleasant and rewarding will she be to visit. Also, she will be less tense when

you visit because she will be confident and secure in the knowledge of your early return.

Phone calls and letters supplement personal visits. For very isolated people a daily phone call or note through the post is very therapeutic. Although not inexpensive, the beneficial effects often make the cost insignificant. The installation and rental of a telephone can be paid for by the Social Services Department. In many parts of the country the social services are so short of money that they cannot pay for a telephone for everyone who requests one. Isolation alone is often not enough to qualify for a phone, and it is often necessary to produce evidence that the old person's isolation puts her at medical risk. For example, if an elder suffered acute attacks of heart failure and could not summon help without a phone, the social services department might consider her a suitable case, whereas they would not if she was only isolated and lonely. It is almost always worthwhile applying, although the elderly person may be disappointed. A letter of support from the GP is very helpful when applying to social services for telephone installation and rental. They do not pay the cost of calls.

More Stimulation in the Home

We have emphasised the importance of clocks and calendars elsewhere (page 116), but there are other ways in which a person who is alone can be usefully and helpfully stimulated. Newspapers and magazines are stimulating even if out of date. A neighbour can be asked if she will hand in her paper after she has finished with it, which provides another visit as a bonus. Magazine subscriptions or payment for a daily paper make welcome presents. Libraries sometimes have volunteers who exchange books for housebound readers, not only providing literature but human contact. Old people should be encouraged to record their memories, either by writing or on tape. A cassette recorder makes a good present, enabling the old person to record and exchange messages with relatives and friends, and there are now a number of tape fellowships whose members communicate with one another by exchanging tapes. These are listed in the *Directory for the Disabled* (see page 43)

The importance of pets in the lives of old people is often underestimated. Old people sometimes do not replace a pet which has died because they fear they will not be able to care for it, or dread the thought of another pet dying, but pets should be considered for isolated people. Dogs do require exercise, but cats and budgies do not and are good companions. Cats are especially good, because they touch and can be touched, giving physical comfort as well as companionship. The risk of old people catching diseases from pets is negligible and the pet's diseases can be dealt with by the People's Dispensary for Sick Animals (address in the phone book).

The Social Services Department can pay for the installation, rental and licences of televisions, and can provide radios. If they cannot help, Wireless for the Bedridden Society (20 Wimpole Street, London, W1M 8BQ) may be able to do so. The Society can also provide television sets.

The advice we have given has been set in very general terms. No two people have the same feelings. The severity of an elder's isolation must be judged in the knowledge of her lifestyle and attitudes, and the steps taken to prevent and reduce isolation depend on her personality and wishes.

Chapter 6
Illness and Disability

HEALTH ADVICE

The primary care team – general practitioner (see page 18), health visitor (see page 21) and district nurse (see page 21) – are most important health advisers. If the problem is mainly one of disability and handicap (see page 85), the domiciliary occupational therapist can be consulted (see page 23).

In hospital the Ward Sister is the person to whom enquiries can be most easily addressed (see page 25). If she cannot answer the question she will find a colleague who can. The medical social worker (see page 95) can be consulted if there are any social problems resulting from the illness.

Take Care of Yourself (Allen and Unwin 1979) by D. M. Vickery, J. F. Fries, J. A. M. Gray and S. A. Smail is a useful guide to the treatment of common symptoms and describes general practitioner and other health services in detail. The problem of incontinence is considered in a book of that name written by Dorothy Mandelstam and published by Heinemann in 1977. *Taking Care of Old People at Home* by John Agate (Allen and Unwin 1978) is a good guide to the management of illness at home. Disability and handicap, and the means by which they are overcome, are also discussed in *Caring for Elderly People: Understanding and Practical Help* by S. Hooker (Routledge and Kegan Paul 1976) and in *Coping with Disablement* (Consumers Association 1974). *The Directory for the Disabled* (Woodhead Faulkner Ltd, in association with the Multiple Sclerosis Society of Great Britain and Northern Ireland 1977) lists, with helpful comments, the full range of state and voluntary services for disabled people, and is an excellent directory of sport, leisure and vacation opportunities. *Help for Handicapped People* (Department of Health and Social Security leaflet HBI) which should be available, free, at major Post Offices and Social Security Offices, summarises the available health and social services comprehensively.

If there are serious difficulties in obtaining any of the services we discuss, you can approach the Community Health Council (see page 29) for advice. In Scotland, the Local Health Council serves the same purpose. The Patients Association is based in London but may be able to help if the Community Health Council is unable to do so (see page 30).

In this chapter our aim is not to describe all the symptoms and illnesses which old people may experience. Self-care books such as *Take Care of Yourself* can be used. If in doubt about the seriousness of a symptom experienced by an old person, the advice of the GP or health visitor should be sought.

Our aim is to discuss the common chronic diseases,

Immobility

Incontinence

Instability

Nutritional difficulties in old age

We do not intend to describe all the features of these diseases, for they affect each individual in a different way, but guidelines can be given on what to expect and from whom to seek advice.

We do not include detailed information on drugs or treatment, but we discuss the problems some old people have in remembering to take the drugs and medicines as the doctor intended and the detection of side effects.

We also discuss nursing at home and the needs of an old person when she is admitted to and discharged from hospital, together with ways in which the disabilities caused by chronic illness can be overcome.

IMMOBILITY

It would be unrealistic for every eighty year old person to expect to be able to walk twenty miles, although some are still able to do so, and more. A decrease in personal mobility is inevitable as we grow older. To expect to be as mobile at eighty as one was at twenty will result in disappointment and depression. However, everyone should expect to be able to walk sufficiently well to care for themselves, to shop and to enjoy leisure activities which are reasonable for their age, unless their muscles or joints, or the nervous system which controls and co-ordinates movement, are impaired by illness. Old age alone is not a cause of severe immobility, although the illnesses which occur more commonly in old age can be, if they are not properly diagnosed and treated.

The elder's GP should be consulted if the old person:

- Has become much less mobile over a short period of time, for example in a month or less.
- Has immobility accompanied by pain in the muscles or joints.
- Has become insufficiently mobile to look after himself, for example being unable to reach the lavatory, do housework, prepare food, reach a phone or enjoy his leisure.

Immobility is a serious problem with serious complications. It leads to joint stiffness and muscle weakness, which cause further immobility in a vicious cycle. Depression can be caused by immobility, and if the elder becomes immobilised in bed very serious complications can ensue.

Causes of Immobility

Never forget that immobility can be caused by depression and that prescribed drugs can weaken or stiffen muscles and immobilise an old person. Certain diseases commonly cause immobility.

Painful feet

Stroke

Parkinson's disease

Breathlessness

Arthritis

Visual problems (see page 52)

Immobility should first be tackled by trying to reduce the effects of these diseases. Even after the best treatment some immobility may remain, but it can often be improved with the help of occupational and physiotherapists.

Painful feet

Disorders of the feet affect old people very commonly. They are due not so much to the ageing process as to the type of shoes which have been worn during the previous six or seven decades. Much can be done to prevent further deterioration if a little care is taken everyday.

The feet should be washed everyday in *warm* water. They should not be soaked for long periods. Nails should be cleaned with a soft brush, not a sharp instrument. Drying is best done by dabbing rather than by rubbing, and a sprinkling of talcum powder is also helpful. It is particularly important to dry the skin between and under the toes, but great care must be taken because this skin is soft and splits easily. Dry skin is best treated by rubbing in olive oil or lanolin cream. Overlapping toes should be separated with cotton wool which should not be wrapped round a toe. Nails must be cut straight across, but if the corner of a nail cuts into an adjacent toe a chiropodist should be consulted. If a nail is very thick, use a nail file on the top surface.

If the old person cannot reach her own feet

you can perform these simple tasks, or the district nurse may be able to help if your elder lives far away from you. He can also apply for chiropody treatment from the National Health Service, but if he only requires simple foot care, such as we have described, he will probably have to wait a long time.

Socks should not be too tight or too short, and shoes should be broad enough to give the bare foot plenty of room. Soft slippers allow feet to spread, and elderly people should be encouraged to wear well fitting shoes in the house in preference to slippers. Remember that eight out of ten shoes are sold on a Saturday, so if you go shopping for shoes on any other day you will receive better attention and advice.

There are certain conditions of the feet for which you should seek outside help and not attempt to treat yourself. If both feet, or any part of a foot, becomes inflamed, swollen or painful or if the colour of the skin becomes white, dusky red or purple, contact the elder's GP as soon as possible, because the blood circulation to the foot may be affected. Other conditions do not require immediate medical assistance, but do require the attention of a chiropodist:

- Corns; we do not advise the use of corn plasters, treatment of the corn with a razor blade or any other implement; consult a chiropodist.
- Cuts, abrasions and ulcers: these should always be seen by a chiropodist.
- Diabetes: the feet of people with diabetes are prone to infection and the skin heals very slowly if it is damaged. The skin on the feet of people with circulation problems is quick to break down and slow to heal. The British Diabetic Association, 3–6 Alfred Place, London, WC11E 7EE offers information to people with diabetes.
- Pain; painful feet should be seen by a chiropodist or doctor even though the skin and nails appear to be healthy.

If you find it impossible to obtain an appointment with a chiropodist ask the GP for help. If the old person has a corn, or the skin is broken or his toenails need cutting, he can ask the district nurse to help.

The National Health Service runs a community chiropody service, with chiropodists working either in specially built surgeries, clinic rooms in old people's homes, health centres or purpose built caravans. They can also make home visits, although it is usually preferable to have treatment in a clinic where the chiropodist has all her equipment to hand. The telephone number and address of the NHS chiropody service is either in the yellow pages of the phone book under 'Chiropody' or in the white pages under the name of the Area Health Authority. You can apply directly, without first seeing a GP.

NHS chiropody is in very short supply. In some areas the waiting list is over two years long, but a long wait is sometimes only necessary if the old person requires NHS transport to the clinic. If you are told that the old person has to wait a long time, ask if it will be any less if you can arrange transport, either driving her yourself, paying for a taxi, or by finding a volunteer to take her.

For many elders a private chiropodist will need to be consulted. The yellow pages contain a list of the private chiropodists but some of them are very inexperienced and unqualified. Anyone can call himself a chiropodist, put a nameplate beside his door and an entry in the telephone book. Some, although not fully qualified, are experienced and skilful, but it is wisest to choose a fully qualified State Registered Chiropodist who will have the letters SRCh after his name. Not only is this a sign that he has had three years training, but it also indicates that he is insured to cover the cost of legal action should he cause any damage, and that complaints against the chiropodist can be made to

The Council for Professions Supplementary
  to Medicine,
York House,
Westminster Bridge Road,
London, SE1.

Social security will not pay any of the cost of private chiropody treatment, but charities may help.

Complaints against the chiropodists employed by the NHS should be made to the Area Health Authority, but such complaints are rare. It is much more common for people to have complaints about the chiropody *service* because it is so inadequate in so many areas. Complaints made to the Area Health Authority, the Community Health Council and the MP will inform them of the deficiencies, and encourage them to try to improve the service.

Stroke

A stroke is caused by interruption of the blood supply to the brain.

The control and co-ordination of muscular movement, including the muscles which are used in swallowing and speaking, is one of the functions of the brain. Like any other organ in the body it requires a steady flow of blood, carrying oxygen and nutrients, and any blockage of a blood vessel which cuts off these supplies for more than a few minutes results in the death of brain cells – a stroke. Doctors sometimes call such an event a cerebrovascular accident or CVA. The exact effects depend on which part of the brain is affected. If the part of the brain which controls balance is affected the result will be instability – unsteadiness or a fall (see page 71). If the part which controls the bladder muscle is deprived of its blood supply and dies, the consequence is incontinence (see page 65). However, the most common area affected is that part of the brain which controls movement.

Because each half of the brain receives its own separate blood supply, usually only one side of the body is paralysed. If one half of the face, and the arm and leg on the same side are completely paralysed the stroke is called a hemiplegia; if the side is only weakened it is called a hemiparesis. Not only is the power to move lost, the affected person also loses the ability to know the position of his joints or limbs unless he can see where they are, and he is sometimes made partially blind as a result of the stroke. The effect is not easy to describe, but if you shut your eyes and move an arm, you will know its position whether it is moving or at rest. People who have suffered a stroke lose this ability, which causes great difficulty when dressing, walking or performing any other action. Speech is sometimes affected (see page 47).

A stroke may have a very serious emotional and psychological effect, in addition to the physical damage caused. People may feel frustrated, angry and depressed as a result of a stroke. Even the ability to think may be affected if certain parts of the brain are damaged, which leads to further confusion and frustration with sudden changes in mood accompanied by weeping.

The aim of the nursing staff is to prevent the skin on the back breaking down and, together with physiotherapy staff, to prevent stiffness of the muscles and deformity of the joints. When the nervous control of muscles is destroyed by a cerebrovascular accident, the muscles do not become flabby and loose, as might be expected. They go into spasm and contract powerfully, pulling the joints into deformed positions. The joints can stiffen and set in such deformities if the skill of a physiotherapist is not employed. The physiotherapist tries to prevent deformity and stiffness so that when the spasm wears off, as it does over time, the muscles and joints can be moved with relative ease. The physiotherapist may ask to see you and show you a few simple exercises so that you can help the elder in his recovery, or you can make an appointment to see her if you are worried or have questions to ask (see page 24). An occupational therapist, is also involved in the hospital treatment of a stroke. She is able to help the elder and his supporters make plans for going home, linking with her colleague the domiciliary occupational therapist, before the person is discharged (see page 23). If speech is affected, a speech therapist can usually be consulted, although their numbers are very few in some parts of the country (see page 47).

As we have said, a stroke is an emotional as well as a physical blow. Don't try to cope with all the emotional upsets yourself. The GP and other members of the elder's primary care team and hospital staff are all there to provide psychological help and advice. In hospital the medical social worker can discuss any particularly difficult or disturbing social, financial or emotional problems.

The domiciliary occupational therapist is trained and able to offer the same type of valuable support for some minor strokes, if the patient is treated at home.

If you have any difficulty which cannot be resolved with the help of these professionals.

The Chest, Heart and Stroke Association
Tavistock House (North),
Tavistock Square,
London, WC1H 9JE.

may be able to provide the answer to the problem, or direct you to an appropriate source of help. It also publishes excellent leaflets on the effects of a stroke and how to cope with them.

Parkinson's Disease

This is a disorder of that part of the brain which controls muscular movement. It may be caused by narrowing of the blood vessels but in most cases no cause can be found. It does not run in families.

The basic cause cannot be treated but the symptoms can be relieved. There are two main symptoms:

1) Tremor, which may affect one hand or both arms, and/or the head, which nods back and forwards.
2) Stiffness of some or all muscles, including those muscles which are used in speech.

There may be a general slowing in movements which causes a small stepping, shuffling walk and the muscles of the face are sometimes affected. Treatment can reduce the severity of these symptoms. The GP may start treatment himself, or he may refer the affected person to a consultant in geriatric medicine for assessment and advice on treatment.

Two main types of drug are prescribed. One sort mainly acts to reduce rigidity and increase the range of movement. The other type of drug reduces the tremor and both types of drug may be prescribed together. Both drugs can produce a number of side effects, and it is important to keep a close watch on the elder and inform the GP if any untoward symptom occurs. As always, care must be taken to ensure that the drug is taken as prescribed (see page 91).

For people affected by Parkinson's disease and their families, we recommend the Parkinson's Disease Society (81 Queens Road, London, SW19 8NR. 01–946 2500.) Its aim is to encourage and raise funds for research and to help patients and their relatives with the problems arising from Parkinson's Disease. Particularly useful are two booklets: *Parkinson's Disease, A Booklet for Patients and Their Families*, and *Parkinson's Disease – Day-to-Day (a booklet for those who are affected)*.

The society has local branches, and the address of the nearest branch can be obtained from the GP, health visitor, social worker, Age Concern or from the main office. Even though you feel that you are being given adequate information by the professionals directly involved, the society is worth joining. It may help you further and you may be enabled to help other affected people or their supporters.

Breathlessness

Disease of the heart or the lungs, or both together, can cause breathlessness.

The heart is a regularly beating muscular pump, with valves at the entrance and exit which allow the blood to flow in only one direction. The heart fails to pump sufficient oxygen round the body when its regular beat is interrupted, when the valves are damaged or when the muscular wall of the heart is weakened. Some old people had rheumatic fever in childhood, which damaged the valves, and many more suffer from narrowing of the arteries which supply the heart muscle itself with oxygen-rich blood, so heart failure may occur in old age.

Breathlessness, which may come on suddenly when lying flat, is only one sign of heart failure, the other important sign is swelling of the ankles or abdomen. Fortunately heart failure is treatable and the usual drugs given are:

- Digoxin, which makes the muscular pump beat more strongly.
- A diuretic drug (water pill), which helps the body excrete as urine the surplus fluid which dams up behind the failing heart.
- A potassium tablet, which is necessary to replace potassium lost in the increased output of urine.

For some people Digoxin alone is sufficient, for others a diuretic drug and potassium may be all that is required. Whatever drugs are prescribed, it is essential that all the medicines are taken correctly.

Also the elder can do much to help herself if she brings her weight down (see page 76). Every pound lost means less work for the heart and lessens the strain on it.

It is important that people with heart disease are helped to adjust and to have enough confidence to enjoy life. If an old person becomes housebound and refuses to go out 'because of my heart' the GP should be consulted. His reassurance, backed up perhaps by that of a hospital consultant, may restore confidence and the ability to enjoy life. People with heart disease have to be sensible, but that does not mean they have to be miserable.

The common lung diseases are bronchitis and emphysema, which sometimes occur together. They cause breathlessness, not only because the damaged lungs fail to absorb enough oxygen, but because lung disease can put such a great strain on the heart that heart failure results, aggravating the breathlessness.

There are not such effective drugs for the treatment of lung failure as for heart failure, but some improvement is usually possible. No matter how long a person has smoked and no matter how old he or she may be, they may benefit from stopping smoking, or at least from cutting down on the amount of tar which they inhale daily. Some people realise that their only hope of improvement is to stop smoking, but are unable to do so or to cut down. The advice of the elder's GP should be taken with regard to smoking. His encouragement may help the old person to stop. If the old person is really addicted, and cannot stop, the GP's reassurance that the dangers of smoking are comparatively minor in old age can help the elder accept failure without feeling guilty. It may be that you feel the old person enjoys smoking so much that it is unkind even to suggest that he should stop or cut down. That is for you to decide, although the advice of the GP or health visitor may be useful when considering what to do.

A reduction in weight will also help people with bronchitis or emphysema.

Those people whose lungs are failing are very severely affected by colds and flu. Any symptom which might be a warning of a cold or flu – sore throat, hoarseness, worsening of cough or increasing breathlessness – should be treated seriously and the advice of the GP sought quickly. If the GP prescribes antibiotics it is essential that they are taken exactly, and for as long as he has indicated. If side effects occur the GP should be informed immediately, as he may wish to change to another antibiotic.

Every autumn a great deal of publicity is given to the danger of influenza and the advantages of immunisation of elderly people, but the Department of Health do not recommend it for all old people. If an old person lives in an old people's home or hospital with lots of other people, and is therefore at greater risk of infection, immunisation may be indicated, but this is a decision which must be made for each individual by his GP.

Arthritis
There are two common types of arthritis:

• Rheumatoid arthritis, which occurs more commonly in women than men, affects the small joints especially those of the hands, feet, ankles, knees and elbows. To be accurate it should be called rheumatoid disease, for it is a disorder of the connective tissue which provides the framework for all the tissues and organs. Treatment can relieve pain and stiffness and can reduce the severity of the disease, which is inflammatory but not infectious.

• Osteoarthritis is not inflammatory. It is probably caused by the wearing through of the low-friction surface of cartilage which covers bones where they meet as joints. It occurs in both men and women and affects the weight-bearing joints – knees, hips and the joints of the spinal column. Treatment does not slow down the disease, but can relieve pain and stiffness.

The first step is correct diagnosis and medical treatment. Some GPs are specially interested in arthritis but many prefer to refer this complex complaint to a hospital consultant. There are specialists in joint disease called consultant rheumatologists to whom the GP can refer an old person, but he may choose to refer him to a consultant in geriatric medicine (see page 22) who is also skilled in management of arthritis.

Aspirin and paracetamol are often effective but a number of new drugs have been developed to relieve pain, and the doctor may try one after another until he finds one which suits the old person best. Other types of drug reduce the inflammation, with the result that more than one type of drug for the treatment of arthritis may be prescribed. Each has a different function however, and care must be taken to ensure the old person takes them as the GP intended.

Because of pain being worse on movement, sufferers tend to keep arthritic joints still. This causes joint stiffness which increases the pain and disability, in a vicious cycle. The immobility of the joints has serious secondary effects, because unused muscles waste and weaken, which further increases the disability. Physiotherapists do much to prevent these secondary effects by teaching exercises which should be continued at home.

There are operations to relieve arthritis, of which the best known is replacement of the hip joint. If it is thought that an operation would help, the GP can ask for the opinion of a hospital consultant. The results of such operations are usually very good.

Even after the most skilled medical and surgical treatment, and the best physiotherapy, some disability often remains and the sufferer from arthritis may be handicapped in caring for herself – in washing or bathing, dressing or cooking – or in getting about her home. The domiciliary occupational therapist has much to offer a handicapped elder and her supporters.

Remember that arthritis can affect the many small joints of the feet very badly, causing fallen arches, hallux valgus with bunions and pain, and the advice of a chiropodist should be sought if any trouble occurs. He not only treats disorders of the feet, but also gives the best advice on special footwear.

The domiciliary occupational therapist should know about every available service – financial, health and housing. The British Rheumatism and Arthritis Association (1 Devonshire Place, London, W1) also gives advice on individual problems.

Increasing Mobility

Once any underlying disease has been brought under control by a doctor, and an old person's feet have been treated by a chiropodist, the physiotherapist is the key person in the fight against immobility.

Her skills help the elder keep his joints mobile, his muscles as strong as possible and develop the co-ordination and control of movement. All this builds confidence. The physiotherapist may concentrate on one or two movements which are particularly important, for example standing up from a chair, walking to the toilet using the furniture for support, or managing the stairs. She will expect the elder's relatives to learn how to encourage the elder in any exercises which she has taught him, and to help him rise from a chair or walk until his confidence and power are fully returned. She may advise the use of a walking aid (see page 71).

The physiotherapist works with the occupational therapist to give the elder as much mobility as possible. The domiciliary occupational therapist can arrange for the installation of handrails along corridors and on both sides of the stairs. She will look at the old person's bed and chair to assess whether they are the correct height. Often the only reason why a disabled person cannot rise from a chair is that it is too low. The provision of special blocks can lift the chair and bed to the correct height. There are special chairs with a spring under the seat which help the elder rise, and 'geriatric chairs', which are higher than the average chair. But we do not think any such chair should be bought before an occupational therapist has been consulted.

The occupational therapist may decide that a wheel-chair would be helpful and arrange for a special wheel-chair assessment at hospital. We do not advise you to purchase a wheel-chair without expert advice – the Red Cross or the medical loans service can lend a wheel-chair if one is needed for a special trip. A wheel-chair cannot negotiate steps, and the occupational therapist will arrange for any necessary alterations of steps to ramps. She can arrange for a lift to be installed if necessary.

INCONTINENCE

There is probably no single symptom which causes as much distress as incontinence. The sufferer feels that she has returned to childhood. She is ashamed and, having sometimes scolded her own children when they were incontinent, may expect a row herself and may try to hide the fact. In our society, body cleanliness and lack of smell are very important for social acceptability.

Someone who becomes incontinent not only feels as helpless as a baby, but also that the uncleanliness and smell of her incontinence will make her a social outcast. Fear of incontinence is almost as big a problem; an elderly person who has been incontinent, even once, can become so nervous of future episodes that she shuns company.

The emotional reaction can make the incontinence worse. We all know that when while waiting for some big event, such as an interview or driving test, we feel the need to go to the lavatory more often. In the same way, worry about incontinence can make the elder wish to pass water more frequently. If she is slow in reaching the lavatory because of arthritis, incontinence is increased. It is well known by hospital staff that some patients who do not feel they are getting enough attention sometimes become incontinent. This ensures that they receive attention, although they may also get scolded. This does not often happen at home, but frequent assurances of a family's love and affection should be given to someone who is incontinent, because incontinence creates insecurity.

Because of the social stigma and shame many people try to conceal incontinence, struggling to wash sheets and clothes or just hiding them away. The sense of smell sometimes becomes less sensitive with age and this, together with the fact that it is normal at any age to notice smells less the longer they persist, leads the old person to believe that she has successfully hidden her incontinence, although the house stinks with the sharp smell of urine or faeces. It is important to bring the problem out in the open. You may find it too difficult and distasteful to do this, because continence and incontinence are subjects which no one in our society likes to discuss. Often it is more acceptable to both sides to ask the GP's help. He may call himself or ask the health visitor or district nurse to visit. If he visits on the pretext of reviewing the elder's general state of health, he can comment on the smell if necessary. Often an old person will reveal this problem to a professional without being asked, although she hesitates to discuss it with a member of the family even in response to a direct question.

Causes of Incontinence

- Stroke; someone who has had a stroke may lose control of the muscles which allow us to close and open the urethra at will, and therefore passes water without warning or control. Strokes also create problems because the affected elder may be unable to reach the toilet or commode, or undress, in time.

- Dementia or any other brain disorder can cause incontinence (see page 106).

- Infection of the urinary tract can result in urgency, frequency and incontinence.

- Any condition which causes acute confusion may also result in incontinence while the person is confused (see page 104).

- Constipation is a common cause of urinary incontinence (see page 77).

- Any drug which affects the mind of the elder, especially tranquillisers and sleeping pills, obviously reduces awareness of a full bladder and the ability to control emptying. Diuretics which are given for high blood pressure or heart failure, increase the rate of urine formation resulting in urgency.

- Immobility; any condition which slows down the rate at which the elder can move, such as arthritis of the hip joints, can cause an elder who suffers from urgency to become incontinent.
  'I feel I have to go very urgently, but I walk so slowly that by the time I've reached the lavatory I've had an accident.'

Prostate disease; the main cause of urinary problems in men is the prostate gland, which is situated at the base of the bladder. In all men it normally grows larger with age; in some it swells to such a degree that it obstructs the flow of urine.

If the prostate is swollen, the stream is slow to start, does not shoot out with the same force as previously and does not finish cleanly but in a dribble. Early signs of prostate trouble can sometimes be seen as stains on the front of trousers and shoes, and on the floor in front of the toilet. Difficulty in passing water may be associated with an urgency and frequency. Most of us can postpone a visit to the lavatory for some time after the first warning or sensation that the bladder is full, but someone suffering from urgency feels a very strong discomfort and desire to pass water almost from the time they feel the first warning. There may also be frequency – the desire to pass water frequently even though very little is passed on each occasion – and an old man may wake to pass water three, four or more times in the night, disturbing not only his sleep but that of his supporters. The prostate swells further if the elder has to stay in bed for a day or longer. If he has difficulty passing water into a bottle when ill in bed, he may find it easier standing up beside the bed. Remember, however, that an old person can be very unsteady on standing up after lying down for a few hours, so great care must be taken. Straining to increase bladder pressure by holding the breath interferes with the return of blood to the heart and this reduces the flow of blood from the heart to the brain. This increases any unsteadiness while standing beside the bed and can cause the elder to faint and fall. This can also happen at any time when the elder is standing at the lavatory trying to pass water.

If the prostate swells quickly, the urethra, the tube from the bladder, may be completely blocked causing an acute retention of urine, which is very painful. The GP should be called immediately.

If the prostate swells slowly, the bladder can increase in size very gradually and painlessly to contain a large volume. It may then dribble all the time as a result of overflow from the distended bladder. Acute retention and dribbling from overflow obviously require medical attention, but so also do the early signs of prostate trouble, and the GP will usually refer the case to hospital.

Prostatic cancer is not very often fatal. It usually occurs in very old men who die of other causes before the prostatic cancer spreads. It is also one of the few types of cancer for which there is an effective drug treatment. The female sex hormones – oestrogens – are given and, although they have side effects, they relieve pain and discomfort.

Stress incontinence is a condition affecting some women. The bladder sits on the muscular floor of the pelvis, the muscles nipping the bladder at the point at which the urethra leaves it. It is these muscles which allow us to hold our water until an appropriate time. During childbirth the baby pushes through the tiny gap beside the urethra, stretching the muscles. In most women the muscles regain their original shape and tension but in some, especially those who have given birth on a number of occasions, the muscles become so stretched that they do not nip the urethra as tightly as they did. Anything which raises the pressure in the abdominal cavity, such as coughing, sneezing or laughing, raises the pressure inside the bladder and pushes urine down the urethra. This is known as stress incontinence and may be associated with urgency and frequency. Stress incontinence is very distressing, but the condition can very often be improved.

Seek the advice of the elder's GP who may refer her to a consultant gynaecologist. There are operations for stress incontinence, but there are also other treatments. One of the advantages of hospital referral is that the gynaecologist can call on the expert help of a physiotherapist. The strength of the pelvic muscles can be regained by special exercises, and many people can be helped without an operation.

If treatment does not completely cure stress incontinence, a sanitary towel may be sufficient to absorb any urine which leaks out.

Tackling Urinary Incontinence

Because incontinence is only a symptom of an underlying disorder, a thorough medical examination is the top priority. The GP may be able to find and treat the underlying cause or he may refer the elder for assessment by a consultant in geriatric medicine, who has the advantage over most GPs of access to special equipment for investigation.

If the doctor cannot offer any effective treatment, it does not mean that the sufferer cannot be helped. Physiotherapists can help not only stress incontinence but can also enable some sufferers to reach the toilet in time by treating their arthritis. Physiotherapy can also help stroke victims to use their paralysed side to its fullest capability. The domiciliary occupational therapist can also be of help. She may advise, and arrange for the fixing of, rails along the hall or up the stairs to allow the elder to reach the toilet. The domiciliary occupational therapist's advice and aids can also reduce the difficulties which some disabled people face in the toilet. A raised toilet seat helps those whose hips are too stiff to sit down with ease.

Rails can help an old person sit and rise. They are placed on the right or left side depending on the side which is stronger.

Horizontal rail

Diagonal rail

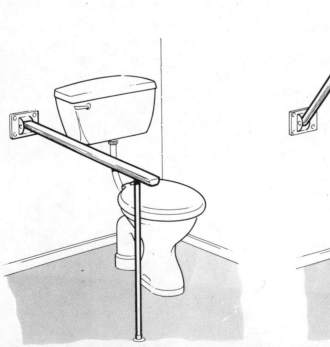

Moveable rail

A frame can be placed round the toilet to give support on both sides.

These are some of the aids which reduce the handicap and allow the elder more control, independence and dignity in the toilet. The occupational therapist can advise on suitable clothing, for example trousers with a velcro fly, or dresses which open at the back.

If it proves impossible to reach the toilet, a commode or chemical toilet can be provided free of charge. In many areas the Red Cross is the source of this invaluable help. The occupational therapist, district nurse or health visitor will know how a commode can be obtained and will be able to teach the elder how to transfer independently from bed or chair to commode.

Both in hospital and at home a nurse's skill is very useful. In hospital, nurses try to help an elderly incontinent patient relearn and regain bladder control by taking them to the lavatory or taking a commode to them regularly during the day and last thing at night. *Restriction of fluid causes dehydration and confusion and only makes problems worse*, but it is sensible to give more fluid in the morning and less later in the day. At home regular suggestions to use the lavatory continue the toilet training started in

hospital. Skin soaked in urine may ulcerate, but both by bathing and treating the skin herself, and by advising what can be done in the intervals between her visits, the district nurse works to keep the skin intact and

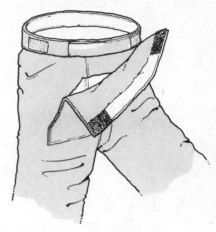

Trousers can be obtained with a drop front

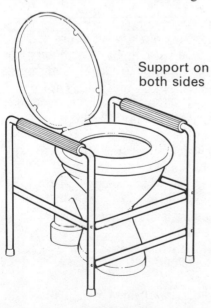

Support on both sides

Toilet aid

A nightdress which opens in front but has a wrapover back is easy to put on and take off. If it has good overlap it will cover the wearer when standing, but can be pulled aside when necessary.

A back opening dressing gown can be worn.

strong. She knows the various types of appliances which are available and can select the one which is most appropriate to the patient, for example a plastic bottle for a man or a small dish urinal, which is so much easier than a bed pan, for a woman.

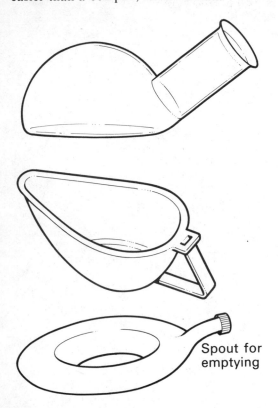

Spout for emptying

St. Peter's Boat

The district nurse can supply free incontinence pads for bed or chair. There are also pants which incorporate small pads to absorb urine and faeces. Ask the nurse's advice on the best way to make the bed. She will help you protect the mattress and arrange the bed linen for maximum comfort and efficiency. The 'Kylie' sheet is excellent and can absorb urine without its surface becoming wet. She will also tell you how to dispose of incontinence pads.

In many areas there is a laundry service which will collect soiled linen for laundering and return it. Ask the home help organiser in the social services department about the laundry service. If the old person does not live with you, the organiser may be able to offer the services of a home help who can wash personal laundry.

Faecal Incontinence

Faecal incontinence may occur with incontinence of urine, or alone. Constipation is a very common cause of incontinence of faeces. The build up of very hard faeces in the large bowel irritates the lining, causing the production of excessive mucus, which leaks past the hard faeces and the sphincter – the ring of muscles which closes the anus – to soil pants and bed clothes. Constipation should always be suspected when someone becomes incontinent of faeces, and their GP should be requested to visit. The district nurse can help people who are severely constipated by giving a weekly enema. However, after the correct diagnosis has been made and the acute problem solved, a recurrence of the incontinence can often be prevented by avoiding further constipation – the nurse can also advise on this (see page 77).

The following general illnesses can also cause incontinence of faeces:

- Stroke; an affected elder sometimes loses control of the sphincter and may also lose the ability to reach or use the toilet independently.
- Dementia or any other brain disorder.
- Infection; food poisoning and dysentery can cause explosive diarrhoea, sometimes accompanied by vomiting. The dehydration which results can be very serious and this condition must be treated as an emergency.
- Any drug which affects the mind, especially sleeping pills and tranquillisers.
- Any condition which causes acute confusion may have faecal incontinence as one symptom, while the person is confused (see page 105).
- Any condition which slows down the rate at which the elder can move, may lead to accidents.

Remember that self-medication with laxatives is a frequent cause of bowel problems. If cascara, magnesium sulphate or any other strong laxative is taken in association with any of the above conditions, or alone, incontinence may result.

The approach to, and management of, faecal incontinence is the same as that described for urinary incontinence – thorough medical examination and treatment; physiotherapy to aid mobility; the advice of an occupational therapist to promote independence; the help of a district nurse to watch the skin and advise on bowel function; and assistance of the home help and incontinent laundry service. Similar psychological factors can cause faecal incontinence as were described for urinary incontinence.

Smell is often a greater problem when there is faecal incontinence than with urinary incontinence. Nilodor, which is available from chemists or directly from Loxley Luxan Medical Supplies, 55–56 Whitfield Street, London, W1A 2BX, is a very effective deodorant for clothing, commode and for other articles.

The psychological consequences of faecal incontinence, shame and isolation, should always be remembered.

For those supporters for whom incontinence is a severe problem we recommend the book *Incontinence* by Dorothy Mandelstam. This excellent book is written by the Incontinence Adviser to the Disabled Living Foundation (346 Kensington High Street, London) which has a permanent exhibition of aids which can reduce the burden which incontinence places on many elders and supporters.

INSTABILITY – FALLING AND FEAR OF FALLING

Causes of Falls

Old people trip more frequently. Failing vision may prevent an old person from seeing a raised paving stone or carpet edge and can cause a fall. Muscle weakness and stiff joints mean that the feet are not lifted so high while walking, so the toe is more likely to catch projecting edges. At home the risk of falling can be reduced by

Better lighting.

Putting rails beside the stairs.

Tacking down rugs, mats and linoleum.

Keeping the kitchen floor clean from grease.

Keeping electric flexes close to walls.

Ask the advice of an environmental health officer or health visitor about safety in the home. RoSPA (4 Priory Queensway, Birmingham) produce an excellent check list – 'Safety in Retirement'.

Outside the house it is less easy to make the environment safer, although a good supply of salt by the front and back door can allow the old person to make frosted paths safe herself. Either an ordinary walking-stick or one with four feet or a walking frame, may be helpful.

Walking aid

71

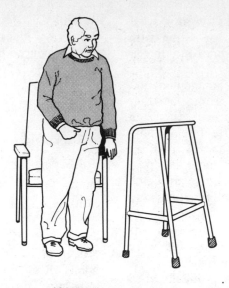

Walking frame

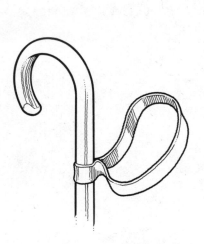

A wrist strap often makes
a stick more manageable

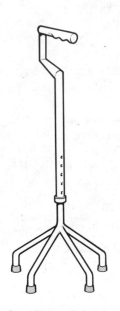

Quadropod stick

Physiotherapists can advise on sticks, but if the old person is not attending hospital or seeing a physiotherapist, ask the advice of the district nurse, health visitor or domiciliary occupational therapist. If the elder thinks using a stick makes him look too disabled, a stout umbrella can be useful. Remember that a stick must have a rubber tip or it can course a fall.

Old people not only trip more frequently, but their powers of recovery may also be less effective than when they were younger. Everyone loses their balance a number of times each day, but most people recover their balance by reflex actions and do not fall. If, however, that part of the brain which controls balance is affected, the ability to recover balance is lost and a trip results in a fall. Sometimes the balancing centre in the brain is so affected that the old person feels unsteady and may fall over even without first tripping.

If an old person becomes unsteady, or starts to fall without tripping, his GP should be consulted. Sometimes the underlying cause can be detected and the GP will try to find such a cause, referring the old person to hospital if necessary. The following are the common causes of instability:

- Arthritis of the small bones of the neck (the vertebrae) can nip blood vessels to the brain which pass through these vertebrae, especially on sudden movements of the neck.
- Disorders of the heart can cause instability. If the blood which leaves the heart is not a sufficiently high pressure to be pumped vertically up the neck and into the skull, the blood supply to the balancing centre is reduced.
- Narrowing of the blood vessels which supply the balancing centre.
- Instability can be due to drug side-effects. Any drug which affects the brain – tranquillisers or sleeping pills – can obviously cause instability if the dose is too great, or if the elder makes a mistake in taking the drug. Drugs which lower blood pressure may reduce it to such an extent that the elder is unstable and liable to fall because the brain is inadequately supplied with blood. The greatest risk occurs when the elder stands up after she has been lying down. It is normal for pressure to drop at this time, and this normal postural change, combined with the effect of the drug, can lead to such a drop in blood pressure – postural hypotension – that the elder falls.

Even if a correctable cause cannot be found, the steps described previously to make the home safer and the provision of a stick for walking should be helpful.

Remember that for several reasons many falls occur at night. An elderly person who has lost his balancing reflex uses his eyes to assess his position in space more than younger people do. In the dark, therefore, he is unstable and if he stands up after lying down for hours, his blood pressure falls. The drop in blood pressure is often made worse because the warmth of the bed has increased the flow of blood to the skin at the expense of the rest of the body. A night light is not necessary if there is a switch that can be easily reached from the bed, preferably one which puts on the main light. The walk to the lavatory can be avoided by the provision of a commode or, for men, a bottle.

Preparation for a Fall

Even after all the measures we describe have been taken, some old people will fall by accident. The first step to prepare for such an accident is to make sure that an old person is able to rise to his feet, should a fall occur. This is possible for most people, even if they are quite severely disabled. For example someone who has had a stroke can learn how to rise after a fall if he has enough strength in the unaffected side.

If the old person is in hospital, the physiotherapist can be asked if the elder is able to rise to his feet. If he is at home, ask the district nurse if she can help him to learn. If an elderly person may require your assistance you should make sure that a physiotherapist or nurse has shown you the best way for you to help. Incorrect lifting can damage the lifter's back.

The warmer the house the less serious are the effects of lying on the floor, because there is a risk of hypothermia if a person is lying immobilised on the floor. This is one reason why it is important to try to warm the whole house, or at least all those rooms and corridors used by the elder.

If someone who has fallen can raise the alarm and summon help quickly he will be

1. Stronger arm on chair

2. Rise to kneeling.

3. Place stronger foot
on ground

4. Stand

Getting up, with a paralysed left side

less anxious about falling. A knock on the wall or floor to neighbours is often effective, provided that the neighbour knows what the knocking means. It is useful to arrange a code, for example four knocks followed by a short silence followed by four more knocks. Even new neighbours may be willing to help if they are approached directly. A bell or whistle is more easily heard, but may be difficult to reach from the position where the fall occurs. This is also the problem with a telephone, but a phone is often helpful and is always reassuring. Someone who lives alone and falls frequently may be supplied with a telephone by the Social Services Department (see page 56), depending on his need and the number of telephones which are available for allocation. It costs nothing to apply, and

the application may be successful if supported by a GP's letter, but in some parts of the country very few phones are available.

In some areas there is a Fish or Good Neighbour Scheme which provides cards for old people to put in their windows if they are in difficulties. There are two drawbacks to this scheme:

- If an old person falls he may find it impossible to reach the window.
- If he lives in an area in which crime is common there is a risk that a sign of difficulty may become an invitation to burglary.

The same drawback is true for flashing alarms which can be attached to an outside wall.

One way round this latter difficulty is to

suggest to the old person's neighbours that they look, not for a positive sign, but for something that has not been done. If a neighbour ensures that the milk is taken in every morning by nine o'clock, or that the curtains are opened by half past eight, and acts if she sees no sign of life, help can be mobilised without signifying that the elderly resident is vulnerable. The milkman or postman can also be asked to keep an eye open for such warning signs.

A move to sheltered housing where there is an alarm bell to call the Warden solves many worries, but even there the tenant may be unable to reach the bell and the move may have disadvantages.

Medic-Alert

As medicine becomes more effective, the number of old people whose lives depend on good medical treatment increases. If an old person who has an allergy, or depends on regular drug treatment, or has an illness which very much affects medical treatment, becomes unconscious, he is at risk. This is because the doctor treating him may not learn of his underlying problem if he does not already know him.

Medic-Alert was introduced into Britain from America in 1963, sponsored by the Lions Clubs. If an elder is:
- Affected by a disease which requires regular treatment or complicates other treatments, for example diabetes;
- Receiving regular drug therapy, e.g. steroids, anticoagulants or drugs for high blood pressure;
- Allergic to drugs;

his life might be at risk if he becomes unconscious if there is no-one present who knows his condition to tell the doctor. It is for these types of cases that Medic-Alert exists.

Medic-Alert provides a bracelet or necklet which is engraved with the wearer's particular condition, for example 'Diabetic' or 'on Steroid Treatment'. If the elder's GP thinks any other information than that written on the bracelet or necklet might be required in

an emergency he can send it to be stored at Medic-Alert Emergency Headquarters. The stored information can be obtained by a phone call day or night to the Headquarters and the phone number is also engraved on the bracelet or necklet.

If you think an old person would benefit write to

Medic-Alert Foundation,
9 Hanover Street,
London, W1R 9HF.

They will send you a form to take to the doctor.

The St. John's SOS talisman is very similar. It consists of a locket in which can be written name, address, blood group and any other details about medical conditions and treatment which might be important in an emergency. Details of the St. John's SOS talisman can be obtained from

PO Box 999,
Kettering,
Northants.

Neither of these is available on the NHS.

Falls and Fractures

Because the bones become thinner with age, old people who fall more often fracture a bone than young people whose bones are naturally stronger. If you or the old person are worried that she may have sustained a fracture, phone the GP, who may decide to send the old person to hospital. If you cannot contact the doctor you can call an ambulance by dialling 999 if it is a real emergency.

When an old person has to attend the hospital casualty department, or the accident and emergency service as it is often called, someone should go with her if possible. The person accompanying can be very helpful both to the doctors, who require information about the old person's medical and social background, and of course to the old person, who may be frightened and bewildered in strange surroundings. If you are unable to go with an old person, it is wise to phone the

Sister of the accident and emergency department or the Medical Social Work Department if you are worried. Sometimes an old person says she will be able to manage at home after a fracture although she knows it is impossible, or says that there is someone at home when in fact she lives alone. If you tell the hospital staff of the home situation it will help them help her better, perhaps by keeping her in hospital overnight, by phoning the home help or district nursing service, or by finding a volunteer to warm the house and make the old person a cup of tea.

We do not intend to try to teach you the first aid management of these fractures or of any other fractures or accidents. We do not think that can be taught using the written word and diagrams. The British Red Cross Society, St. John's Ambulance Association and Brigade, and in Scotland the St. Andrew's Ambulance Association, run excellent first aid training courses. The medical lecturers and trained instructors who teach on such courses provide excellent tuition by a combination of lectures and demonstrations. The first aid taught is applicable to people of all ages and is, in our opinion, excellent preparation for someone looking after an old person. The courses are also enjoyable and can lead to further work with these voluntary organisations.

NUTRITIONAL DIFFICULTIES IN OLD AGE

Serious cases of malnutrition are rare but dietary imbalance is not uncommon. Dietary imbalance can cause:

Obesity

Constipation.

Piles.

Deficiencies of essential dietary elements.

However, dietary problems can often be prevented by curing the underlying causes:

Depression (see page 98)

Isolation (see page 43)

Financial worries (see page 79)

Ignorance (see page 80)

Dental problems (see page 80)

Remember that any illness and disability can result in nutritional problems if the elder's ability to care for herself is affected.

Problems

Obesity

Although slimming magazines and books often give tables showing the 'ideal weight' for people of different heights, no-one needs an expert or a chart to tell them whether or not they are overweight. All that is required is a mirror and honesty. Someone who is overweight or obese is prone to many diseases which would not affect her, or would be milder, if she were not obese. Diabetes, osteoarthritis and problems of the feet are all made much worse by obesity. An obese person will recover much more slowly from illness, even if the illness itself is unconnected with her weight; for example it takes a fat person much longer to recover from any surgical operation, her wound is slow to heal and chest infections are more common.

The cause of obesity can be simply stated – more energy is taken in than is required for the day's work, and the surplus is converted to fat.

Ageing by itself has little effect on an individual's fatness, but if an elder takes less exercise, and therefore uses less energy, she may put on weight as she grows older. It is often difficult for an old person with a tendency to fatness, who is immobilised by arthritis, to lose much weight and she may get depressed if she sets herself an unrealistic goal. There is little point in an old person being permanently miserable because of keeping to her diet, unless there are strong medical indications for her to do so, but if an old person wants to lose weight she should be helped.

- Check with her GP that dieting would be sensible. Some illnesses cause people to gain weight and he may wish to examine her to exclude such diseases as the cause of her being overweight.
- Buy scales and use them once a week; daily weighings are unnecessary.
- Try to help her modify the diet so that it includes:
  - less fats,
  - less sugar and foods containing sugar,
  - more fibre.

Advice can be sought from the health visitor, or a dietitian if the old person is in hospital. There are many good books on slimming which list the fat, sugar and fibre composition of different foods. These books are suitable for old people as well as young slimmers. Weightwatchers clubs have no upper age limit.

Encourage the old person to take more exercise. Retired men often fail to realise just how much energy they used to expend getting to and from work, and at work itself, and put on weight quickly after retirement. It is a reasonable rule for an old person to decide that he or she will take a certain amount of exercise each day, perhaps a fifteen or thirty minute walk. Such a routine of regular exercise helps prevent obesity, and plays a part in its cure. Any type of exercise is beneficial. Walking is the cheapest, but many Local Authorities offer special concessions to elders who wish to swim, or learn to swim, play bowls, study yoga or take up some other form of exercise. Although very few old people will come to any harm if they increase the amount of exercise they take gradually, it is wise to check with the GP before starting a new form of exercise.

Finally, remember that eating may be one of the few pleasures left to an old person, so don't be too hard on her if she says she can't lose weight.

Constipation

The British are a bowel conscious people. Frenchmen worry about their livers, Germans are concerned about their circulation, but for Britons it is their bowel function which is important. This was even more so when today's elders were young. When they were children, tremendous importance was laid on regular bowel movements, and castor oil and other laxatives were administered frequently. The result is that some of them pay particular attention to the regularity of their bowels and take a laxative if there is the slightest delay. Many take laxatives regularly, and have done so for years, with the result that the normal function of the bowel is lost.

Taking all these factors into consideration it is very difficult to define constipation. There is no rule of nature that man should have three, two, or even one, bowel movements daily. The frequency is individual, and so is the regularity. Some people open their bowels with clockwork regularity and become agitated if they cannot do so, while others have never had such regularity. As people eat less food, there is obviously less material in the bowel, and the bowels need not open so often. Because the amount of food consumed usually decreases as people age, the bowels do not need to open so frequently.

Constipation becomes a problem when the elder considers it is a problem. Even if it is normal for an elder not to have a bowel movement for two days because he has not been eating, his worry is a problem which should be tackled, otherwise it can build up and he might start dosing himself with laxatives with unpleasant side effects. The most common cause of constipation is a faulty diet, and the prevention and cure of constipation is by changing the balance of the elder's diet.

The human bowel has evolved to process and digest large amounts of food. It was not until the turn of the century that energy-rich refined carbohydrate – sugar – became widely available and people were able to obtain enough energy for daily life from much smaller volumes of food. The other change in the diet is that the unrefined carbohydrate – flour – which is eaten is usually white flour, lacking the fibre of wholemeal flour. A consequence of this diet is that the bowel does not have so much material to process. The result, rather surprisingly, is that material takes longer to pass through, resulting in constipation, and the pressure inside the bowel increases, causing pain, especially in the lower abdomen. If the pressure rises high enough pouches of bowel lining pop through the muscle wall of the bowel to form little cul-de-sacs. In these side pockets undigested food stagnates and bacteria grow, causing diverticulitis.

When the problem of constipation first occurs we advise a consultation with the elder's GP, so that he can exclude serious illness. If constipation develops over a short period of time, for example over a period of a week or a month, without any change in the diet to explain it, the possibility of a general illness must be considered. Depression can cause constipation. It can occur as a side effect of drugs, particularly those containing codeine, and drugs used to treat Parkinson's disease. Dehydration, due to fever, may lead to constipation.

Doctors now believe that constipation can be prevented and cured by increasing the amount of fibre in the diet. There is fibre in vegetables but it is the fibre of cereals – wheat, oats and sweetcorn – which is more effective. A helping of All Bran or Bran Buds every day will prevent constipation in most people, but other whole grain cereals – porridge, breakfast cereals and wholemeal bread – also contain fibre and are equally useful. The only laxative which we would advise for use, without first consulting a doctor, is Milk of Magnesia.

Although infrequent bowel movements and constipation appear to be minor problems, they are of major significance to many old people and must be taken seriously.

Piles

Piles, or haemorrhoids, are varicose veins round the anus which develop in people who sit a great deal, and are aggravated by constipation. The common symptoms are pain, itchiness and bleeding. Although there are simple reasons for passing blood or black motions we recommend that the doctor be consulted whenever blood is seen. His diagnosis is doubly important because it not only allows the correct treatment to commence, but the elder can be reassured that he does not have cancer. Fear of cancer is common after bleeding from the back passage has been seen.

Many treatments for piles are advertised but, in our opinion, you should follow the GP's advice. If the old person has confidence in a favourite remedy which he has used for years, his doctor will probably advise him to continue to use it. Just as important as treatment of the piles themselves is the prevention of constipation and general skin care. It is essential to keep the skin between the buttocks as clean and dry as possible, because the itch may not be caused by the piles themselves but by the skin around them. The district nurse can give both advice and practical help to minimise discomfort. Do not apply creams or lotions to this sensitive area without the nurse's advice. A bidet is excellent, although expensive, for self-care; for those who cannot afford one, a spray attached to the bath taps will often be satisfactory. Surgical removal of piles is possible, but is hardly ever necessary, except for piles which bleed so heavily that they cause anaemia.

One of the elder's main difficulties with piles is that he cannot talk freely about them. They are an embarrassing, as well as a painful, subject and this is another reason for involving the elder's GP or a district nurse, for he may be able to talk to them more easily than to you.

The GP should be consulted if diarrhoea develops because there is always an underlying cause.

Diarrhoea

The commonest cause of diarrhoea is constipation. The presence of hard faeces at the lower end of the bowel irritates the sensitive lining of the bowel, causing it to produce protective mucus which leaks out of the back passage and gives the appearance of diarrhoea on the elder's pants or bedclothes. Sometimes the problem can only be prevented by weekly enemas given at home by the district nurse, but the prevention of constipation by the dietary measures we have described is usually sufficient.

The diarrhoea of food poisoning is sudden and watery, and may be accompanied by vomiting. A bowel which is affected by diverticulitis may suffer diarrhoea, sometimes alternating with constipation. Drugs can cause diarrhoea, the most common culprits being laxatives bought by the old person himself, but other drugs can cause diarrhoea as a side effect.

These are the common causes of diarrhoea. There are others, and a medical opinion is always advisable if the diarrhoea persists for more than two days or if the elder becomes confused due to dehydration.

Deficiency diseases
The following elements may be deficient in an old person's diet.

Protein – found in meat, fish, eggs and chicken.

Iron – found in red meat; deficiency can cause anaemia.

B Vitamins – found in vegetables, meat and wholewheat food; deficiency can cause anaemia.

Vitamin C – found in fresh fruit; deficiency can cause easy bruising and weakness.

Vitamin D and calcium – found in milk and milk products; deficiency can cause bone disease.

Fluid – immobile old people may not get enough to drink; at least three pints of fluid, including one pint of milk are required daily.

Fibre

If an old person is consuming at least a pint of milk, one cooked meal and fresh fruit every day, it is unlikely that she is malnourished. If an old person develops food fads, for example refusing to eat meat, fish or eggs, she may become malnourished. If in doubt ask the opinion of the health visitor. She may ask the GP to visit or arrange an appointment at the surgery if she is worried that the elder is malnourished.

Preventive Measures

If you suspect that someone has a nutritional problem you should ask for the opinion of the health visitor or GP. However, problems can be prevented. Certain factors predispose to nutritional problems:
- Depression (see page 98).
- Excessive intake of alcohol (this can be very difficult to detect).
- Isolation (see page 43).

Financial worries
Although pensions are much lower than wages or salaries, poverty is not a common cause of malnutrition, in our experience. Poverty certainly limits an old person's ability to choose freely, but it is possible for pensioners to select an adequate and nutritious diet. What can be a problem is an old person's *belief* that she is impoverished and cannot afford meat, fish, fruit or other foods which she defines as 'too expensive'. There are two reasons for this – decimalisation of the currency and inflation. Some old people still convert the price of goods to pounds, shillings and pence and then think of the price they used to pay. They say 'I'm not paying nine and six for a chop' or 'I won't buy eggs at twelve shillings a dozen' not appreciating that their pension has been increased to take account of inflation. It can be very difficult to correct this mistaken assumption, to restore the old person's confidence that she has enough money to provide adequately for herself. The assistance of the home help organiser, district nurse, health visitor or any professional who is trusted may be necessary to persuade her that she can

afford to eat. This attitude could become even more common because metrication will further disrupt the dimensions of the world the elder has known for decades, but it can be prevented.

Old people should be as closely involved as possible in budgetting and household planning. Although it may be quicker to take over all the financial management of the household economy, this may cause problems in the long run. If an old person loses touch with prices for six months she may never be able to regain an ability to assess value for money.

Exceptional circumstances additions are available for supplementary pensioners who have to have a special diet for medical reasons, for example because of difficulty in swallowing, or obesity. A letter from the GP or hospital doctor should be sent to Social Security (see page 138).

Ignorance

A large number of pamphlets, leaflets and books have been produced for elderly people, advising them which foods are nutritious and how they can enjoy a balanced diet. It is our opinion, however, that ignorance is not a major cause of malnutrition in old age, and many of the old people who are given this information share this opinion. They feel that as they have already managed to survive for seventy or eighty years on the basis of the knowledge acquired from their parents, their knowledge of what is good must be adequate. Widowers are an exception. Although men who marry nowadays often know how to provide for themselves, the custom was very different forty to fifty years ago. Men were working longer hours, and expected to have all their food prepared by wives who shared this expectation. Consequently some men rarely prepared any substantial food during forty or fifty years of marriage. Bereavement therefore leaves them not only desolate and depressed but ignorant of food preparation and cooking. For some widowers depression is the main reason why they do not eat properly, but others would cook if given the

right support and advice. There are a number of cookery books written specially for elderly people, but any simple cookery book will be satisfactory if the old person can understand the instructions. We would emphasise however that although most elderly people do know a great deal about food, they usually do not know enough about the nutritional causes of obesity, or the importance of fibre in the diet, to prevent constipation and bowel disorders.

Easy Cooking for One or Two by Louise Davies (Penguin) is an excellent book for older people.

Dental Problems

Teeth are important for eating, speaking, and for their appearance. If an elder has no teeth she will most probably forego meat and vegetables, which are valuable sources of iron and vitamins, so that deficiency diseases may occur, especially constipation because the diet is low in fibre. The teeth play an essential part in the formation of letters and words, and someone who has no teeth or whose teeth fit badly, is placed in an awkward social position, and may become isolated. Finally, an attractive set of teeth can improve morale, and the converse of this is that an early sign that someone is becoming depressed or is losing interest in life, is that she no longer bothers to put in her dentures.

The first set of dentures which people acquire is an important symbolic step, a sign of degeneration, and the old person with her first set has both emotional and physical problems to face.

A new set of dentures always causes some discomfort, but if the discomfort is severe the dentist should be consulted again. The face, mouth and lip muscles must learn to do their part in the support of the dentures. Soft food is best to start with, to be followed by food cut into small pieces. It is usually better to wear dentures day and night until the mouth is accustomed to them, after which they can be worn day and night, or be taken out at night, depending on the dentist's advice.

The person wearing a new set of dentures is almost always nervous, because she does not feel comfortable and confident immediately, so she should be encouraged if she is making progress and helped if she is not. The fitting and making of the set is only the first step in a long learning process. Confidence can be improved if the person practises reading aloud from a book; a mirror is very helpful for this practice.

A greater sense of security can be given by the use of a denture fixative, and a dentist can advise on the most suitable preparation. Unclean dentures are uncomfortable, but cleaning requires much more than steeping overnight in water. A special brush and denture paste are required. Ask a pharmacist if you are unsure what to buy. Remember that someone can have bad breath even though his dentures are clean, and a little toothpaste whisked up in a cup of water makes a refreshing mouth wash.

Discomfort and pain of the tongue, mouth and lips may be caused by dentures but there are other causes; most commonly mouth infections and vitamin deficiencies. If the symptoms cannot be explained by a new set of dentures seek the GP's advice.

Every adult is allowed two free examinations by a National Health Service dentist each year, but false teeth do not need to be replaced as often as this. The gums shrink quite quickly while someone is wearing her first set of dentures and they may need to be replaced after only a short time. Subsequently, dentures may have to be replaced every two years, but this varies from one person to another. Anyone who still has her own teeth should, of course, attend for a twice yearly check-up, if they can find a dentist who is willing to treat them as an NHS patient.

This is now a major problem. In many parts of the country dentists are refusing to treat patients unless they are prepared to be private patients and pay the full cost of their treatment, because they make a loss on many of the treatments for which the NHS pays. An individual is not registered with a dentist as she is with a GP. Each new course of treatment is a new contract between dentist and patient, and the dentist is at liberty to refuse to treat someone on the National Health Service, no matter how many times he has treated her in the past. This is very upsetting; not only does the old person lose the service of the dentist whom she has known for years (unless she is willing and able to pay for private treatment) but she may experience difficulty in finding another dentist who will accept her as an NHS patient. Ask your own dentist if he will accept your elder as an NHS patient. If he will not, you will have to phone a number of dentists listed in the Yellow Pages. If you are still unable to find a dentist, write to the family practitioner committee of the Health Authority in which your elder lives. They may be able to suggest a dentist known to them who is accepting NHS patients, but if they cannot help, write to the area dental officer of the Health Authority. He cannot order any dentist to accept a patient (neither can the family practitioner committee) but he may know a willing dentist. If all this fails, the elderly person will have to seek private treatment or attend a dental hospital, if she is fortunate enough to live near one. The treatment at a dental hospital is usually done by students, but they are very closely supervised and the standard of treatment is high.

Those who receive a supplementary pension are entitled to free dental treatment, and those whose income is above this level may be eligible for help, the exact amount being determined by their income. Ask the dentist for Form F.1D which has to be completed and sent to Social Security. Full details are given in *Your Guide to Dental Treatment Under The National Health Service* (Leaflet NHS4) and *Free Dental Treatment – how to claim even if you're not on supplementary benefit* (Leaflet M.11) which are available from Social Security and Post Offices.

The charge for a course of treatment

covers the cost of any subsequent *minor* adjustments to dentures which might be necessary. As mentioned above, it is not uncommon for the first set of dentures to require replacement in quite a short period of time. The *replacement* of these first dentures is regarded as a new treatment and a charge is made for the second set of dentures.

It is essential to ensure that the dentist understands that an individual wants NHS treatment, and agrees to provide this, before he treats her. The only way to be certain is to sign the NHS contract form, which requires the NHS number, before treatment starts. If this is not done the dentist can ask for private fees.

Repairs to dentures are done by dental technicians, a number of whom are listed in the Yellow Pages. To choose one that offers a reliable service, we suggest that you ask the dentist to recommend one.

If the old person finds it difficult to reach the dentist's surgery, it is possible for the dentist to visit her at home, but, it is our opinion that it is better to try to help the elder get to the surgery, because the dentist is usually able to offer better treatment there. If you are unable to take her yourself, phone or write to the local branch of Age Concern or Council for Voluntary Services (see page 13) and ask if they can provide the name of a voluntary driver, or recommend a volunteer scheme which you can approach.

If you feel you have a complaint, discuss it first direct with the dentist concerned. If you are still not satisfied you can write to the Family Practitioner Committee if the treatment was given on the National Health Service. If you are dissatisfied with private treatment you will need legal advice because there is no procedure for making complaints.

Illness and Disability

Any disabling physical or mental illness can increase the risk of nutritional problems.

If physical disability is still the cause of the elder's inability to feed herself adequately after she has been assessed and treated by a doctor and physiotherapist, she will need help with shopping, with preparing and cooking food, and with eating. A trolley can make shopping easier, but old people may find shopping too difficult even if they do not have to carry food. A nearby shop-keeper can be asked if he will deliver and collect orders; many will do this for a housebound elder even if they do not run a delivery service. Alternatively, a neighbour can be asked if she will shop for the elder when she does her own shopping. If the old person is supported by a home help she can do the shopping.

If the elder is handicapped in preparing, cooking or eating food, new ways must be found for her to perform the household tasks which disability has made impossible. There is much that you and the elder can do together to overcome her handicap, by experimenting and using common-sense. By trial and error you and the elder together can solve many of the minor problems, and expert help is available for those you cannot resolve.

Some wall tin openers can be used with only one hand. Most ironmongers sell a metal plate – the Unduit – which can be screwed to the underside of a shelf and allows jar lids to be removed easily. Cellophane wrappings and cardboard can be cut if the packet is held firmly and safely. It is usually possible to find a potato peeler which suits the elder's remaining abilities, among the types available in the ironmongers. (Household gadgets and utensils are expensive, but they can often be borrowed for a trial period from friends.) If potatoes cannot be peeled, they can be scrubbed while impaled on a spiked board.

An electric mixer is a useful gift. The small Moulinex mixer is ideal but a one-handed beater is just about as effective and is very much cheaper to buy. One of the most common problems is that bowls and dishes slip while a disabled person is trying to work. The most effective non-slip mat is a Dycem plastic pad (available from Dycem Plastics, Parkway Trading Estate, Bristol, BS2 9YB). A bread board with one raised side is very useful. A piece of bread or a biscuit can be laid against the raised side so that spreading

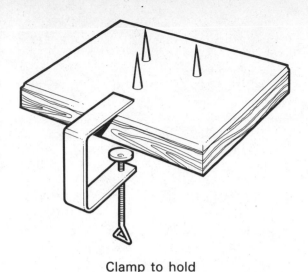

Clamp to hold
board onto table

Walking trolley

can be done with one hand. Boxes and
packets can also be steadied for opening on
such a board. Kettles which switch off
automatically are safe but still have to be
lifted for pouring. Wall mounted water
heaters boil water which can be poured
straight into the teapot and are very much
safer. Vegetables can be cooked in a chip
basket, metal sieve or a steamer. These
methods avoid the most dangerous part of
cooking, pouring off the hot water. An
electric frying pan offers great scope for
cooking and is easy to operate while seated.
If the elder can stand to operate the cooker,
she will find oven-to-table ware saves work
and reduces the risk of burning. Oven gloves
should cover the wrist — motor cycle
gauntlets are very good for the job, provided
they are not plastic, but they are expensive.
A shoulder bag or a basket or bag hung on a
walking frame allows an elder to carry a
thermos and food from the kitchen to where
she wishes to eat.

Cutlery with thick handles is easier to grasp.
Sponge rubber tubing can be obtained from
the Red Cross to adapt ordinary cutlery.

Alternatively, special cutlery can be
bought, for example a knife and fork combined, or the utensil can be strapped to the
hand with a Velcro band.

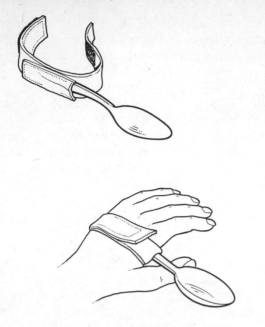

It should be possible to find plates of modern design which have an adequate side against which food can be pushed to aid lifting, but special plate sides are available to adapt flat plates.

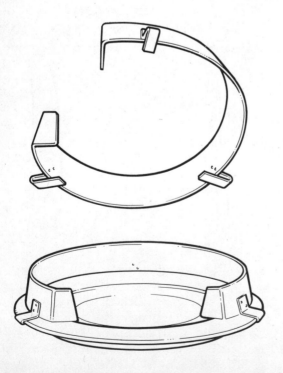

Liquids present special problems, but a teapot pouring stand can make life much easier.

Two handed soup cups are easier than conventional teacups for some people. Others will need a special cup, a straw or plastic tube.

Almost all the nutritional needs can be met by liquidised food if the elder is too disabled to manage solid food or has difficulty swallowing. A liquidiser makes an excellent present, or it may be possible to borrow one for someone who has difficulty swallowing. The dietitian should be approached, either by asking the health visitor, if the elder is at home, or the Ward Sister if she is in hospital. Slow eaters finish up with cold food, but a dish-warmer set at the lowest setting keeps food warm longer.

Whenever problems appear to be insoluble, or the right aid cannot be found, or when some action becomes dangerous, for example pouring from a teapot, the occupational therapist (see page 23) should be consulted. She will usually be able to see a way round the problem, either by suggesting that the elder uses a different approach and method, or uses an aid, or that the working surface be raised or lowered and the kitchen working area rearranged. We suggest that an occupational therapist should always be consulted before structural alterations are made to the kitchen.

If an old person is still too handicapped to be able to cook with all these aids, home helps can do the cooking, with meals-on-wheels when the home help cannot come. The meal service is usually very limited at weekends; some Social Services Departments pay neighbours of elders whose family live far away to cook for them on Saturdays and Sundays. Most meals-on-wheels services are only able to give a meal on all five weekdays to those most in need.

It is our opinion, and we cannot emphasise this strongly enough, that isolation is the cause of malnutrition most often overlooked. For most people eating is not only a nutritional, but a social process. The appetite fades away when meal after meal is eaten alone. Food becomes tasteless and eating boring. Even the basic hunger drive becomes dulled by isolation and depression. Lunch clubs are better than meals-on-wheels for some people, because the old person is given the most effective aperitif of all – the companionship of other people. There are now lunch clubs in most towns and the local Age Concern office should know where and when they meet. Instead of cooking *for* an elder, those who are trying to help should eat *with* them or, better still, ask the elder to cook for someone else as well as herself.

DISABILITY AND HANDICAP

There is no easy definition of disability. It would be unnatural for a man to be as able at eighty as he was at twenty, or for a woman aged seventy-five to be able to work as well as she could when she was thirty-five. Anyone who expects to avoid disability as they grow old will be disappointed. Neither is it possible to define disability by comparing an old person with all others of the same age. Although an old person can always think of a contemporary who is more able than he is, there are always those who are worse off. There is no definite standard of disability against which an old person can be assessed. He must be judged, and must judge himself, in the light of his past abilities, his age and any diseases from which he might suffer.

However, anyone who feels frustrated that he cannot do something, which it is reasonable to expect of someone of his age and background, requires help to deal both with the frustration and the disability which gives rise to it. Sometimes an old person is frustrated because he is unrealistic in his expectations. As we have said, some loss of ability is inevitable but some old people cannot accept this. It is often difficult for family members to discuss this with an elderly relative, and the help of the elder's GP can be invaluable. He can bring out the cause of the frustration, help him adjust to his decreasing power and manage the depression which sometimes follows the acknowledgement that old age has arrived. In most cases, however, the frustrations can be reduced by helping the old person overcome the disability which is the underlying cause. When an old person is prevented from looking after himself, i.e. when he is unable to wash or dress, do housework, get to the lavatory or feed himself independently, he is said to be handicapped by his disability. Similarly, if he is so immobile that he cannot look after his affairs – for example, going to the Post Office for his pension, or enjoy the social and leisure activities which are reasonable for someone of his age and background, he can be said to be handicapped. We have discussed the problem of immobility (see page 59) and here discuss the management of disability which handicaps the elder in his ability to care for himself.

Emotional Problems

Disability is not only a physical problem. Disability can cause depression even if the affected person was previously of a cheerful disposition. It can also cause anxiety. People who are unable to look after themselves are often anxious, not only because they are never completely sure their helpers will turn up, but also because they often fear that they will have to go and live in a home or hospital some day. Disability is a cause of isolation which in turn causes many serious mental problems.

Not only does disability affect the mental wellbeing of a person, but mental factors can cause disability. Some people who cannot leave their wheelchairs are able to work, drive cars and lead a full family and social life. Others, whose physical disability appears to be identical, achieve little in comparison. The same can be observed with all types of physical disability. No two people respond in the same way to an identical impairment in ability. In general, people who were alert and had strong motivation before becoming disabled manage to overcome their disability to

85

a greater extent, and are less handicapped than those whose approach to life was not so positive. Sometimes someone who was well motivated and tried hard to succeed in all aspects of life is severely handicapped by a small degree of physical impairment. If this is the case, depression should be suspected. Depression, whether caused by the disability or not can result in apathy and loss of motivation. For example, an active old person who is told he has arthritis may be so depressed, imagining his future, that he stops trying to help himself. If depression is suspected the elder's GP should be consulted (see page 98). Isolation can also contribute to disability. An old person who is isolated and receives company and attention from home help, nursing and other services because he is disabled, may not be inclined to struggle to overcome his disability. The 'reward' for someone like this who makes the effort and overcomes disability is that he loses his companions. This process is unconscious, the old person does not realise he is not trying as hard as he can to become independent. If you feel that the disability has psychological causes or consequences, you need the opportunity to discuss it with someone. Either the GP, health visitor or any other professional who knows the old person well, for example an occupational therapist or social worker, should be approached.

The key to the management of disability is adjustment. The elder must be given help to adjust to his decreasing ability and so must his supporters. Disability is not only something physical 'in' the old person, it is the physical effect of his physical impairment, his reaction to it *and* the effect these two influences have on his interactions with other people. He may become frustrated and angry towards his disability, and this may surface as anger towards his helpers. He may be bitter that fate should have singled him out for physical impairment, and this bitterness can colour all his interactions with other people. The people helping may feel angry towards an elder they feel could do more than he does. Disability does not only pro-

duce sympathy and compassion but also tension and anger, both of which are normal. Adjustment takes time, and the advice and support of professionals. Any professional who knows, and is trusted by, the disabled elder and his supporters can counsel effectively, but occupational therapists are particularly experienced in helping people and their families adjust to physical impairment, and social workers are skilled in the management of anger or tension in families.

Overcoming Handicaps

We will describe the aids and adaptations which are available (outlined in much more detail in *Coping with Disablement*, available from the Consumers' Association and most public libraries) but the emphasis will be on the professionals who are there to support and advise you. We would not like you to rush out and spend money on aids, because the real solution to the problem might lie in better medical treatment, the retraining of muscles or the relearning of an old skill with the help of a physiotherapist.

When disability develops, the solution to many small problems will be found by you and by the elder himself, by the use of common sense. By trial and error one type of comb or bath brush is found which is more suitable than others. However, if you are considering spending more than a pound or two, or altering the structure of the elder's dwelling, you may wish to consult an occupational therapist.

Dressing and undressing
If an old person is still unable to dress or undress independently after he has had appropriate medical treatment and physiotherapy, he can still be helped to manage his clothes independently. He can be taught new ways of performing old tasks. For example, an elder affected by a stroke can often put on a pullover if he uses the good arm to pull it over the affected arm first, laying the

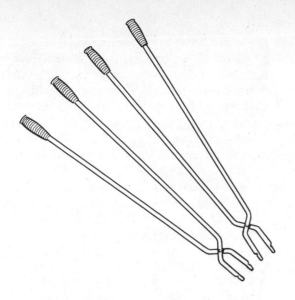

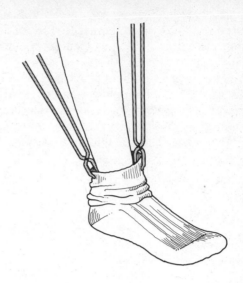

Sock tongs in action

affected arm on a table for support. Teeth can be used to pull on or off a glove or cuff. If it proves impossible to teach a new skill, simple aids can be given which allow a disabled person to pull up a zip, lift on a jacket, pull on a sock or perform other dressing or undressing actions.

These aids are available from the Red Cross, which publishes a good catalogue *Aids for Disabled People*, but you should consult the occupational therapist as to their

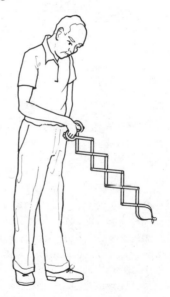

Dressing stick (hanger with rubber page turner on end)

suitability. It is also possible to adapt clothes. Zips are usually easier than buttons and Velcro fastenings are often less difficult than zips. A different design of clothing may be less handicapping, and this does not necessarily mean clothing designed only for disabled people, although some firms do design for disability. Clip-on braces rather than those which have buttons, wrap-around skirts or dresses which fasten at the front, can make all the difference between dependence and independence. Specially designed clothing may be required, for example trousers with a drop open front, or a made-up tie with elastic at the back. The WRVS produce a guide to help people adapt clothing for slightly disabled elders, and occupational therapists have catalogues of new clothing for all degrees of disability.

Pick-ups are invaluable for dressing.

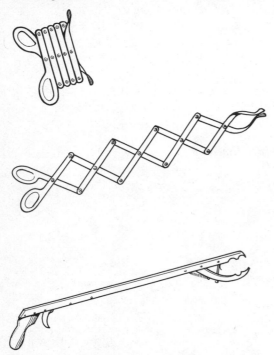

The Disabled Living Foundation (346 Kensington High Street, London) has a clothing advisor whose advice can be asked on all aspects of clothing. The Shirley Institute (Didsbury, Manchester, M20 8RX) publishes a catalogue listing both the designs of special clothing available and their suppliers.

If the old person is too disabled to dress or undress himself independently despite these aids, the district nursing service can help him both in the morning and the evening, although the amount of help available is variable. Home helps are not always employed to help old people dress, although many do, and wardens of sheltered accommodation are not meant to help with dressing, although some will help in an emergency.

Washing and bathing

If the old person is mobile enough to walk to a basin this should be encouraged. The bathroom floor should be free from mats; a fitted carpet is better and can be laid quite cheaply. If he is prone to falling, or unsteady on his feet, the basin can be a dangerous place for an old person, who has to close his eyes, bend over and splash water on his face. A seat of the correct height is very useful as is a rail beside, or round, the basin.

Any rails put up should be fixed with screws which are at least two inches long.

Shoulder stiffness is common and limits the person's ability to wash the back of the neck, back and hair. A sponge on a piece of string, or long narrow piece of towel can be used to wash the back of the neck and trunk. A long towel attached to the wall can be used to dry parts of the body which cannot be reached in a conventional manner.

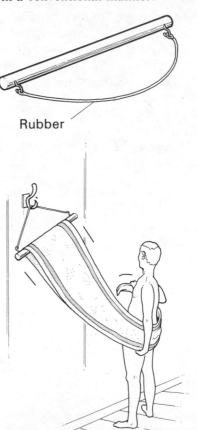

Rubber

If the taps are difficult to turn, ask the occupational therapist whether she thinks a tap turner is indicated, or whether the tap should be changed to one with a lever which is easier to turn.

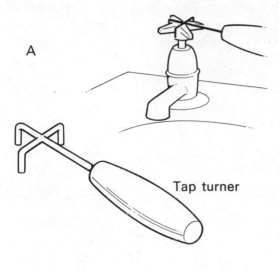

A

Tap turner

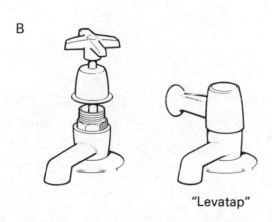

B

"Levatap"

It may be possible to find a hairdresser to pay a home visit at least once a month to wash and set hair. Brushing and combing can be made possible by the use of a long handled comb or brush. If a home visit cannot be arranged, a volunteer can often be found to take an old person to the hairdresser periodically. This provides company as well as hairdressing and is preferable if the elder is isolated.

Sponge sticks are available for washing legs and feet.

Eyes, ears and nose are difficult to clean if the ability to control movements accurately is lost. Ask the advice of the domiciliary nurse on keeping these areas clean.

The use of a towelling mitt to make soap less slippery and easier to hold, or a nail brush attached to the basin with suction cups for people who have lost the power of one hand can be helpful, and by experimenting you will find ways of washing which suit the elder, but remember that the district nurse and the occupational therapist are there to advise you both.

Many old people find bathing particularly difficult. The height of the bath and the need to squat right down make getting in difficult, and getting out is just as great a problem. The bath can also be dangerous. A bath mat which attaches to the base of the bath, or adhesive treads are essential aids for all old people. A handrail attached to the wall with two inch screws, or a top-rail offer security and support.

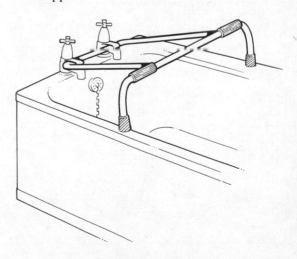

'Economic' safety rail

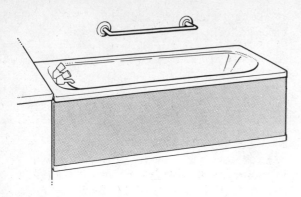

Bath board and seat

Sometimes an old person who has fallen becomes too nervous to bathe alone. The presence of yourself or a friend in the house, if not in the bathroom, may bolster the elder's confidence sufficiently for him to bathe. If you are willing and able to help your elder into and out of the bath, you should ask the district nurse to teach you both how best to do this, because it is very easy for a helper to damage her back. She may suggest that a more elaborate aid would be helpful, either a bath seat, a board and seat, a vertical pole or a hoist, or perhaps a combination of these.

The nurse may ask the domiciliary occupational therapist to call to assess the

Hoist

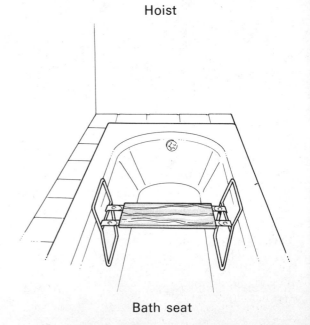

Vertical rail

Bath seat

situation and advise. Or you can approach the domiciliary occupational therapist yourself.

A shower can help an elder remain independent, who could not otherwise do so, but we would advise this only if the shower has an effective thermostat and is not simply attached to the hot and cold taps. A shower unit is also useful for some disabled people who cannot use a bath independently, provided that it has a non-slip floor, a seat on which the elder can sit while showering and a thermostat on the shower unit. We think that it is always wise to consult an occupational therapist before installing a shower or modifying the bathroom.

Remember that some elderly people manage to work out ways of 'washing up as far as possible and down as far as possible' and that a bidet can often allow them to complete the process and become clean all over without a bath.

If an old person is unable to bathe herself even with these aids and your help, you can ask her doctor if he can arrange for the domiciliary nurse to visit regularly, usually once a week, to help the elder bathe. The nurse will give a bed bath or a chairbath if she cannot help the elder get into and out of the bath. It is also possible for an old person to attend a day centre or a day hospital to be bathed.

Independence in personal care is very important. If it is lost, not only does the elder become dependent but she loses her dignity. To be helped with lighting a fire is one thing but to have someone else, no matter how nice they may be, wash your bottom or comb your hair is quite another. Some old people enjoy it; others find it distasteful and upsetting and will be very gratified if they can gain as much independence as possible in personal care.

Advice Centres

There are three important centres which can provide advice and help for a disabled person and her supporters.

Disabled Living Foundation
(346 Kensington High Street, London, W14 81VS. 01–602 2491) has a vast store of help and information for the disabled. It runs an Aid Centre and has an information service which covers a broad range of subjects concerning disabled people such as clothing, aids to prevent incontinence and aids for housework.

Scottish Information Service for the Disabled
(18 Claremont Crescent, Edinburgh, EH7 3QD. 031–556 3882) provides an information service and advice with special facilities for professionals such as social workers, and has a reference library available.

Wales Council for the Disabled
(Crescent Road, Caerphilly, Mid Glamorgan, CF81 1XL. 0222 869224) acts as the national co-ordinating body for organisations for the disabled, both statutory and voluntary. The organisation comments upon proposed legislation on all matters affecting the disabled and seeks to encourage their support on amenities and facilities for the disabled. It is also able to give advice.

DRUGS AND MEDICINES

Old people are frequently prescribed drugs and medicines by GPs and consultants in hospital, and they buy and consume many others without prescription. Every drug has more than one effect on the body; the effect for which it is taken is called its therapeutic action, the others are called side-effects. Aspirin, for example, is taken because its therapeutic action as a pain-killer (an analgesic) is very good. But aspirin also has side effects; for example it can irritate the stomach causing nausea, pain and sometimes bleeding, and it can cause buzzing in the ears. Usually the side effects of a drug are mild and unimportant at the dose necessary to achieve a satisfactory therapeutic action, but no two people are the same, and a minority experience side-effects after taking a dose which causes no problems for the majority. They are said to be sensitive to the drug's effects. In general, people become more sensitive to drugs as they become older, because the liver and kidneys, which inactivate drugs, become less efficient.

Side-effects can occur even when drugs are taken exactly as prescribed. They are more common if the old person does not take them as the doctor intended. An elderly person may become confused by the frequency with which he should take different drugs, taking the 'three times a day' drug only once and the 'once a day' drug three times. He may take all his drugs with the same frequency, for example, taking all four of his prescribed drugs three times a day, although that instruction applies only to one drug, or he may take a dose, forget he has taken it and repeat the dose an hour later. Some old people make all these types of mistakes, and make different mistakes on different days.

There are a number of reasons why people make mistakes with drugs:

- Failing memory. Doctors know that very many people of all ages forget to take the drugs prescribed after the first day or two of treatment. When people get older and experience loss of memory this tendency is increased.
- Failure to comprehend instructions. An old person who is hard of hearing or nervous may not catch the doctor's spoken instructions and his vision may be too poor to read those written by the pharmacist.
- Failure to appreciate the importance of the prescribed drug. Particularly with diseases which cause few symptoms, an old person may not understand why he has been prescribed a certain drug and may not appreciate how important it is to keep taking it. People sometimes stop taking a drug if they develop a symptom even though that symptom has nothing to do with the drug.
- Self-medication. Not only do old people buy their own drugs, some keep any prescribed drugs which are left after a

course of treatment, taking them again from time to time without consulting the doctor again. *Drugs which are no longer necessary should be disposed of.* Ask at the health centre or surgery how best to do this.

There are two occasions when mistakes are particularly likely to occur for the first time, thus setting a pattern of mistakes which will be repeated every day.

1) When an old person is prescribed a new drug, with a new set of instructions by his GP, this can upset his established routine of medicine taking. It can cause not only errors in the way he takes the newly prescribed drug but can upset the accuracy with which he has been taking his other drugs.

2) When an elderly person is in hospital he is often given new drugs. In the ward his drugs are usually kept in the drug-cupboard, and the correct dose handed to him at the right time of day when the nurses take the drugs round to the patients. When he goes back home he has suddenly to take over all this control of his medication, and mistakes are not uncommon at this time. He may also mistakenly recommence taking the drugs he left at home when he went into hospital, although they were discontinued when the new drugs were prescribed by the hospital staff.

If a drug has been prescribed by the GP, he is the person to consult, or the health visitor if he is not available. If a drug is prescribed in hospital, the Ward Sister can be consulted and she can ask one of the medical staff if she is unable to answer your questions. You can also consult a pharmacist in the pharmacy or chemist's shop which dispensed the GP's prescription. Not everyone wearing a white coat behind the counter in a pharmacy is a pharmacist; there is usually only one in each shop, so you have to ask to see the pharmacist if you are in any doubt at all. Pharmacists are highly qualified in all aspects of the effects of drugs on the body, and very well prepared to advise an old person or his supporters.

The following questions are those which are most important:

- What is the dose?
- How many times each day should the dose be taken?
- Are there any special instructions relating to food?
- Should it be taken before, after, or with food? Are certain foods to be avoided while taking the drug?
- Can the old person take alcohol on the same day he takes the drug?
- Will the drug react with any other prescribed drug or any medicine the elder has bought himself?
- Are there any side-effects to watch for?

If any new symptoms develop while the old person is being treated with a drug, the elder's GP should be informed, but, if you cannot make contact with the GP, the pharmacist should be consulted.

Even if you and the old person know all about the drugs and their properties it can still be a problem to ensure that they are taken as the doctor intended. It is too much responsibility for a neighbour or volunteer to give drugs to an old person regularly, although some will do it well and without anxiety. The wardens of sheltered housing are usually forbidden by their employers to take on this responsibility. If a domiciliary nurse is going in every day to treat an old person, she will see that he takes his medicines, but in most areas the district nursing services is too busy to visit daily just to give drugs, except for insulin and other drugs which have to be given by injection. An old person can be helped if his day's drugs are laid out in egg-cups, if instructions are written in large print, or if he is phoned to remind him when it is time to take his drugs, but these methods are no substitute for time spent in explanation. The old person has to understand why and how he is to take his drugs if he is to remember them, and that takes time in discussion with doctor, nurse or pharmacist.

Homoeopathic Medicine

Homoeopathy is a branch of medicine practised by doctors. Homoeopathic doctors choose the remedy for a particular patient according to the totality of the symptoms, rather than on the basis of the diagnosis. The diagnostic criteria are only a part of this whole symptom picture.

For treatment medicinal substances are used. These are all natural mineral, plant and animal substances, unaltered by chemical processes. The medicinal substances are diluted many times so that treatment is in minute quantities. This is very different from modern medicine in which new and artificial chemical substances are manufactured to make drugs. Modern drugs are often very effective because they are very powerful. However, they also have many side-effects, some of them very serious, which medicinal substances do not have.

If the elder is worried about the drugs used in medicine, homoeopathy with its emphasis on the natural source of its remedies, may be more attractive. If the homoeopathic doctor finds a disorder which would be better treated by surgery or by modern drugs, he will refer the problem to a surgeon or use conventional drug therapy.

Homoeopathic medicine is available on the National Health Service, but there are very few doctors specially trained in homoeopathy. If the elder wishes to choose a GP who will offer homoeopathic treatment, write to:

The Faculty of Homoeopathy,
2 Powis Place,
Great Ormond Street,
London, WC1.

They will inform you of doctors who practise homoeopathic medicine in the locality. If one practises nearby you must approach him to see if he will accept the old person as a NHS patient. If there is no doctor living near enough, the elder will have to rely on a local GP but should tell him that she prefers homoeopathic treatment whenever possible. If she breaks a bone or has varicose veins, he will refer her to the local general hospital for treatment, which is just what a homoeopathic doctor would do. However, if the GP agrees that a second opinion is needed she can be referred to:

The Royal London Homoeopathic Hospital,
Great Ormond Street,
London, WC1.

This applies even for those who do not live in London. If the cost of travel will be a problem, write to the medical social worker at the hospital to see if help with the fares can be obtained.

NURSING AT HOME

Although most serious illnesses are managed in hospital, many of the minor illnesses of old people which confine them to bed are managed at home. Supporters of elderly people should know the basic principles of home nursing because they will almost certainly have to do some nursing for one or two days each year, sometimes more often. Some nursing tasks are highly skilled and require years of training, but the basic techniques of caring for ill people are fairly simple to learn, although they may be difficult to apply in practice.

There are four main types of nursing task:

● Making a comfortable bed.
● Keeping the ill person clean and comfortable – care of the skin and pressure areas, mouth, eyes, ears, hair and nails.
● Helping the ill person to change position in bed, to move from bed to chair and back, and to perform such other movements as are necessary.
● Personal care and treatment – giving medicines and pills, helping the patient to eat and enjoy her food, ensuring an adequate fluid intake, and giving a bed pan.

We could cover page after page with descriptions and drawings of how to help a person move in bed, or sit on a bed pan; however, it is our opinion that such skills cannot be adequately taught by word and picture. No two ill people are the same and the abilities and strengths of each helper are different. We believe that such skills have to be taught by a qualified teacher.

If illness strikes, the domiciliary nurse is the ideal person to give both practical help and advice. She can not only give the ill person a bed bath, but she can show the helpers how best to keep the elder clean between her visits. The domiciliary nurse does not only make a patient comfortable. She is willing and trained to teach those who will be with the elder all day to perform the simple tasks which lead to comfort. The elder's GP may suggest that the domiciliary nurse should call as soon as he has diagnosed the illness, or the domiciliary nursing service can be phoned directly (see page 21).

The Red Cross lends aids such as bed pans, commodes and back rests, to people who are being nursed at home. Before any equipment is bought the domiciliary nurse should be asked whether or not it could be borrowed.

Nurses can also be engaged privately for nursing at home by contacting a nursing agency (see page 21).

It is more satisfactory to prepare for illness before it happens, and we would advise everyone to enrol for one of the home nursing courses run by either the Red Cross or St. John Ambulance Association and Brigade, or the St. Andrew's Ambulance Association (in Scotland only). The courses are excellent and prepare people for nursing patients of all ages. The three associations produce a very good manual called *Nursing*, and the British Red Cross Society produces a helpful set of cards called *What You Need to Remember about Nursing for the Family*. The manual and cards, however, are best used after the skills have been taught by a trained instructor.

Although home helps are not allowed to nurse people, the difference they can make to the housework of either the elder or the person helping her can make the nursing task much lighter.

CANCER CARE

In some parts of the country the Health Service has set up terminal care units, sometimes called continuing care units to help people affected by cancer. Even though the cancer cannot be cured, expert help can greatly diminish both the suffering from physical symptoms and the psychological strain felt by both the patient and his relatives.

Two charities offer special help to cancer sufferers.

Marie Curie Memorial Foundation,
124 Sloane Street,
London, SW1X 9RF.
01–730 9157.

The foundation can help provide a night nurse – ask a domiciliary nurse for details. It can also help financially and has a small number of residential homes.

National Society for Cancer Relief,
Michael Sobell House,
30 Dorset Square,
London, NW1 6OL.
01–402 8125.

This society provides financial assistance, e.g. grants to help pay fuel costs or buy extra bedding.

Both these charities, like all others, need financial assistance themselves.

HOSPITAL CARE

In-patient

More serious illnesses are better managed in hospital, although even strokes and heart attacks can be well managed at home, providing the elderly person and her supporters are given the appropriate type of help.

The change of environment following hospital admission is sometimes very disturbing to an old person who is physically ill, and as much detail as possible should be given to the nursing staff so that they can attend to her needs. If it is her custom to have a commode by the bed, or a nightlight, tell the Ward Sister. If you have always made sure that she went to pass water every night at eleven, make sure the nursing staff know as this can prevent her becoming agitated and incontinent. The Sister is the person on whom you should rely. Inform her of the elder's Social Security arrangements as soon as she is admitted. If there are any social problems, you can ask the Sister to make an appointment with the medical social worker for you. If ever an old person needs contact and engagement with those she knows and loves, it is when she is removed from her familiar environment. Visits are vitally important.

If you feel that the amount of notice given before discharge is too short for you to make the necessary arrangements, tell the medical social worker immediately. If that has no effect, phone the elder's GP and tell him why you think it is impossible for her to be discharged. He can then use his influence to try to persuade the hospital to keep her in until suitable preparations can be made. If nursing is necessary, the domiciliary nurse should be consulted. If the elder has become disabled during her illness, the hospital occupational therapist should be consulted before discharge.

It is not always easy for the GP to find a place in hospital for an old person. Sometimes there are just not any empty beds in the geriatric hospital. On other occasions there may be an argument between the hospital and the Social Services Department – the hospital staff saying she is 'not ill enough' to be admitted to hospital, the staff of the Social Services Department maintaining that she is 'not fit enough' for an old people's home. In either case the GP may be powerless to put more pressure on the hospital, and the specialist in community medicine for social services, a doctor working in the Health Authority offices, may be approached by the GP and asked to try to resolve this difference of opinion.

Sometimes an old person is so disabled

that her relatives think she should stay in hospital and not return home. Hospital staff are not keen to take people to live in hospital. Even though an elder has been in hospital for three or six months, or even longer, the aim of the hospital staff will still usually be to rehabilitate her sufficiently to go home or be transferred to an old people's home. However, there are a few beds in each hospital unit for old people to live in until they die. The places are few so that there is often a very long wait for a bed to become vacant.

If there is danger of loss or damage to the furniture or goods of an old person who is admitted to hospital or to an old people's home, the Social Services Department can take steps to prevent such loss or damage. Action can be taken using the power vested in Section 48 of the National Assistance Act 1948, but if the Social Services Department feel that this will not be sufficient they may discuss the possibility of application to the Court of Protection with the elder's supporters.

Day Hospital and Intermittent Admissions

If an old person cannot be admitted to hospital to give permanent relief to the family or friends supporting her, regular temporary relief can be offered by attendance at day hospital and by admission for a short stay at regular intervals.

An elder is taken to and from day hospital by ambulance, if necessary being dressed by a domiciliary nurse before she is collected. At a day hospital the elder's medical condition can be kept under review by doctors, and physiotherapists can prevent her disability becoming more severe. She can also be nursed, for example she can have a bath, be given an enema, or have her hair washed. At the day hospital occupational therapists

organise craft work (which the old person may be able to continue at home) and can assess her disability and try to overcome her handicaps. The staff of day hospitals also try to relieve the elder's supporters as well as helping the elder. The consultant in geriatric medicine can sometimes offer care on all five weekdays to enable a son or daughter to work. Although Social Services or voluntary day centres do not offer such intensive treatment, some have staff and facilities to bathe those old people who attend. An old person can attend both a day hospital and a day centre (see page 55), if the day hospital doctors accept the GP's referral and the day centre organiser has a vacant place to offer.

As an alternative, or in addition to day hospital attendance, the consultant in geriatric medicine may offer intermittent admissions to the elderly person. This means planning admissions at regular intervals over the next six months or year, for example, for three days every fortnight, or one week every three months, or at whatever interval suits the elderly person, depending on the demands made on the hospital by all the other elderly people and their supporters who need help. This series of planned admissions can also include a two week break to enable the elder's supporter to have a holiday.

The hospital may suggest that the elder would benefit from a series of planned admissions, but if you feel that *you* would benefit from such regular relief ask the GP if he can request the consultant in geriatric medicine to consider your problem. You can make the suggestion yourself if you make an appointment to see the medical social worker at the hospital. She may also be able to arrange for relief admissions to an old people's home if the old person is not too severely disabled.

Don't allow yourelf to be broken by the burden of caring. Everyone needs to recharge their batteries.

Chapter 7
Mental Health in Old Age

MENTAL HEALTH ADVICE

The elder's general practitioner (see page 18) and health visitor (see page 21) are the first people to approach for advice and support. If a social worker is involved, she too will be a useful source of help. If the elder is attending a psychiatric hospital, either the psychiatrist or psychiatric nurse, and the hospital based social worker can be approached.

If you feel that the services are unsatisfactory or appear to be unavailable, the Community Health Council (see page 29) or, in Scotland, the Local Health Council, can be consulted. They may seek the help of MIND, (22 Harley Street, London, W1) which is a specialist advisory body interested in the problems and rights of people who are mentally ill, and the problems and rights of their relatives and friends. The Mental Health Foundation (8 Wimpole Street, London, W1) is also interested in those problems and in the improvement of mental health services.

WHAT IS MENTAL ILLNESS?

To understand mental health and what is called mental illness in old age, it is necessary to consider the concept of mental illness which prevails in our society.

When the term 'mental illness' was introduced to replace the idea of possession by evil spirits as an explanation of disorders of mood, thinking or behaviour, and treatment replaced exorcism, a great advance was made. It has been very useful to consider mental illness and physical illness as two similar phenomena which should be treated with skill and sympathy, but there have been drawbacks. For example, the cause of the mental illness was often sought *in* the patient, concentrating especially on his development and upbringing, whereas mental illness, like physical illness, is often caused or aggravated by factors in the environment *around* a person. Treatment cannot cure if the patient has to return to the same environment which caused his problem.

Another drawback is that, just as it has become the practice to regard people as being physically 'ill' or 'not ill', with a sharp distinction between the two states, so has it been common to regard mental illness as a completely separate state of being. There are some types of mental condition which no-one would dispute are abnormal, just as no-one would dispute the abnormality of a broken leg, but many people receiving treatment from GPs are experiencing mental symptoms which are qualitatively normal. It is normal to be anxious and depressed at times, to feel persecuted and out of joint with one's friends and family periodically, but it is not normal for those feelings to reach such an intensity as to interfere with the family and social activities of daily life.

People have developed the same attitude to mental symptoms as to their physical symptoms, coming to believe that doctors will be able to diagnose and cure them. They seek out the doctor not only because of their faith in the expert, but often because he is the only person to whom they can turn in times of trouble. Because relatively little is known about the thoughts and feelings of people in the past, it is not known whether mental symptoms are more common or more severe nowadays than in times past. What is certain is that the sources of help in times of trouble are, for most people, much fewer. Respect for the church and confidence in the minister have diminished; people are much less likely to live near relatives; and the increase in population mobility makes the development of close friendships more difficult and splits many of those which form, as people move about the country in the course of their career. People who go to see doctors with mental symptoms, and even those who are given drugs, are not necessarily 'mentally ill'. Many are not so much those who are *more* disturbed, but those who are *less* well supported in society.

When we consider the lives of many elderly people, it is obvious that they are less well supported than younger people. Work is itself a form of group therapy, whatever the nature of the job. Many minor worries are resolved and depressions lifted by colleagues at work, and by the activity of work. Younger people are more frequently able to go out and meet other people in pubs, clubs, churches and other group activities. Because of their low income and immobility, elderly people are denied these opportunities to divert their minds with the ideas, stimulation and sympathies of other people. Friends die, children often move away and – the most shattering blow of all – the spouse sometimes also dies. Bereavement affects many old people, leaving them alone, so it is not surprising that elderly people often take their mental symptoms to the GP, solely because they have fewer alternative means of psychological support than young people.

The tranquillity of the mind is probably upset more often in old age, but in our opinion the number of problems taken to GPs reflects not an epidemic of mental illness in old age, but the nature of our society in which old people are often isolated and unsupported. If an elder is receiving treatment from his GP for some disorder of the mind, or even if he is visiting a psychiatric hospital, it does not mean that he is 'insane' or 'mad'.

Symptom and Diagnosis

A symptom is what a person feels wrong with himself. A diagnosis is the name the doctor gives to what he decides is wrong. Sometimes both are the same, for example depression can be both the elder's feeling and the doctor's diagnosis. Or they may be different, for example when an old person feels worried that her memory is failing and the doctor's diagnosis is dementia, or when an old man does not know where he is and wanders about his house feeling upset, and the doctor diagnoses an acute infection as the cause of his confusion.

Both symptom and diagnosis are important, but a third factor must also be considered. When an old person is mentally disturbed, the feelings and problems of his helpers, *their* symptoms, have to be identified before the problem can be completely defined.

DEPRESSION

It would be abnormal for people of any age not to feel depressed on certain occasions. Depressing events and trends occur with increasing frequency as a person grows older:
- Retirement is a depressing blow for many people.
- Life on a low income can be demeaning and depressing. Not only is decision-making dominated by money rather than the individual's choice, but low income is a depressing reminder of low status. The need to apply for financial help and undergo means tests is felt by many people to be degrading and depressing.
- The frequency and enjoyment of sexual intercourse may be affected or completely curtailed by physical disability or feelings of guilt.
- Isolation frequently causes loneliness and depression (see page 43).
- Deteriorating housing conditions are very disheartening, especially for an owner occupier who has struggled for decades to buy and look after his home.

- Physical disease and disability affect even the most resilient and optimistic character.
- Deaths of friends cause depression, and the death of a spouse desolation. The effect of a death on an elder is both direct, due to the loss, and indirect because each death of a contemporary reminds an old person of his own inevitable death (see page 196).
- Dependence is depressing. It is not just that a dependent person was previously independent, but he had other people – children, spouse, neighboursand friends – dependent on him, so dependence is a double loss. It is a loss of independence and the dependence *of* others, both now replaced by a dependence *on* others.

When all these factors are considered it would be surprising if some elderly people were not depressed more commonly than young people. It is normal for an elder to have an afternoon, day or even a longer spell of depression, and this must be respected. There is no point in telling an elder to 'snap out of it' or to think how lucky he is. On the other hand it is not right to make no effort to lift the depression. The best way to do this is not to argue with the depressed person, but to let him talk about his fears of death, or his dependence on you, or whatever is the underlying cause. Try to understand not only his doubts, fears and worries, but the reason why he is depressed by them. Rather than telling him he 'should not' be depressed, agree that it is reasonable for him to be depressed and that he is not mentally ill, for many people fear depression itself.

When should the help of an outsider be sought? There is no general rule which can cover all cases, but we suggest that an outsider can be helpful when the depression is felt to be a problem by the elder or his supporters.

This can occur when:

- The cause of the depression cannot be found by discussion within the family or with friends.

- He is worried that he is becoming mentally ill.
- He loses interest in life and becomes apathetic.
- The depression is upsetting the balance of family life.
- He says the reason for the depression is that he is bad or unworthy, or that it is a punishment for past sins.
- He wakes depressed earlier in the morning than is usual for him, or when his appetite is affected and his weight starts to decrease.

If he says or even hints that he is considering suicide, this should be taken very seriously and referred to the GP immediately. Suicide is more common in old people, especially in older men. Although it can be argued that people have the right to commit suicide after they have been offered and tried to find comfort from all the helping services available, it is a tragedy if people commit suicide before anyone has tried to help them.

If the cause for the depression can be identified, you can immediately involve the outsider who could solve the problem, for example a social worker, if the elder is going to be evicted. However, we think that it is appropriate to ask the GP's opinion at the same time, because of the risk of suicide.

Depression does not always make itself clear as a symptom, even to the depressed person. A person who is depressed may not realise it, perhaps because he is ashamed of the cause of the depression. Depression can present itself in the following ways:

- As constipation. The constipation may be a result of the reduced intake of food due to decreased appetite, but it can occur even with a normal intake if a person is depressed.
- As listlessness. The elder may feel tired or 'washed out', or complain that he has no energy or doesn't enjoy life. These symptoms can be caused by depression or by physical disorders, so it is important for the GP to be consulted if they persist for longer than a few days.

- As physical symptoms. Depression can cause physical symptoms, headaches and neuralgia, pains in the joints or any of a host of other minor symptoms. A depressed person may have more than one type of symptom and attend his GP time after time with different minor complaints. Sometimes he is accused of being a hypochondriac, but this is untrue. He really feels these symptoms, although the underlying depression goes undetected both by himself and his GP.
- As agitation and confusion. Although it is usual for depression to slow people down, it can have the opposite effect. Someone who is depressed can become very agitated and more active, rushing about from one task to another without completing any, and talking in a disjointed manner, leaping from one topic to another without discussing any single topic coherently.

Remember that someone who suffers from dementia can also become depressed and show any of these symptoms. It is particularly important not to forget this because someone who does suffer from dementia (see page 106) may be unable to express himself clearly and declare his feeling of depression in words.

The Alleviation of Depression

We are all experienced in the management of mild depression, because we manage and alleviate our own depressions and those which affect our family, friends and colleagues. Even when the GP, psychiatrist or one of his team is involved, you have a vitally important part to play. Ask the GP or psychiatrist how you should discuss the old person's depression with him, and continue to treat him as normally as possible. Affection, companionship and love are always useful 'treatments', and the elder may need more physical affection than usual while he is depressed. Touching is supportive and helpful, even if it is only holding the elder's hand while talking with him.

Professionals have a number of different ways of tackling depression. The first is to solve the underlying problem. Once the GP is satisfied that the elder is not seriously depressed, he may ask the health visitor to take over responsibility for solving these problems, and the related depression; alternatively, he may ask a social worker's help. Social workers are particularly useful when the cause of the depression is not obvious or when it lies in the family. For example, if an old person feels guilty about his dependence and the demands he makes on his children, he can become depressed. If this depression is not alleviated by the family's assurance that he is not a burden, a social worker may be able to help. This requires the co-operation and involvement of the whole family in honest and frank discussion. If it is felt that isolation is a cause of depression, the provision of home help and the offer of transport to a day centre can be arranged by the health visitor or social worker. Remember that the Samaritans are always there in emergencies.

The GP can prescribe anti-depressant drugs, but he may be reluctant to do this because of their side effects. Depressed people are sometimes so disinterested and apathetic that they do not take the drugs prescribed for them, so the advice we give on drugs (see page 91) is very relevant for anti-depressant drugs. The GP may decide to refer the elder to a psychiatrist for one or more of the following reasons. He may be unsure of the diagnosis, whether the elder is depressed or suffering from something else; he may be unsure how severe the depression is and want the psychiatrist's opinion on the risk of suicide, or his advice on treatment. Psychiatrists cannot prescribe any different anti-depressant drugs from those which GPs are able to prescribe, but they can manage depression in other ways. If the psychiatrist is fortunate enough to be well supported and works with a psychiatric nurse and a social worker, one of the team is able to spend more time with the depressed person than is possible for the GP or health visitor. The psychiatrist can ask the elder to come to the day hospital, to spend the day with trained staff, being taken to and from hospital by ambulance.

A psychiatric day hospital not only overcomes isolation, and makes it possible for the team to spend more time with those who attend than they could if they had to travel to every individual's house, but it allows them to meet, and be treated, with other people with a similar problem. Group therapy, in which the affected individuals share their problems and help one another can be very helpful. Electro Convulsion Therapy (ECT) is sometimes used to treat depression and it can be effective. It is painless because a general anaesthetic is given, and it has few side effects in young people, but doctors are sometimes reluctant to use this treatment on old people unless there are clear indications for doing so. It should not be given without the patient's permission. The psychiatrist may decide to admit the old person to hospital if he cannot find a cause for the depression, or considers that there is a real risk of suicide. A stay in hospital allows all the staff on the ward to get to know the elderly person and his problems.

Even the most highly trained professional requires the help and co-operation of the depressed person and his supporters if his depression is to be lifted. Family and trusted friends have a vital part to play. Remember that the priest or minister can often be very supportive to the elder in the management of depression. The objective of management is not so much to 'cure' depression, which implies it leaves the person completely, but to reduce it to normal levels which the individual can manage himself.

ANXIETY

Everyone is anxious about something almost every day. The level of anxiety does not only depend on the magnitude of the problem; some football managers and surgeons are very cool, others are anxious; some housewives and gardeners don't worry whatever happens, others are anxious continually, even when affairs are running smoothly. The common factor in situations which cause anxiety is uncertainty. The person who has to make a decision which is not clear cut or who has to wait helplessly in fear of something happening, is in a position of uncertainty, and uncertainty breeds worry and anxiety. As people grow older their lives become more uncertain:

• They may be uncertain whether they will be able to pay all their bills or run up debts.

• They may be afraid of being mugged or attacked.

• Those who have fallen once or are unsteady may have the fear that they will fall again and lie helpless and unhelped.

• Those who are dependent on others may be uncertain whether they will be able to continue living in their own home or will have to go to live in a home or hospital.

• Those who have been incontinent are often uncertain of their ability to remain continent in company.

• Those who have been ill may be uncertain whether illness will strike again; fear of cancer is a very common cause of anxiety.

Although death is certain, its moment of arrival is not, but it becomes more probable every year, and this is another uncertainty in old age. It is a tribute to the resilience of the human spirit that old people are not more frequently anxious than they are, when all these uncertainties are considered. The ability to cope with uncertainty is an individual characteristic. No two people are alike. In general those who were frequently anxious when younger are anxious old people, and those who were placid and unflappable when young show the same characteristics in old age, but exceptions are common. Some people who were very anxious during their working life become philosophical in old age, feeling that there are no decisions to be taken in old age which can affect the inevitable changes of ageing. Others become more anxious as they grow older, perhaps due to attacks of illness or the death of a spouse.

Anxiety may focus on one specific fear, for example the fear of falling; it may arise from a number of different fears; or the elder may be unable to identify any specific factor to explain his distressing anxiety.

Anxiety can affect an old person in many different ways:

- He may talk about his anxiety or anxieties freely. Sometimes one source of anxiety comes to dominate an old person's life so that he thinks and talks about it to the exclusion of any other topic. It becomes an obsession with him. The anxiety may influence his actions. If the influence becomes excessive it is sometimes called a phobia by doctors. For instance, if someone has been mugged, then it is reasonable for him to be too anxious to return to the area in which the crime took place. If he refuses to leave his house, even to go into the garden, then he is said to have developed a phobia. The advice of a locksmith or the police about making the house secure against intruders by a *well-fixed* chain, locks and window bolts, can be very reassuring. In the same way it is reasonable for an old person to worry about the price of electricity, but if he refuses to put on his heating at all, although he has plenty of money, he can be said to have a phobia of debt.
- Anxiety can make the person depressed and apathetic, but it can also make him tense and irritable.
- Anxiety can prevent someone from sleeping.
- People who are anxious often suffer from physical disorders. There are two reasons for this. We all suffer from symptoms which we know are trivial and will pass off without medical attention. However, if someone is anxious he may worry about a physical symptom which he would not otherwise notice, especially if he is anxious about cancer or some other serious illness. An anxious person may

suffer from only one symptom or from a number of different symptoms. In either case treatment of the symptom or symptoms will not give relief, if the underlying anxiety is not recognised and relieved. Some old people who are called hypochondriacs are in fact people whose real problem is anxiety.

Anxiety can also cause physical symptoms directly. Headaches, stomach pains and aches in other parts of the body are all forms of psychosomatic illness which can result from anxiety. (They are called 'psychosomatic' because the mind affects the body, and *psycho* and *soma* are Greek for mind and body respectively.)

The Relief of Anxiety

Anxiety becomes a problem when either you or the old person consider it to be a problem. We say either you *or* the old person, because he may be so taken up with his anxiety that he cannot see how big a part of his life it has become. When anxiety becomes a problem in its own right, distinct from the problem which is the underlying cause of the anxiety, it is time to do something about it. The first step is to try to solve the underlying problem, if it can be identified. The anxiety may persist even while the basic problem is being tackled, but you can do a great deal yourself to relieve the anxiety.

It is usually not sufficient just to say 'don't worry'. Listen to the elderly person and tell him that you appreciate why he is still anxious, even though the cause is being dealt with. He may still be uncertain that you and he can solve it and need reassurance that, although there is still some cause for anxiety, the end of his anxiety is in sight.

You should consider asking for help from an outsider if the elder:

- Is very worried even after you have identified and started to tackle the basic cause of his anxiety.

- Cannot identify any underlying cause with your help.
- Has a number of problems about which he is worried.
- Thinks and talks of little else or is acting abnormally, that is if he has developed an obsession or a phobia.

The elder may be prepared to confide in an outsider things which he would or could not reveal to his family, and some professionals are trained to deal with anxiety. If a professional is already visiting an old person, his anxiety can be discussed with her, even if the professional is attending him for some other purpose; for example if the district nurse or domiciliary occupational therapist is visiting, it would be appropriate to ask her advice initially. If there is no one visiting, it is probably best to ask his GP or health visitor to call to see him. Alternatively, you could write to the Social Services Department to ask if a social worker can call, but this will usually take longer to arrange than a home call from the health visitor.

Perhaps less important than the type of *service* from which you seek help is the *person* who comes to give it. If the old person is close to and trusts someone, that person should be asked to help. This might be the GP, the vicar, the health visitor or social worker, or some other person already known to the elder.

If anxiety is severely disturbing the elder, his GP should be consulted. He can prescribe a tranquilliser – Valium is the one most commonly prescribed – but will usually prefer to try to relieve the anxiety by discussion and psychological support. However, Valium does relieve anxiety and reduce tension and, as it is relatively free from side-effects, it is often prescribed. If the GP cannot relieve the elder's anxiety, he can request a psychiatric opinion.

The best form of management of both anxiety and depression is prevention, which is often the prevention of isolation.

SLEEPLESSNESS

No two people have the same sleeping pattern, and there is no consistent change in sleeping pattern as a person grows older. Some sleep more, some sleep less. Many old people sleep less because they are less physically and mentally active, and because they often doze once or twice during the day. Old people often worry about their inability to sleep for the same length of time as they did when younger, but there is no evidence that their health suffers in any way from lack of sleep, and the GP's reassurance that an old person does not need more sleep is often sufficient to allay this anxiety. Inability to drop off to sleep may be a sign of hidden anxiety, and early morning waking can occur in depression. Physical illnesses, such as indigestion, painful joints and breathlessness, can also disturb sleep. The opinion of the elder's GP should be sought when sleeplessness becomes a problem so that he can exclude these disorders.

If an elder lives with you his sleeplessness may aggravate you, although he is not in the least upset by it. Even if he does not come into your room his movements can waken you, and if he tries to make a cup of tea or light a fire you may be worried. It is important to decide whether sleeplessness bothers you, or the elder, or both of you, before consulting the GP. Some simple solution can often be found if the main problem is the effect that it has on you. It may be sufficient to give him a flask of tea and an easy chair in his bedroom to prevent your rest being disturbed.

Although there are effective sleeping pills, GPs regard them as the last resort and prescribe them only after all other measures fail. The first step is to try to increase the amount of physical and mental activity in the elder's day. Encourage him to walk to the shops with you or go for a walk on his own every day. Encourage him to read or take up some other leisure activity. One of the great benefits of day centres and day hospitals is that they offer an opportunity for the old person to be busy and to grow tired. If he sleeps a lot during the day, and sleeplessness at night is a problem, come to some arrangement that you will wake him if you see him nodding off, except at certain times, for example after lunch. It may be possible to prevent him dropping off to sleep during the day by making his daily life more interesting. Television and radio can be stimulating, and therefore tiring, but they can also cause agitation and aggravate sleep problems.

A warm drink at night is soothing and relaxing, but the elder should be reminded to empty his bladder before retiring because a full bladder and a constipated bowel can prevent sleep. Finally, the bedroom and bed should be warm enough to promote sleep, but not so hot that discomfort is caused. Old people who find it difficult to remember to take drugs as prescribed sometimes take the prescribed dose, drop off to sleep for a brief period, wake again and take more tablets, because they cannot remember having taken the first dose. *The bottle of sleeping tablets should always be kept far from the bed.*

Sleeping tablets can make an old person very unsteady if he wakes in the night to pass water, but it is possible to prevent falls by providing a light and a commode or urinal often the prevention of isolation.

whatever the elder fancies, is as effective as a sleeping pill for many people. Alcohol can interact with some prescribed medicines, so check with the elder's GP before suggesting such a nightcap.

There is a buzzer-nightlight due to come on the market which indicates to the carer when the old person gets out of bed (to be sponsored by United Drug Ltd of Ireland). This will be particularly useful in caring for mentally confused dependants.

CONFUSION – DISORDERED MENTAL FUNCTION

The term 'confused' is often used to describe elderly people, but there is considerable confusion about the meaning of the word 'confused'.

The many processes of the mind can be divided for convenience into four major types of operation:

- Memory – the ability to retain new facts and to recall them when required.
- Mood – the balance between happiness and sadness which varies continuously, normally staying within a narrow range and avoiding big swings into either elation or depression.
- Orientation – the ability to know who one is, where one is, and to have a sense of time accurate enough to know not necessarily the date or day of the week, but the month and year, and which friends and family members are alive and which are dead.
- Logical thought – the ability to analyse problems and deduce solutions.

The adjective 'confused' is often used when any, or all, of these mental functions are impaired. It is not a term which we recommend because it implies that the whole range of mental functions is impaired. That is very rare. Usually some functions are less affected than others, and it is very important to determine which are affected and which are not, to allow you to concentrate on the elder's strengths. This is both comforting and helpful to him. Also, when discussing an old person's problems with someone, for example the matron of a nursing home, it is preferable to state exactly what is wrong with his mental functioning. For example, rather than saying an old person is 'mildly confused', it is better to say that 'he sometimes forgets where he is and makes mistakes when he is dressing, but he can remember his children and grandchildren and is usually cheerful'.

The most important fact to remember is that disordered mental function is not a *disease* like pneumonia or measles; it is a *sign* like fever or a rash. Doctors do not diagnose 'confusion'; they recognise it as a sign that something is affecting the brain of the elder, which in turn is affecting his mind. There are many underlying causes of disordered mental function but, from a practical point of view, it is important to classify and consider it according to the rate of onset of the disorder; in some people the disorder develops rapidly, in others the onset is slow.

Disordered Mental Function of Rapid Onset

If in less than one month the mind of an old person develops signs of disorder, in one or more of the four primary functions, there is usually an underlying physical illness which can be treated successfully. The onset can be very rapid: within a day or an even shorter period of time.

The following are the common causes of disordered mental function of rapid onset:

• Drugs. Obviously tranquillisers, sleeping pills and other drugs which affect the mind can cause disorder if they are taken incorrectly. Some elders are very sensitive to the effects of these drugs and can be affected even if they take them as prescribed. Many other types of drug can upset mental function, and the elder's GP will probably review all the drugs which he is taking at a very early stage in the investigation. Remember that some old people are very sensitive to the effects of alcohol, especially in combination with sedatives or tranquillisers, and that alcohol is a not uncommon cause of a disorder of very rapid onset.

• Infection. A high fever and the other toxic effects of a generalised infection can cause delirium in people of any age. As the brain ages it becomes more sensitive to the toxic effects of infection and fever. Its function, and that of the mind, becomes disordered at a temperature which would not have caused any upset when it was younger. Chest infections, such as pneumonia or bronchitis, and urinary tract infections are the most common causes, but any infection can have the same result. Even if the elder's temperature is not elevated he may have an infection, so do not rely on your home

thermometer to exclude an infection. Ask the GP's advice if you are in any doubt.

• Stroke. It is usual to associate the term 'stroke' with the paralysis of one side of the body, but some strokes cause no paralysis. The proper medical term for a stroke is a cerebrovascular accident (see page 61). This means an accident to one of the blood vessels leading to the brain, which therefore interrupts the supply of blood and oxygen. If this happens to a blood vessel which supplies the part of the brain which controls muscular movement, the result is paralysis. Cerebrovascular accidents can also occur in those blood vessels supplying parts of the brain which control memory, mood, orientation and logical thought.

• Constipation or retention of urine can so upset the body's metabolism that the brain and mind are affected.

• Heart disease. It is often thought that heart disease causes either breathlessness or pain in the chest, but this is not always so. The normal function of the heart is to pump adequate amounts of blood, enriched with oxygen, from the lungs to all parts of the body. Any failure of the normal function of the heart interrupts this essential supply of oxygen. If the blood vessels to one part of the body are narrowed by disease, that part of the body will be affected before any other when the heart starts to fail. The blood vessels to those parts of the brain which control the four primary mental functions are often narrowed by hardening of the arteries, and therefore a heart attack, or any interruption in the normal regular rhythm of the heart, can cause disordered mental function, even if there is no other sign of heart disease.

These are only the more common physical causes of disorders of rapid onset. *Even if the elder appears to be physically well, his GP should be consulted as soon as mental function is upset. The earlier the underlying physical illness can be detected and treated, the sooner will normal mental function be restored.* The GP may be able to diagnose the underlying cause immediately, or he may have to send blood samples for laboratory examination and arrange for other tests. If he feels in doubt about the diagnosis, either when he first sees the elder or after he has tried to diagnose and treat him, the GP may ask for a second opinion from a consultant in geriatric medicine. He can do this either by referring the elder to hospital, or by asking the consultant to pay a domiciliary visit to see the elder at home. If the elder is also physically unwell the domiciliary nurse will be able to help you (see page 21).

Don't forget that mental disorder of rapid onset can be caused solely by psychological or emotional pressure, such as depression or grief. Sometimes, in the search for the physical disorder, which is the most common cause, this is overlooked.

Disordered Mental Function of Slow Onset

When there is a slow deterioration in the functioning of the mind over a period of months or years, a different approach is required. The loss of function may be so slow that it is not perceived by those who see the old person frequently, and is only noticed by someone who has not seen him for some time. It is worthwhile emphasising this, because it sometimes happens that the person caring every day for an elderly person is criticised for allowing a deterioration to take place without asking the GP's advice. However, it is well known that the closer you are to someone, and the more frequently you see him, the more difficult it is to notice slowly developing changes. Just as parents are less struck by changes in their children than those who see them once or twice a year, so it is with those who care for elderly people.

The first difficulty is to decide whether a disorder in mental function is abnormal. In spite of what we have said about the myths of ageing – that many of the characteristics ascribed to old people are based on society's prejudice rather than hard facts – there are changes in the four primary mental functions as the brain ages and a person grows old:

- The ageing brain is less able to retain new information and to recall recently acquired facts.
- Because of the uncertainties and misfortunes which so often accompany old age, mood swings may be greater than in youth.
- Retired, housebound people are sometimes less well orientated than younger people at work; probably because people of working age received more reminders of who they are, where they are and what time it is through the media of letters, phone calls, appointments, working hours, holidays and all the other demands of employment and bringing up a family.
- The ageing brain is sometimes less able to carry out logical thinking with the same skill and speed as it could when younger.

All these changes occur normally, that is, within a normal range. When should you consider a change to be abnormal and request outside help? In our opinion the decision should not be based so much on the degree of disorder as on the effect it has on the elder's life. For example, it is relatively unimportant if he cannot remember the names of all his grandchildren, but it is important if he forgets to light the gas once he has turned it on, or forgets to take his key when he goes out. It does not matter if the old person does not know which month or year it is provided he knows the difference between day and night, and does not knock on his neighbour's door to borrow a cup of sugar at 3 a.m. It is immaterial if an old person can no longer do a crossword, but it is a matter of concern if he cannot think logically enough to dress properly. As with the other mental symptoms, it is wise to ask the advice of a professional as soon as either you or the old person are worried. Sometimes the reassurance of the GP, health visitor or social worker that an observed change is within the normal range is enough to relieve tension, and allow the old person to enjoy life once more.

The cause of disordered mental function of slow onset is usually a physical disorder which affects the brain, either directly or indirectly, by upsetting the balance of the body's metabolism. Unfortunately, the underlying cause cannot be cured so frequently as in disordered mental function of rapid onset. There are curable physical diseases, such as thyroid disease and vitamin deficiency, which affect the brain in a slow and insidious fashion. Prescribed drugs can lead to a slow deterioration of mental function if the old person does not take them as the doctor intended (see page 91). However, in many cases the underlying physical disease is a failure of the brain itself, and this cannot be cured or even influenced by doctors.

The medical term 'dementia' is often used, but many doctors now prefer to use the term brain failure. This is not a diagnosis, it is merely a statement that the brain is not functioning with its former efficiency, and this inevitably results in disordered mental function. There are two common causes of brain failure:

- One is atherosclerosis – hardening of the arteries. We have said that a cerebrovascular accident is one cause of disordered mental function of rapid onset. If, instead of such a sudden accident happening, the arteries to the brain progressively harden and narrow, the supply of blood and oxygen to the brain is steadily reduced and the brain fails slowly. This steady process is interrupted, in some people, by one or more cerebrovascular accidents, each of which may cause either a sudden deterioration in mental function, paralysis of part of the body or both. High blood pressure can aggravate this process, and the correct diagnosis and treatment of high blood pressure is very important in the management of brain failure caused by hardening of the arteries, which is sometimes called atherosclerotic dementia.

- The other common cause of brain failure is a degeneration of brain tissue of unknown origin. Because no cause is known to explain the death of the brain cells, other than old age, this type of degeneration is sometimes just called senile dementia.

There is no treatment which can cure either senile or atherosclerotic dementia, although the correct management of high blood pressure is very important if it is present. There are drugs which it is claimed can reduce the severity of dementia, but only a small number of cases benefit from them and doctors are very careful in their use of them. The GP is the key person. He may be able to find an underlying, treatable cause. He may be able to exclude the possibility of any such cause by his own examination and investigation, or he may request a second opinion from a consultant in geriatric medicine or psychiatry. Of course, the GP has much more to offer than merely the exclusion of correctable physical causes. By his interest and concern he can lighten the problems you have to face and he can request the help of other services to lighten your burden.

HELP

How Others Can Help

If the old person is incontinent, the district nurse can help. If the elderly person lives alone, far away from you, the nurse may also help him dress and bathe. Although some nursing services are very hard pressed, especially in winter, it is sometimes possible for a nurse to visit twice daily to help an old person dress and undress. If the old person lives near you, you will probably be helping with bathing and dressing, but if you are feeling the strain of regular daily care and would like a night away or a long lie in, ask the GP or the nursing officer if the nursing service can give you relief on at least one day a week (see page 21). If the old person lives with you, and if you find that bathing him is upsetting or embarrassing for either you or him, or a physical strain, ask for nursing help.

A home help can be a great support for someone who lives alone. If you live near the elder, the home help organiser may expect you to help with his housework. She may be able to provide a home help if you make it clear that you wish someone else to go to help the elder, not just for your convenience but because you are finding daily care a growing burden and strain. Because old people whose minds are not working properly can present problems, the organiser may send an experienced home help. The first few days are sometimes very difficult; the old person may not even allow the home help to enter his house, and it can be a great help if you can be there to introduce the old person to the home help, perhaps staying in the house for her first few visits. The home help can help in very many ways, especially with day to day financial management, but this is the source of one problem – accusations of theft. Old people who are forgetful sometimes lose their purse or money and assume that it has been stolen, often accusing the only person who has been in the house – the home help. This is very distressing for the home help, and you should immediately discuss such a problem with the home help organiser. (see page 16).

Much of the care for mentally disturbed elders does not require training, only compassion and kindness. Neighbours and volunteers can help by driving the elder to a day centre, or by keeping him company if you want to go out for an evening. In some areas there is an evening sitting service and an overnight sitting service, which can give tremendous relief if the old person lives with you. A night or even an evening away allows you to recharge your batteries and regain strength. Ask the district nurse or the local Age Concern office if there is such a service, run either by the Health or Social Services or by a voluntary organisation such as the Red Cross.

Social service support

Although your difficulties can be lessened, they are often not completely resolved and they can still weigh heavily on you. If the elderly person lives on his own, the strain of providing and arranging daily help, and the worry during those times he is alone and isolated, can be very considerable. If he lives with you, his constant presence can be very wearing and small irritants can become sources of major annoyance. Social Services Departments are now offering short stays in old people's homes to give relief to elderly people and their supporters.

The stay may be only for the day. The old person is usually collected for day care by Social Services transport in the morning, arriving at the home between nine and ten o'clock, and staying there until about four o'clock when the transport service takes him home. The Social Services Department prefer to arrange this on a regular basis, on the same day or days each week, because it allows them to plan the best use of their transport fleet. The amount of day care offered varies from one part of the country to another, but some departments now offer care five days a week, to allow supporters to go out to work. If you would like one day's relief so that you can attend a special event, the Social Services Department may be able to help you, provided that you give them enough notice. Day care is usually offered only on weekdays because homes are so short-staffed at weekends, but if you have a good reason for requesting a day's relief on a Saturday or Sunday the Social Services may be able to help, although transport to and from the home is often more difficult to arrange at weekends. A small charge is sometimes made for day care.

Remember that it is often more economical to leave a low level of heating on in the elder's dwelling while he is away for day care, because it is more expensive to heat up a house which has been allowed to cool down during the day, than to leave heating on at a low level. This is especially true if it has not been well insulated.

Although day care can relieve the elder's isolation and your anxieties, it can also be upsetting. Change is difficult for most of us to cope with, and for someone whose sense of orientation is not functioning efficiently it can be very disturbing. The travelling to and from the home can take an hour or more each way, and this imposes additional physical and psychological strains. Many Social Services Departments now offer regular admissions, for example a fortnight every three months, planned to give you as much relief as possible within the limited resources which Social Services have at their disposal. All departments offer two week admissions to allow you to go on holiday. You will have to book such a period very early in the year, or even a year in advance if you wish the home to admit the old person during a peak holiday period. You do not need to be going away to qualify for relief. A charge is usually made for all admissions.

To request day care or a short stay in an old people's home, write to the Social Services Department. If one reason for your request is that you are under strain and feel a need for relief, make this clear in your letter as well as describing the elder's need. Sometimes Social Services Departments are a little reluctant to offer short stays to old people who live with families, because they fear that the families with whom they live will not have them back. Make it clear that it is not your intention to unload the responsibility for the elder's care permanently, but that you would be able to care with greater strength if you were given a break.

After you have written to the Social Services Department to request day care or a temporary admission, a social worker will make an appointment and visit you to discuss the way in which you and the Social Services Department can share the care of the old person. The social worker can, of course, do much more than make arrangements for day care. We have described the skills of the social worker (see page 15); she is trained to help families bring to the surface and resolve hidden tensions. When an elder is mentally disturbed he may also be more disturbing, and the tensions which exist in every family are heightened, putting both you and the elder under strain. When you ask a social worker to relieve the strain on you, she may think that she can do more than merely arrange for the elder to spend time in a day centre or home. She may feel that it would also be supportive to try to help you deal with some of the underlying tensions. This means that her visit may result in an interview in which your feelings for the elder and his for you are discussed. It is essential for the social worker to build up as full a picture of the elder and his supporters as possible, and this will require your co-operation.

Health service support

The GP can also call on the expert opinion of the psychiatrist and his team if he is uncertain of the diagnosis or best management, or if he thinks that hospital treatment would be appropriate (see page 96). Only the psychiatrist can make the decision to offer an old person hospital treatment, either by admission or attendance at a day hospital. Like a social services day centre, the day hospital relieves the old person's isolation and your burden, but it also offers treatment. At a day hospital, nursing staff try to discover the reasons for an old person's depression, anxiety or agitation. The occupational therapist will try to assess his strengths and weaknesses in activities of daily living, for example his ability to manage a gas cooker safely, or to shop; and the medical staff can investigate his physical and mental health, and supervise his drug treatment. If the hospital staff feel that they have assessed the elder's capabilities fully and are satisfied that his physical and mental state is stable, they may suggest that he can go to a social services or voluntary day centre. However, this is sometimes impossible because there are so few day centres, and they may decide to let him continue attending just to relieve his isolation or your burden. No financial charge is made for attendance at day hospital and the ambulance service arranges transport.

If it is felt that the travelling to and from day hospital is too tiring and upsetting, or if the hospital staff would like to assess the elder over a longer period of time, they may decide on his admission for a week or two. Psychiatric hospitals also offer admission when supporters wish to go on holiday, and can plan a series of admissions to provide relief at regular intervals. The amount of help you can expect from the psychiatric hospital depends upon your needs, the number of places in the day hospital and the number of beds which are at the disposal of the psychiatrist to meet all the demands made on him. Many hospitals try to offer care on all weekdays to those whose need is greatest, but less help is offered at weekends because of shortage of staff.

It is quite possible for an elder to attend both a psychiatric day hospital and a day centre, or be admitted both to an old people's home and a hospital at regular intervals. Unfortunately, there is a gap between psychiatric hospitals and homes as well as this overlap. If the elder for whom you care is said to be 'too confused' for an old people's home, but 'not disturbed enough' for admission to a psychiatric hospital, then you may feel disheartened and angry. Speak to the old person's GP to see if he can get one or other to care for the elder. If he is unable to help further, he may write to the specialist in community medicine for social services of the Area Health Authority.

Financial Help

Financial help is also available. Social Security can pay an Attendance Allowance (see page 140) or an Invalid Care Allowance (see page 142), and some Social Services Departments may now pay allowances to people supporting elderly relatives at home.

Harnessing Outside Help

This is obviously a complicated system of services and you may find it difficult to make all the necessary contacts yourself, when your attention and energy is taken up in caring. Either the elder's GP, health visitor or a social worker should act as a guide and supporter through the maze of services, and over all the obstacles. As with all problems, the services are inadequate in many areas and often appear to be insensitive to the needs of the old person and yourself. There is another problem that can be very upsetting, which is created not by a shortage of the service, but by the way you ask for outside help.

If an old person has painful joints, is breathless or feels depressed, he will usually welcome expert help as a means towards curing his symptom. If, however, he feels no symptom, then he may well be angry and bitter if people start coming uninvited to his house, to arrange for him to go to a day hospital or a day centre. One feature of disordered mental function of slow onset, which creates particular problems for an elder's supporters, is loss of the ability to have insight. Insight is the faculty of knowing about one's self; for example, knowing that one has made a mistake or knowing that one is angry or depressed. Not only do some old people forget things, have extreme mood swings and think illogically, but they are not aware that they have developed these tendencies. They still feel 'all right' and tell their supporters not to worry when concern is expressed and help suggested. If the person who is looking after an old person feels he needs help and calls in outside help, although the elder himself says he does not want it, the consequences can be serious.

The elder may see the 'help' in quite a different light. Think what it is like to be assessed by an expert who has been called in to judge if you are mentally disturbed:

One or more people come to your door and enter the house. They introduce themselves, but in the excitement of the moment you do not catch their names and where they come from. They start to question you. 'What is the date?' 'How many children has the Queen?' 'Count backwards in sevens from one hundred.' (These are questions sometimes asked in the diagnosis of dementia.) 'Can you dress yourself?' 'Are you worried about anything?' 'Do you feel depressed?' 'Can you manage at home?' You suspect that these people will make notes about you when they leave and store them in government offices as a basis for having discussions about you. You sense that your future hangs on the answers to these questions, some of which are difficult, all of which are upsetting.

Being assessed is a daunting enough procedure for an old person when he has asked for outside help, but when the helpers come to him without his prior knowledge or agreement he may feel very frightened, or even persecuted, which can make his mental disorder even greater. Even if the suggestion that the elder should see a psychiatrist is made by his GP or health visitor, the old person may suspect, and perhaps correctly, that you have played some part in it, and feel betrayed.

If you are to prevent the development of bitterness towards you, it is essential to be as open and honest as you can. If the elder's mood or behaviour is worrying you, tell him of your anxiety. If he tells you 'not to worry' or says that he is 'all right' but you are not relieved, make this clear to him. Tell him that people of all ages often fail to recognise that they are unwell and that you are going to ask his GP to see him. There is a place for firmness in all relationships, and we think that this is a time to be firm. Even if he becomes angry when you make it plain that you are going to ask the GP to call, he may welcome a visit, for old people are often secretly worried about illness. If the GP says that he is going to ask the opinion of a hospital doctor, the elder may be upset, but at least your part in the referral to hospital will be obvious and not hidden. This may cause temporary anger but is unlikely to lead to lasting resentment and bitterness, which

not infrequently develop when the elder feels he has been betrayed by those he thought he could trust.

Remember that an old person with a poor memory may forget that he has agreed to see a doctor, and be very upset when the doctor arrives. It is useful to remind him that a doctor is coming from hospital to see him, and ask if he would like you to be present. Even if an old person has asked for help, the initial interview can be alarming and your presence either in the house or in the room can be very supportive.

Someone who is severely mentally disturbed, but refuses to see a doctor or accept treatment, can be admitted to hospital against his wishes, provided that the appropriate legal steps are taken. The Mental Health Act of 1959 authorises procedures for the compulsory admission of people to hospital, either for observation or for treatment. The duration of admission is determined by law. Applications for compulsory admission under the Mental Health Act must be made by a social worker or the nearest relative (except in an emergency when any relative can do so). We think it preferable for a social worker to do this, as it reduces the risk of any subsequent bitterness towards the relative. The application has to be accompanied by medical recommendations. The Mental Health Act is very complicated and contains a number of different sections covering different types of problem. If the GP or social worker thinks that compulsory admission would be appropriate, they will discuss it with you.

Coping on Your Own

Even if there are adequate services and you are able to obtain help without alienating the elder, you will still have to carry much of the burden yourself. Obviously the type of problem you have to face is determined by whether the old person lives with you, whether you are single or married, and whether there are other brothers and sisters living nearby. But the same types of problem are faced by everyone and they can be related to the four aspects of mental function – rational thought, memory, orientation and mood.

Illogical thinking

We have previously emphasised the importance of conversing with an elder as though he were capable of logical thought, as the great majority still are. Correct his mistakes as you would correct those of a younger man; look for meaning in every statement. Although a statement does not appear relevant to the previous statement, it may be very relevant to an idea in the elder's mind which relates to some past event.

Try to seek out the connections of his apparently unconnected statements. No matter how illogical an old person appears to be, he will have some areas of thought in which he can still think logically. It may be gardening, football or some topic which involves the knowledge he acquired while he was employed. Work in these strong areas; introduce them to the conversation whenever you feel he is getting lost.

There are two types of faulty thinking which cause particular concern – thoughts of persecution and self-neglect.

Persecution

We all feel persecuted occasionally either by life in general or by one specific individual or organisation. Sometimes there is good reason for our feeling, at other times there is not. Such feelings are normal and occur normally in old people as well. If the feeling of persecution is unrelated to any real threat, and lasts for more than a few days, doctors call it a state of paranoia. If an old person has paranoid thoughts it can be very distressing, not only for him but for other people. He feels threatened, persecuted and frightened, and those whom he accuses feel hurt and bitter. Other people, who are not accused, may be sympathetic; but they may also gossip and say 'there's no smoke without fire', which adds to the distress of those accused. An old person who repeatedly for-

gets where he has put his purse, or his pension book, may accuse the home help or a daughter either of theft or of hiding things from him, each time his money is lost. From his belief that he is being robbed or fooled time after time comes a general suspicion of all people at all times. One event, such as a burglary, can be enough to make an isolated disabled person feel helpless and persecuted. The event need not be criminal – an interview with an unsympathetic official can trigger off paranoia. Even if a social security officer is sympathetic, as most are, one question innocently worded in a way that frightens the elder can leave him suspicious not only of social security but of all officials. Paranoia has been defined as being a state of persecution 'unrelated to any real threat', but it is important to remember that there is often more than one reality in any situation. To the elder's supporters and the professionals involved the reality of the situation may be that the elder 'is in need of help'. To the elder himself the reality may be very different – that 'everyone is trying to get me out of my home'. The supporters think they are trying to help him, but all he remembers from their conversations is that they are worried about his ability to remain at home.

It is important to distinguish a feeling of persecution from a feeling of fear. Old people sometimes grow very frightened by the newspapers and TV, and come to believe that crime and violence will soon overwhelm them. It is also important to distinguish paranoia from anger. Old people may appear to be suspicious and hostile to those who are trying to help them. However this does not stem from paranoia, but from the anger and frustration which result from dependence. It can also be a sign of depression.

If you cannot allay his fears by discussing his thoughts of persecution with the elder, you will need the help of an outsider. For many old people the GP is the most trusted person because he has often known the elder for a long time, and he should be consulted. The GP can refer a person who feels persecuted to a psychiatrist if he thinks that the feeling of persecution is a sign that there is some more serious underlying problem. It is essential to remember that great care must be taken in the way you seek outside help, if the old person is not to be made to feel that you too have become an ally of his persecutors. Be honest and frank.

Self-neglect

Another very distressing development is self-neglect. A small number of old people become increasingly dirty and unkempt, either in their dress, in their housekeeping, in personal cleanliness or in all three. In some, this is part of a general deterioration in mental function, occurring together with failing memory and disorientation. More puzzling are those whose mind seems to be functioning well in every way, except for their refusal to maintain previously accepted social standards. Some appear to have lost insight; others are well aware of the concern of family and friends and disapproval of the neighbours, but don't seem to care.

In considering such behaviour, it is important to ask whether this is a new facet to the elder's personality or just a continuation of an old trend. Many people are collectors, not just having formal collections like coins or antiques, but collecting and storing almost everything which comes their way; perhaps a better name for them would be accumulators. Someone who has accumulated books, china, newspaper cuttings and other objects for twenty years will have a cluttered house. If this accumulating process continues for another thirty years, the result can be chaotic. If in addition they have always been untidy and not too interested in cleaning and dusting, the chaos can become very dirty. The problem is much more worrying if the elder was houseproud and tidy when he was young.

There are a number of possible reasons for such a change in behaviour in an old person:

- He may be depressed and, although he does not say anything or perhaps even realise it himself, this results in apathy and a careless attitude to himself and his appearance.

- He may be physically unwell and too weak to do his housework, or the physical illness may be affecting his brain.

- In some people self-neglect is a sign not of medical breakdown, but of a social disorder. A widower may be completely incapable of self-care, having been waited on hand and foot during all his married life. Some widows neglect themselves, not just because of depression but because it was their husband's demands which kept up their standards.

- Most of us keep up appearances to impress other people, and if an old person becomes very isolated and does not see many other people he may not bother to keep himself or his house clean and tidy.

This can be a difficult problem to tackle. The first step is to discuss it with the old person himself. If change takes place gradually, over a long period of time, it is less easy to detect than if it occurs rapidly. An old person who has been progressively neglecting himself over a period of months or years may be completely unaware of his slowly slipping standards. It is probably best to be direct, to say that it appears to you that he does not seem to be coping as well as previously. Old people sometimes appreciate a direct approach rather than hints or suggestions, and in response to such a statement the elder may agree that he is finding self-care more of a problem. If he realises that he is not coping, but says that he will manage now that he is aware of the problem, you should allow him a chance to take action, offering practical help if necessary. If he has not taken any effective action after a week, we think that you should suggest that he asks the GP to look in to see him. Explain that physical illness can develop without warning symptoms and that his inability to keep up his previous standards might be due to a curable physical illness. Once more we would advise firmness in this approach.

If the old person does not admit there is

any problem, your approach has to be different. You will then have to make your anxiety clear to the elder and say that you would like him to agree to the GP seeing him, to relieve your anxiety if nothing else. The GP will try to find any underlying physical or mental illness, with, if necessary, the help of a consultant in geriatric medicine or a consultant psychiatrist.

To help the old person with housework you can ask for home help. If the house is very dirty, however, the home help organiser is entitled to refuse to send in a home help (see page 16). The Environmental Health Department should then be approached (see page 26). Some departments are willing to clean out dirty houses, but others use outside contractors and either you or the old person has to pay for such help. The Environmental Health Department is also the source of practical help and advice on the control of pests. If the elder refuses to accept such help, it may be because he fears that some of his precious possessions will be thrown out or he may simply be unable to face the upheaval. It is almost always possible to overcome such resistance, but you may need the help of a health visitor or social worker to persuade the old person that such a move is really necessary, and this should not be rushed. It can take months to win the elder's confidence and the clearing up can gradually be started as his trust is gained. If the cleaning of the house will benefit other people, for example yourself or neighbours, this must be honestly stated, and the suggestion should not be presented to the old person as being solely for his benefit.

The Environmental Health Committee of a local authority can issue a court order against a house-holder, requiring him to cleanse his dwelling and the surrounding ground. Although environmental health officers occasionally receive petitions from angry neighbours about badly kept houses and gardens, they rarely take legal action. If the neighbours have complained to the council, write to the Environmental Health Department describing all the conditions of the case and ask for their advice on how you can deal with the problem.

If the old person is attending a psychiatric hospital, the occupational therapist can be an invaluable source of support, because she is specially trained to help people cope with the activities of daily living. She is sometimes able to pay a visit to the old person at home, although she may have difficulty finding the time from her duties in hospital. If the old person is not coping, you can write to the occupational therapist of the ward which cares for him, and ask if you can meet her to discuss his and your problems.

Remember that the elder may be so ashamed of the dirt that he neither wishes to recognise or discuss the state into which he has fallen. Remember also that some people appear to be happy in dirt and disorder, even those who were previously clean and tidy. Whatever you or other people think, it is the old person's opinion which is most important.

Failing memory
If an old person whose memory is failing has insight, and recognises his waning power, he may be very distressed. Although we advised you to correct any mistakes in logical thinking, it is often difficult to tell whether an elder has made such a mistake, or whether it is his memory which has let him down. If, for example, he says you came to see him three days previously, when it was in fact the day before, you have to decide whether he has made the sort of error which we say you should correct, or whether his memory has failed. The importance of correcting errors of logical thinking is that the old person can often correct the error you have pointed out. However, if you point out failures of his memory, he may not be able to do anything about them, and can become anxious and depressed, so it is sometimes as well to let them pass if they are unimportant.

Doctors cannot treat failing memory, although it is always important for the GP to be asked to examine an old person whose memory has started to fail, to exclude a correctable physical illness, but you can do much to help. Memories do not just lie in the brain in a haphazard arrangement, they are ordered in a definite way with a system of indexing and cross-references, which allow us to find the one we want, just as we find a book in a library. When we want a particular memory, for example someone's name, it may come quickly or we may have to refer to other facts, what he looks like or who introduced us to him, before we find his name from our store of memories.

It is this ability to make cross-references which fails first. The memory is still there, but the old person cannot retrieve it so easily. You can help by giving more information. For example, instead of saying 'I saw old Jack today' you should say 'I saw old Jack Robinson, the butcher, today'.

A different approach is required when you cannot be present to help the old person retrieve the appropriate memory. For the elder to remember to take the drugs prescribed for him in the way in which the doctor intended, we offer advice elsewhere (see page 93). But there are many other occasions when memory-jogging is also necessary to ensure that an old person remembers to light the gas once he has turned it on, or remembers to eat, or to pay bills promptly. It is useful to write down instructions as well as giving them verbally. Leave the written instructions by the telephone so that you can phone to remind the elder to look at the instruction. If he is not on the phone, it may be effective to set a cooker timer or an alarm clock to ring at the time at which the old person wishes to eat or to do something, and to place the written instruction beside the timer.

One type of memory defect which can be aggravating is repetitive behaviour. The old person asks the same question time after time, apparently forgetting that you have answered as soon as you have finished speaking, or makes the same complaint, about pain or the need to pass water, repeatedly. Some old people develop the habit of repeating the same action, walking to the door, going to the sink or taking off some item of clothing, without ever realising that the action is useless or that they have done it before. Repetitive behaviour is due to a memory defect in some old people, but in others such actions are a means of gaining attention.

In hospital it is not uncommon for staff to recognise that a patient is repeatedly behaving in the same way to gain attention. A patient who says he has a pain soon discovers that this attracts staff and arouses interest in him. After the cause of pain has been cured, some people continue to complain because they find that they receive much less attention and company when they are without pain than when they had it, so they say they feel pain. Staff who realise they have no pain may stop being sympathetic, but for some old people this is unimportant. People who feel neglected may draw attention to themselves, for example by repeatedly making a noise or wetting the bed, even though this may result in their receiving a scolding rather than sympathy. A similar pattern or behaviour can develop at home. If you are very busy looking after an old person who is ill you may find it a relief to have a rest when he is not calling for you. This is obviously sensible and right. If, however, he thinks that he only receives attention when he calls and that you do not come to see him if he does not, he is tempted to call and call again. If he finds that one type of call will bring you with greater speed and certainty than any other, he will tend to repeat that call. We emphasise that this type of repetitive behaviour to seek attention is usually unconscious – the old person does not realise what he is doing.

If an elder repeats the same action time after time, we think that you should consult his GP. The GP may be able to understand the cause of the repetitive behaviour and suggest a consistent method of dealing with it, or he may ask for a second opinion from a consultant psychiatrist. Either the psychiatrist, the psychiatric community nurse or the psychologist in the team will then act as your adviser.

Excessive swings in mood

Swings in mood, from depression to elation, are normal. It would be unnatural not to respond to changes in the social environment. As the brain fails, the emotional response to an event tends to be of a greater degree, and is sometimes not appropriate to the event. For example, if someone speaks sharply to a young person, his response will usually be to become tense but not to make any outward signs. If an old person whose brain is failing is spoken to in the same manner, his response might be either to burst into tears, to become angry and shout or, occasionally, to laugh. To prevent emotional outbursts, you will have to be even more cool and patient than you would be with someone of your own age. Be consistent, try to remember how you responded to a situation on one occasion, and respond in the same way on the next similar occasion. If you feel your own emotions becoming too upset to remain cool enough to calm the old person for whom you are caring, you should discuss the problem with either the health visitor, a social worker or any professional who is known to the old person. An occasional argument is normal, and it is normal for someone who is caring for an old person to lose her temper, or for an old person to lose his; but if the emotional upsets are very frequent or last for days, then you should seek help.

Disorientation

For an old person to be well orientated, he has to be able to see, hear and communicate to the best of his ability. He also requires to have the markers which active people use but so often take for granted. Ensure that he has a clock which works and which he can see and a calendar which has print big enough to read. Disorientation can be a sign of depression as well as a sign of brain failure (see page 98). A depressed person is apathetic and no longer cares about the date or time, and if an old person suddenly stops winding his clock or crossing off the day on the calendar, it may be a sign of depression.

Orientation is more than merely knowing where one is and what time it is, it involves a sense of social position. This sense of position is determined, not by clocks or maps, but by the demands other people make on us and their expectations of us. An old person who feels himself useless to anyone else is disorientated and will be helped by being given the opportunity to help others. An old man may still be able to advise on gardening; an old woman may still be able to make pastry or knead dough. Find an opportunity for an old person to contribute successfully to you and to society and you will improve their mental well-being.

Wandering is one aspect of disorientation which can be very worrying. If an old person wanders, a reason for his doing so should be sought. Is he trying to find his way back to a home he has left? Is he looking for someone? One risk of wandering is that the old person will be run down, but this risk can be reduced. Wandering is worrying to neighbours and can be annoying if the old person knocks on their door at night when he can't find his way home. When wandering is first evident, the GP's opinion should be sought. Even if he cannot find a curable disorder as the cause of the tendency, he can refer the old person for day hospital or day centre attendance, which often provides so much stimulation and activity that the elder is too tired to want to wander.

If the old person is just going out for a stroll because it has always been his custom to go for walks, he may be annoyed if someone tries to restrain him by locking a door or by other means, and this can lead to even greater problems. The most serious risk to someone who wanders is road traffic. The importance of road safety drill should be impressed on old people who do not realise that their speed and ability to react is slowing. If someone is unable to appreciate this, then care should be taken to ensure that they wear light coloured clothes, perhaps an off-white top coat and luminous armbands, although it may be difficult to persuade an old person to use these. For women a light coloured shopping bag or handbag is also useful in twilight and at night.

If an old person has been seen by a doctor, and if you have taken all possible steps to ensure his safety from traffic, then it is his right to be at risk.

Disturbing Behaviour and the Use of Tranquillising Drugs

We realise, of course, that the symptoms of brain failure rarely fall neatly into one of the four disorders described. More than one is very often present, sometimes all of them. The type of behaviour which such disorders of the mind produce can be very disturbing. Restlessness, wandering, agitation and aggression can occur either singly or together, or sometimes one follows the other during the course of the same day and night.

Those who try to help you will always look for a psychological reason for such behaviour, and suggest ways in which the old person's social life can be altered in an attempt to reduce the disturbing behaviour. If this fails, tranquillising drugs can be prescribed by the GP or consultant psychiatrist.

Tranquillisers are classified according to their strength as either minor (the weaker drugs) or major (the stronger drugs). Minor tranquillisers, such as Chlordiazepoxide (Librium) or Diazepam (Valium), are commonly prescribed and are free from serious side-effects if taken correctly. They are very useful in the control of anxious agitation and can help the elder to sleep if anxiety is keeping her awake.

The major tranquillisers used are almost always drugs called Phenothiazines which is the name of the basic chemical formula. The basic formula has been altered to give a number of derivatives which have different names but similar properties: Chlorpromazine (Largactil), Promazine (Sparine), Prochlorperazine (Stemetil), Trifluoperazine (Stelazine). These drugs have serious side-effects if they are not taken as prescribed. They may make the old person unsteady on his feet. They upset the thermostat which

controls the body's temperature and put the old person at extra risk of hypothermia. Phenothiazines can aggravate Parkinson's Disease, with stiffness of the face and muscles. In some individuals who are sensitive to the action of these drugs these side-effects can occur, even if the old person takes them as the doctor intended.

Because these drugs affect the mind and are only prescribed for people whose minds are disordered, particular care has to be taken that they are taken correctly.

TAKE CARE OF YOURSELF

Caring for an old person who has disordered mental function can be very demanding. Don't allow yourself to become run down. It is normal to feel depressed and dispirited, angry and frustrated from time to time. Many supporters probably feel violent towards an old person who is being aggravating, even though they feel it only for a few seconds, and then feel ashamed but never admit it to anyone else. If you feel desperate, ask for help and let the person you are asking know just how tense or tired you are. Most professionals now realise that those people who look after the old people need relief and help just as much as their elders. They appreciate that you are the most important supporter, and that your health must be maintained for the good of you and the old person. If the first person you consult is unsympathetic, try someone else.

We have given advice which we hope will help you maintain the old person at home, with temporary admission to an old people's home or hospital. Although the number of beds which are available to admit an old person permanently are limited, it is possible for an old person to spend the rest of his days in a home or hospital. You can be caught in an awkward position if the Social Services Department says that the old person is too disturbed for one of their old people's homes, but the psychiatric hospital staff say that he is not disabled enough for long-term admission to hospital, although both agree he is too much for your care. The elder's GP should try to persuade one of these services to accept responsibility, and he may write to the specialist in community medicine for social services of the Area Health Authority to see if he can sort out the problem.

Don't feel guilty – take care of yourself so that you can continue to care for your elder.

Chapter 8
Hypothermia and Heating Problems

HEATING ADVICE

The elder's health visitor (see page 21) or the home help organiser (see page 16), if the elder is receiving home help, are the best people to approach with general enquiries. Questions about gas, coal or electricity should be addressed to the respective fuel board (see page 125). Any housing problems, such as dampness, condensation or poor repair, which aggravate heating problems are best taken to the environmental health officer (see page 26). If none of these services can offer appropriate advice the Citizens Advice Bureau, (see page 14) or Age Concern office (see page 14) should be approached for help.

Poverty is such an important cause of heating problems that this chapter should be read in association with the chapter on financial affairs.

WHAT IS HYPOTHERMIA?

Body temperature varies by as much as 1°C during the day. This variation is within fixed limits, usually between 36.5°C and 37.5°C, although these limits vary slightly from one individual to another. If the temperature rises above the upper limits of normal, the person suffers from fever. If it falls below the lower limit of normal, the person is said to suffer from hypothermia. Doctors usually make the diagnosis of hypothermia only when the body temperature is less than 35°C, which is well below the normal range.

Anyone can suffer from hypothermia – shipwrecked sailors, mountaineers and school-children in exposed countryside – but in our society it is most common in old people for two reasons:

- Our temperature sense, like the sense of vision and hearing, becomes less sensitive in some people as they age. An elderly person whose ability to sense cold is failing will not know she is cold and will not therefore take any appropriate action, such as lighting a fire, putting on more clothes or walking about. She will continue to sit, feeling well, but getting colder and colder.

- Normally, when the body temperature falls corrective measures are automatically taken. In the centre of the brain there is a thermostat, just like that in a central heating system. When the body temperature drops, the blood temperature drops and there is a flow of cold blood through the part of the brain in which the thermostat is situated. The thermostat then goes into action by increasing heat production – releasing hormones to create energy, causing the muscles to shiver, and reducing heat loss by cutting off the blood supply to the skin, especially the skin of the hands and feet. In old age this part of the brain may be affected by disease, so the person may be able to feel cold but is not able to respond normally. Some people lose both their ability to be aware of a cold environment and their ability to respond to, and correct, a drop in body temperature. Barbiturates and Phenothiazine drugs such as Chlorpromazine (Largactil), Thioridazine (Melleril), Prochlorperazine (Stemetil), Trifluoperazine (Stelazine) predispose to hypothermia, as does alcohol.

Hypothermia can be fatal but is not necessarily so. People can be warmed slowly back into the normal temperature range, provided that the hypothermic person is treated before their temperature has dropped too low. Hypothermia is not easy to recognise. The affected person may not feel cold and, in many cases, may not even look pale, often being flushed. Hand temperature is not a reliable sign of hypothermia. It is normal for hands to be cold in a cold environment, but if the skin on the abdomen, which is always warm, feels cold to touch, hypothermia should be considered. As the ordinary clinical thermometer does not measure temperatures below the normal range, it is not helpful in diagnosis. *If you are in any way suspicious, call the GP immediately and say that you think that an old person has hypothermia.* Ask the GP what steps you should take before he comes. If you cannot speak to the GP directly you will have to act yourself:

- Make the room as warm as possible, but do not direct heat straight at the elder.
- Give warm drinks only if she is alert and fully conscious, otherwise give nothing by mouth.
- Help the old person put on more clothes or, if she is able to walk, help her to bed and give her a hot water bottle or turn on the electric blanket at the lowest temperature.

The treatment of hypothermia requires care and is best done by doctors and nurses. What you can do best is to prevent it.

THE PREVENTION OF HYPOTHERMIA

A Safe Temperature

A room temperature of 21°C (70°F) is usually safe and acceptable. This may be too low for some people, too high for others, especially in the bedroom, but always try to ensure a temperature of 18°C (65°F). A room thermometer is useful in helping you maintain the room temperature at the desired level. If you are worried that the room temperature is falling too much at night, you can buy a maximum/minimum thermometer, which is inexpensive and records the highest

and lowest temperatures reached, but this is rarely necessary. Try to buy a thermometer which the old person can read; although this may be impossible as most have very small numbers and scales. The hall and passage ways should not be allowed to drop below 18°C (65°F).

Meeting the Cost of Heating

The first objective is to ensure that the elderly person has the highest possible income. We have described financial benefits elsewhere (see page 132), and here discuss in more detail only those benefits which are specifically designed to help with heating costs.

Supplementary pensioners can claim an Extra Heating Allowance which is a weekly addition to their pension. Full details are given in the Department of Health and Social Security leaflet *Help with Heating Costs* (Leaflet OC2). There are three levels of allowance, called 'low', 'medium' and 'high', the level given being determined by the needs of the pensioner, as specified in Table 8.1.

To apply for an Extra Heating Allowance the old person must write to her social security office. Include as much information as possible, describe the housing conditions and state clearly why the dwelling is difficult to heat. If there is a health problem ask the GP if he will write a letter to Social Security. If he thinks that there is a risk of hypothermia it is important for him to state this. If heating bills are high, include copies of them (many libraries now have photocopiers). If the heating bills are low because the old person is scared to use her heating due to its cost, explain this, otherwise the visiting officer from Social Security who assesses the application may not realise how high the costs would be if the dwelling was adequately heated.

If the claim is refused, an appeal should be considered (see page 140). The same sort of evidence as was used to support the initial claim should be collected and presented in more detail.

Table 8.1 *Extra Heating Allowances for Supplementary Pensioners*

Need for Extra Heating	Level of Allowance Granted
If the old person has restricted mobility or any condition which requires extra heating, (e.g. bronchitis, heart disease, rheumatism, arthritis) *OR* her house is difficult to heat adequately because of large rooms, high ceilings, stone floors, rising damp or draughts.	LOW
If she has *both* the conditions already described as being necessary for low level allowance to be granted *OR* if she is housebound or remains at home almost all the time, or is seriously ill *OR* if her accommodation is *exceptionally* difficult to heat.	MIDDLE
If she has all conditions already described as being necessary for a middle level allowance to be granted *OR* is bedridden or spends most of her time in bed *OR* requires a constant room temperature both day and night because of serious illness.	HIGH

(We have not expressed the three levels in financial terms because they are increased periodically.)

EVERY supplementary pensioner who lives in a centrally heated dwelling is entitled to and should claim an Extra Heating Allowance. (Electric storage heaters are considered as central heating if they are the main form of heating used.) The level of allowance depends on the number of rooms occupied. The kitchen is counted as a room, but the bathroom or toilet is not.

Only supplementary pensioners are eligible for these financial benefits. This is a source of bitterness to many elderly people who are ineligible for supplementary benefit because they have saved, or have a small pension. If the old person has a low income, and finds her heating costs difficult to meet, she should consider whether to apply for supplementary benefit and an Extra Heating Allowance. Many people who receive a retirement or widows pension from social security and a local authority rent and rate rebate would qualify for a supplementary pension, including an allowance for rent and rates. But they do not claim because they would be no better off, as the amount of financial help given by the State is about the same in both cases. However, some people who are in receipt of a retirement or widows pension and local authority rent and rate rebate, and who would qualify for an Extra Heating Allowance on account of health or housing conditions, would be better off becoming a supplementary pensioner. Ask the opinion of the rent and rates rebate officer. If he cannot advise you, ask the Citizens Advice Bureau or local Age Concern office. Both are listed in the phone book.

In very few cases would an old person become financially worse off by changing, and if so it would only be by a matter of pence. There is the disadvantage that applying for supplementary benefit entails undergoing a means test; but if there was a chance that an elderly person would qualify for an Extra Heating Allowance, which might entitle her to an extra pound or two a week, any apprehension she feels about the means test may be worthwhile overcoming.

In 1976 the government introduced a scheme whereby supplementary pensioners and those elderly people receiving rent and rate rebates were eligible for help with electricity bills presented in the first three months of the year. The future of this scheme cannot be predicted with certainty, but it will probably be continued in some form. Because the regulations may change from year to year it is important for elderly people, and those

who help them, to be aware of the need to collect an explanatory leaflet from electricity showrooms early in the winter. Any queries should be addressed to electricity offices and showrooms.

Fear of fuel debts

Even if extra financial help is obtained, fear of debt may prevent the elder from using her heating apparatus. This attitude can be very difficult, or even impossible, to change, but the fear of a large quarterly fuel bill can be greatly reduced. The fuel industries provide a wide range of facilities to help save towards the quarterly bills: you can buy saving stamps, make weekly cash payments or monthly payments by standing order. Ask about easy payment schemes at your local electricity and gas showrooms. Some coal merchants still run a scheme which allows weekly payments to be made to a credit account. A separate Post Office or savings bank account can also be used for fuel bills. In cases of genuine hardship, where other payment arrangements are not appropriate, the board may install a prepayment meter provided it is safe and practical. Fuel purchased by pre-payment meter costs more than fuel purchased quarterly, so we advise you to use a quarterly tariff with regular savings. If the old person does not buy gas or electricity direct from the supply authority but from a landlord, the amount which landlords can charge for fuel is limited by law, but it is not the responsibility of the gas or electricity board to ensure that the landlord does not go above the maximum legal price. Each fuel board has a Consumers Consultative Council which can give a ruling on the price which a landlord can charge. If you think that a landlord is overcharging, you can approach the Consumers Consultative Council directly for a ruling, or you may prefer to ask the advice of a Citizens Advice Bureau, or Housing Aid Centre. The electricity and gas industries have published a very useful, and simple, leaflet entitled 'Electricity and Gas Bills for your home – How to pay them, How to get help if there is real hardship' which should be available in all gas and electricity showrooms.

Sometimes elderly people do run into debt and may be threatened with disconnection. Under the Fuel Industries' Code of Practice, before they disconnect for debt, the industries will take steps to remind the consumer that the supply will be continued if he enters into (and keeps) arrangements for regular payments, such as to ensure clearance of arrears within a reasonable period. The Code also states that disconnection will be delayed for at least fourteen days where the consumer applies for help to the local social security office or the Social Services Department (see page 14).

This procedure only delays disconnection and you must act quickly. It is not enough to pay off part of the bill. What the board requires is that the elder either repays the debt completely or makes an arrangement to pay off the debt by agreeing to make weekly payments to the fuel board. If the weekly sum required by the board is beyond the means of the elder, ask the social security office if they can help.

Premises will not be disconnected between the beginning of October and the end of March where it is shown that all members of a household in receipt of income are pensioners over retirement age, unless it is clear that they have adequate financial resources. Again the advice we would offer is that you should try to prevent a crisis arising in the first place. If you expect difficulty in paying the fuel bill you should immediately seek advice from electricity or gas showrooms on how payment can best be effected. Staff can give advice and help to a consumer who is in difficulties. Debts and hypothermia can both be cured, but are better prevented.

Choosing the Most Suitable Method of Heating

The choice of the type of fuel and fire greatly influence the cost of keeping warm, because there is a wide variation in cost of different fuels and the efficiency with which different types of fire burn each fuel. Although we recommend certain types of fuel and give a list of fires ranked according to efficiency, we do not expect you to choose the cheapest and most efficient as 'the best'. You will need to decide with your elder what is best for her and the choice has to be made within two constraints:

- The old person's preference. If an old person likes an open fire and finds it both companionable and a comfort, it is obviously wrong to change. If keeping a coal fire going is proving too much for you, for example if you have to visit her home three times daily to do this, you must tell her so. Rather than taking away the fire for this reason it may be possible to find someone to share your burden, either the home help service or a neighbour. A neighbour may be happy to take in coal once a day if you ask her. She may find it easier to do so if you offer to pay a small sum of money weekly – some people find it easier to help if they are employed to do so.

- The types of fuel available. If there is gas in the street it is often not too expensive to lead it into the house, but if there is no gas in the neighbourhood it is not a feasible choice. Bottled gas is expensive and we do not advise it except for emergencies. It is not easy to generalise about comparative fuel costs, but we offer here our opinions on the common types of fuel.

- *Gas* is the cheapest form of energy, especially if burned in a convector heater. Always choose a fire with controls on the top which are easy to turn and buy a fire which gives convected heat, either alone or combined with radiant heat. Special taps are available for people with a weak grip. Make sure that the old person is on the most economical tariff.

- *Coal* is most efficient when burnt in a closed stove but such a stove precludes the possibility of burning wood. If the elder lives in an area which has been designated a smokeless zone then she will be offered a grant by the council to cover the cost of installing a smokeless fuel closed fire or any other type of heating apparatus, including gas or electric fires. It is wise to discuss the choice with a representative of the Solid Fuel Advisory Service. They may advise you to spend a little more money to buy an efficient fire, and one which the elder can understand and operate. Smokeless fuel is more expensive, and the special types of fire have to be carefully managed, or else the cost of heating can be greater than it was with the old open grate.

- *Electricity* is the most expensive form of energy to buy, but it is 100 per cent efficient in use. We do not recommend, except for short periods, the use of radiant 'bar' fires. Electric heaters of any type using day rate electricity should be used for no more than three hours of heating. Storage heaters are less expensive to run and they provide continuous warmth, which is an advantage to elderly people. Many people make electric heating cost more than it needs to by being on the wrong tariff. The tariff system may seem complicated, and we recommend you to seek the help of the local electricity board.
- *Paraffin* is not as comparatively cheap as it once was. New paraffin heaters are very much safer than old heaters, but it is essential to have any heater serviced regularly. The other main drawback is that paraffin and bottled gas heaters produce large amounts of water vapour and can result in condensation, and both require increased room ventilation.

The Department of Energy produce an excellent booklet called *Compare Your Home Heating Costs*, which should be available in Citizens Advice Bureaux and Housing Aid Centres. The leaflet provides up-to-date information on the cost of different fuels.

Central heating is commonly already installed when an old person moves into a new dwelling and is not a matter about which you have any choice. The most important step you can take is to ensure that both you and she know how to operate the thermostat and time-switch. Ask the fuel board if someone can come to the flat to show you the most effective and efficient settings. In sheltered housing schemes the warden should be able to advise.

This is especially important if the dwelling has ceiling heating, because careful control of this type of central heating is crucial to its success. Another common type is electricaire storage heating, consisting of a large storage heater. All storage heaters have become more expensive, but they are still a useful source of heat. The bricks in the heater store heat, which is then blown into the room by a fan. The amount of heat released, and therefore the cost, can be controlled in a number of ways:

- Don't switch the heater off unless it is to be off for a week or longer. If you do the bricks cool down.
- Turn the fan switch off at night.
- Use the booster switch for as short a period of time as possible.
- Don't block the warm air outlets.
- Ask the advice of the electricity board concerning the setting of the thermostat.

Efficiency league table
The efficiency of different types of heater – the amount of heat they produce for each pound spent – cannot be given precisely because it is affected by the elder's understanding and use of them. However, we can set the heaters out in an economy league table with Division 1 the most economical and Division 4 the least economical. Remember all open heaters should have a guard for safety reasons.

The fires in each division are *not* listed in order of efficiency.

DIVISION 1 (MOST ECONOMICAL)
Gas convector heaters
Closed anthracite stoves

DIVISION 2
Gas radiant/convector fires
Electric storage heaters
New solid fuel fires

DIVISION 3
Gas radiant fires
Old solid fuel fires
Paraffin heaters

DIVISION 4 (LEAST ECONOMICAL)
Bottled propane and butane gas
Electric fires

It is one thing to choose a more efficient means of heating, but another to pay for the change. Many people are able to identify what would be a more suitable form of heating but are unable to change to it because of the expense involved. It may be cheaper to insulate rather than to change the heating system.

Supplementary pensioners can apply to social security for an Exceptional Needs Payment to cover the cost of:

• Repairing existing appliances.
• Replacing appliances which are broken beyond repair, inadequate, hazardous or too expensive to run. For example, supplementary benefits can pay for the replacement of a radiant (bar) electric fire if it is the elder's only form of heating.

An Exceptional Needs Payment – ENP – will cover both the purchase and installation of a heating appliance, but not necessarily a new appliance. It cannot be given to pay for the installation of central heating (see page 138).

The Social Services Department can pay for the replacement of a heater which the elder cannot manage because of disability. For example, if she is too disabled to obtain adequate heat from a coal fire because she cannot make and maintain the fire, Social Services can pay for the replacement by a self-igniting gas heater with top controls, using the powers given to them by the Chronically Sick and Disabled Persons Act. They can also pay for the alteration of a gas or electric fire if the elder is too disabled to operate it. Ask the domiciliary occupational therapist's advice.

If the area in which the elder lives is to become a smokeless zone, she will receive a grant for conversion of her open fire. *Before you or she pay out any money for the replacement of a fire, ask the Environmental Health Department if such a programme is planned for her area.* It is very annoying to spend money, then to find that the council would have paid for the work if only you had waited another six months. Money will not be reimbursed for work done before the scheme was introduced, or without approval.

If none of these methods of raising the money is applicable, follow the suggestions we describe to raise a lump sum (see page 139).

Before you buy any heating appliance, ask the fuel boards or the Solid Fuel Advisory Service if they have any special offers for pensioners.

The Fuel Boards – How They Can Help You

Electricity
Your local electricity board can be contacted at the board's office or any of its showrooms. The staff can advise you on:

• The choice of the most suitable tariff.
• Easy payment schemes.
• Appliances.
• How to operate and set the controls on heating and other appliances. (Ask for a home visit if you are uncertain.)
• Insulation.
• Aids for disabled people.

Remember that queries about bills should be discussed as quickly as possible with your local electricity board. If, after raising the matter with the board, you are still dissatisfied, you can contact your local Electricity Consultative Council who are there to help you. The address of the Consultative Council can be obtained from the electricity board's showroom.

Gas

The gas regions also have area offices and showrooms. They offer similar services to the electricity board and advise on:

- Easy payment schemes.
- Appliances.
- How to operate and set the controls on heating and other appliances. (Ask for a home visit if you are uncertain.)
- Insulation.
- Aids for disabled people.
- Free safety checks for elderly people living alone.

The Gas Consumers Council is there to help you with any complaints or queries which you feel have not been well handled by the area office.

Solid fuel

Advice on solid fuel and appliances can be obtained free of charge from the Solid Fuel Advisory Service. If required, they will visit the home to give on the spot advice on all aspects of solid fuel heating. Many builders' merchants are Approved Appliance Distributors and some have Living Fire Centres where appliances are on display and advice is given. Choose a coal merchant who is a member of the Approved Coal Merchants Scheme (ACMS) and talk to him first if you have a complaint about solid fuel. If necessary, take the matter up with the Regional Secretary of the ACMS. Failing satisfaction from either of these you can refer the matter to the Domestic Coal Consumers Council (DCCC). The Citizens Advice Bureaux will be able to provide you with the address of your Regional Secretary and that of the Secretary of the DCCC.

Warmth Conservation

Having raised the income to as high a level as possible and burned the money as efficiently as you can, the final step in the prevention of hypothermia is to minimise the amount of heat which is lost.

Keep the old person warm

It is surprising how often an old person who is at risk of hypothermia, or who is cold, is inadequately dressed. Sometimes the problem is that she does not have sufficient or adequate clothes. If money is the problem, remember that supplementary pensioners can claim an Exceptional Needs Payment for new or extra clothes. Another difficulty elders face is that many shops stock clothes for young, slim people. This applies particularly to warm sensible underwear. If you cannot find a good haberdasher, we recommend that you use one of the mail order firms which advertise in women's magazines. Sometimes the elder does not wear the clothes she has, either because she forgets to dress properly (in which case she needs help in the mornings to remind her what to put on) or because she is too physically handicapped. If physical disability is the main dressing problem, ask the advice of the domiciliary occupational therapist (see page 23).

Encourage the elder to wear as many layers of clothes as possible.

Encourage her to wear wool – still the best warmth-giving material.

Remember that quilted material makes an excellent coat lining.

Remember that anoraks and trousers suit and flatter people of all ages.

Thick tights are also excellent, provided they do not affect the circulation.

Remember that a hat prevents a great deal of heat loss.

A 'Spacecoat' is a housecoat which is made of material insulated to a very high degree, and which will not catch fire. It is an attractive, safe and warm garment for all elderly people at home. Available from Spacecoat, Rawlings House, Rawlings Street, London SW3 2PU, 01–589 0551.

Food provides energy and energy provides internal warmth. Hot food is no more nutritious than cold food, but it is warming. It takes heat into the elder and does not take heat from the body during its digestion. Almost every elder can be taught to make herself a bowl of soup and a boiled egg, no matter how disabled she is – ask the advice of the domiciliary occupational therapist. A flask is very useful as it can be filled by any visitor, providing a hot drink for emergencies.

Keep the room warm
If the elder spends most of her time in one room, this can be insulated. Consider the following actions:

- Block off the fireplace if not in use. Leave half-penny size holes in the screen for ventilation.
- Seal any gaps between floorboards and lay a carpet underlay or old newspapers to insulate the floor.
- Seal draught gaps round windows and doors with adhesive insulation tape.
- Line the curtains. Curtains should be so thick that it cannot be seen from outside whether there is a light on in the room or not. Heavy curtains not only stop draughts but act as a form of double glazing.
- Hang a curtain at the door of the room.
- Double-glaze the window either with a new window unit or with clear cellophane food wrapping, which is especially suitable for windows with small panes. Seek the advice of an environmental health officer.

Never make the room airtight. If there is a paraffin or bottled gas heater it could be dangerous, because they use up oxygen while burning.
Supplementary pensioners can apply for an Exceptional Needs Payment to cover the cost of these insulating materials.

Before discussing house insulation, we wish to make some specific points about bedrooms. Many people prefer their bedroom cooler than the rooms in which they live during waking hours. Many like to have an open window no matter how low the air temperature outside, and it can often help to emphasise that this practice is not essential for health. If the old person refuses to have heating in her bedroom, all through the night, try to ensure that there is some source of heat in the room for an hour before she retires to bed. Although electric bar and fan heaters are expensive to run, this is one occasion on which we recommend their use because they are ideal for taking the chill off a room. Although people like a cool bedroom, a warm and cosy bed is necessary for comfort and safety. Because impairment of the power to regulate body temperature occurs as part of the ageing process, old people need a warmer bed than they had when young. Thick pyjamas and nightdresses are essential. Bedsocks are easy to knit and make a tremendous contribution to comfort in bed, and the old fashioned bed cap is also useful. Many old people are in fact well acquainted with measures to keep warm, having been brought up in an age during which central heating was unknown. But they may need some encouragement to return to old-fashioned sensible practices.

Bedclothes grow thin and should be replaced. An Exceptional Needs Payment can be made to supplementary pensioners to replace bedding. Continental quilts have many advantages. They are light, warm and make bed making easy, but it may be necessary to lend one to an elder before she will be convinced of its worth.

Rubber hot water bottles are difficult to fill with shaky hands. To reduce the danger a neck holder which allows the holding hand to be kept away from the hot water should be used – ask the domiciliary occupational therapist if she thinks that one would help. Metal hot water bottles which stand upright for filling without being held and keep warm all night, if they are in a knitted cover, are still available and the old stone hot water bottle is also safer to fill than a rubber bottle. There are new electric blankets which run on 'extra low voltage' – E.L.V. – which can be left on all night while the elder is in bed. The extra low voltage results in a much safer blanket. Even when the elder has been incontinent and the bed is wet they are still safe. Ask the Social Services Department if they can lend one. If an E.L.V. blanket is not available on loan, we recommend either a Halcyon CU3 or a Dee Gee G5 for a single bed, and the Safesleeper SL or the Dee Gee SUB24 for a double bed. These blankets were reviewed in *Which*, November 1977.

Leave a flask of tea by the bed, offer the elder a bottle, pot or commode to pass water in the bedroom, and you will have provided for both comfort and safety.

Keep the house warm
It is not enough to warm and insulate one room – the whole dwelling must be considered. If the rest of the dwelling is too cold, there will be a tremendous rush of cold air into the warm room through any gaps in the room's insulation or when the door is opened. We therefore advise some heating in parts of the house other than those lived in by the elder. It is important to heat the hall. Not only does an old person have to cross the hall on the way to kitchen or toilet, but to have a cold hall and a warm room is a recipe for unstoppable draughts. An excellent form of heating for a hall is a gas convector heater, provided there is an external wall for the flue. There is no visible flame and the heater is a metal box fixed on an outside wall with cold air being drawn in the bottom and hot air rising from the top. It is both safe and economical.

Heat produced in the hall rises and a great deal can be lost up the stairwell. A heavy curtain hung across the stair can reduce this heat loss, but it is no bad thing to have some heat pass to the upper parts of the house to prevent damp and mould, and to provide a layer of warm air over the rooms in which the old person lives. The same problem arises with unused rooms. Although it is wise to close the doors of such rooms to prevent loss of heat, the effect on these rooms and the whole house must also be considered.

The first and cheapest step in insulating the house is to seal all gaps round doors and windows. Remember to leave some ventilation for paraffin, gas and coal fires, and *never cover insulation bricks*.

The next step – which is essential – is to prevent heat loss through the loft by laying at least four inches of insulating material, glass fibre or mineral wool. Council tenants can ask the housing department to do this, although they may refuse if they have spent all the money set aside for house improvement in the current year. If this is the case, ask for the job to be considered for the next financial year. A letter from the elder's GP may be helpful. Many councils now purchase insulating material which can be laid by the tenant, his friends or volunteers. Ask the housing department if they will supply the material if you supply the labour. If you are unable to do this yourself ask the local Age Concern office if they can supply a volunteer. Owner occupiers can apply for an Improvement Grant from the Local Authority (see page 158) for insulation of lofts, water tanks and pipes in lofts, and hot water tanks wherever they are located.

Even if you cannot raise the money from an official source, it would be financially worthwhile to pay for the material yourself if the old person is going to stay in the house for at least three years. From the point of view of the elder's comfort, it may be worthwhile to insulate whatever the cost.

It is not difficult to lay insulating material. Remember to insulate *over* the water tank, after building a simple hardboard box round it. Do not put any insulating material under it, so that some heat reaches the tank in cold weather. Glass fibre and mineral wool are irritating substances: Gloves and a mask should always be used when they are handled. A metal and gauze mask can be bought cheaply in most ironmongers.

When the work and expense of loft insulation is over, the next decision is whether or not to insulate the walls. This is a much more difficult decision. The decision depends on two factors: the length of time the elder expects to live in that dwelling, and the type of wall construction. The cost of loft insulation material takes about one year to repay, but wall insulation is usually more expensive and takes five years or longer to recover in terms of energy saved. However, wall insulation increases the value of the dwelling so that, when it is sold, some of the cost can be recouped even if the elder did not enjoy its benefit for five years.

Modern dwellings have 'cavity walls', two layers of brick with a cavity of air sandwiched between them. This air barrier insulates the interior of the dwelling, but the insulating power of the wall can be increased by filling the air space with insulating foam. This procedure can have unsatisfactory results, but the risk of this is minimised if a well established firm which has an Agrément Board certificate is employed. Ask the Environmental Health Department for a list of local firms which have this certificate or contact the National Cavity Insulation Association, 178–202 Great Portland Street, London W1N 6AQ (telephone 01-637 7481), for the name of the member company which operates nearest you.

An environmental health officer can be asked to visit the elder's dwelling to advise on the suitability of cavity wall insulation, and we advise you to ask for such help if the walls are exposed to wind and rain, are in bad repair or if you are in any doubt at all. Firms prefer to insulate the whole dwelling, because it is often difficult just to insulate the walls of one room.

Older brick built dwellings have solid walls which are composed of two bricks laid side by side nine inches thick, with no cavity between them. (If you do not know how the wall is constructed, ask an environmental health officer.) It is possible to insulate a solid wall by attaching battens to the inside of the wall to which insulating panels can be nailed. These panels have, of course, to be redecorated and there are other problems – you should ask an environmental health officer for his opinion before starting work. It is impracticable to insulate a whole house or flat using this method, but if the elder lives in one room it may be worthwhile. It is simpler to buy an insulating layer such as 'Warmalene', which is hung like wallpaper.

Very old brick built dwellings sometimes have walls which are only one brick thick ($4\frac{1}{2}$ inches). If this is the case, we recommend you to consider this type of insulation.

Neither Improvement Grants, nor Exceptional Needs Payments are paid for wall insulation.

HOT WATER

If there is a double heating element, use the top element for heating water for general washing purposes. Only use the long element to heat the whole cylinder for baths and washing clothes. Heating water by gas circulation or solid fuel is often no cheaper than by immersion heater in a properly insulated cylinder.

If the cylinder has only a single element it is probably wise to leave the element on all the time if the elder uses hot water twice or more a day, but the cylinder must be insulated with at least a 3 inch lagging jacket. Ask at the electricity showroom if you are uncertain whether the tank has a single or double element. Ask also to see if you can use off-peak electricity. If the water from the tap is too hot for your hand to be held in it, turn down the setting on the tank thermostat (if it has one) to 60°C (140°F) and certainly to no higher than 70°C (158°F). A time-clock can be fitted to the hot water system. Dripping hot taps waste money, and worn washers should be replaced.

Make sure that the tank has three inches of lagging, no matter what type of element it has or what fuel you use.

CONDENSATION

Damp and running walls are a common cause of distress, especially if mould grows on them. The basic cause of condensation is simple. Water vapour, which is often invisible, becomes liquid water again when it touches cold walls. The cure for condensation is to reduce water vapour and to heat the walls. Water vapour is produced as steam from boiling kettles and pans.

As cooking without pan lids produces large volumes of water vapour which saturate the air, boiling water should always be covered. Water vapour is also produced by gas cookers, paraffin heaters or calor gas fires. The production of some water vapour is inevitable, and it is important to provide plenty of ventilation so that the vapour can escape. To warm the walls it is necessary to warm the air in the room by the means we have described. We realise that ventilation reduces room temperature, so the two measures we advocate to reduce condensation act, to some extent, in opposition to one another. You have to decide the most appropriate balance between warmth and ventilation.

There are other causes of dampness – penetration of rain from outside, rising damp and leaking pipes – and the opinion of an environmental health officer at the Town Hall should be sought if you are in any doubt, or fail to dry the dampness using the advice we have given.

WANT AND NEED

Although these practical problems are often difficult to solve, the most difficult problem is not practical but psychological, when the old person's definition of what she *wants* differs from what other people thinks she *needs*. An old person who refuses to use her heating appliances even though she has enough money to pay her heating bill presents a problem to those trying to help her. To understand this reluctance it is essential to remember that:

- Many of our elders were brought up in days when fuel was paid for *before* it was used, either by paying the coalman on delivery or by putting coins in a meter. Using fuel which has not been paid for makes them nervous of debt.
- Many such people were brought up to budget on a weekly basis and find quarterly bills and budgeting impossible to manage.
- To someone who has been brought up in fear of debt using coal, which can be seen and measured by the shovelful, electricity and gas are unknown, and even frightening, invisible commodities.
- Having been brought up in cold houses, some elders actually feel uncomfortable in warm dwellings or warm bedrooms.
- A few believe that there is virtue in being cold and uncomfortable, rather than being warm and comfortable.

What else can you do if you have increased the elder's income, ensured that she used her money as efficiently as possible, and adapted her environment to retain the warmth created, but she still refuses to turn the fires on? There is no simple answer to this. You will have to emphasise again that she need not fear debt, that she needs more heat than she thinks and that you and her other supporters are very worried and upset. The authorative opinion of a trusted outsider, for example the GP, can reinforce this advice. In the long run, however, the decision is her own and if an old person wishes to live at risk of hypothermia and suffer discomfort, that is her right. When you have done all that can be done, you have to live with your anxieties, sharing them with other people – a social worker, GP or health visitor – and allow the elder to lead her own life in the manner she chooses.

PREVENTING FIRE

The possibility that an old person will set fire to his dwelling is a common cause of worry to all who know him, and of course to his neighbours. Paraffin heaters are usually considered to be the greatest risk, and they can be dangerous if the old person's hand shakes while he is filling the heater or if the heater is not properly serviced. The main causes of fires are not, however, paraffin heaters but cigarettes, pipes and matches. The risk of fire spreading from these sources is markedly increased if the elder drinks alcohol heavily while smoking. He may fall asleep while smoking, or become forgetful and leave a pipe in his chair, or not smell burning because of the effects of the alcohol he has drunk.

To reduce the risk of fire:

● Remind the elderly person of the risks of fire. This is necessary for people of all ages but particularly so for older people because their sense of vision and smell may be less sensitive.
● Try to persuade the elder to use a lighter, instead of matches.

● Try to discourage him from smoking in bed. If he continues to do so try to make sure that he has woollen bed covers, which are less inflammable.
● Try to buy flame resistant nightwear.
● Buy a small fire extinguisher and a fire blanket for the kitchen and for any other room in which the elder regularly smokes. Inform the neighbours where the extinguishers are kept, if they are anxious about the possibility of fire.
● Consult an Approved Electrical Installation Contractor if the wiring is old or suspect. A Roll of Approved Contractors should be available in Consumer Advice Bureaux and Electricity showrooms. If re-wiring is necessary, a maturity loan can be applied for – ask an Environmental Health Officer for details.

Chapter 9
Financial Affairs

A knowledge of pensions, financial benefits, taxation and how to increase one's income is essential. This book is not designed to provide detailed information in any one of the foregoing areas; all space will permit us to do is to provide guidelines.

The social security system is very complex, and has been referred to as a 'tailless crocodile'. If, consulting the information we have provided, you are not clear on any point, do not hesitate to refer to those whose job it is to advise on the system. The elder's health visitor may be able to answer questions about social security (see page 21) as may a social worker if the elder is being currently in touch with one (see page 14). Social workers are unlikely to involve themselves in a problem which is solely financial, and will probably refer complicated financial problems to the Citizens Advice Bureau (see page 14) or Age Concern (see page 14). If your elder is in, or attends hospital, the Medical Social Worker (see page 14) can be consulted. If the elder has a home help, the home help organiser is a useful service of advice (see page 16). For the social security benefits related to disability, the occupational therapist will be able to give advice (see page 23) and complicated problems can be referred to the voluntary organisation D.I.G. (Disablement Income Group) Attlee House, 28 Commercial Street, London E1 6NS. Remember also that social security officers and offices are a source of help, advice and support and the officers can pay home visits to disabled people. *Your Rights*, which is published annually, is a clear and excellent guide to social security (price 25p), Age Concern, Bernard Sunley House, 60 Pitcairn Road, Mitcham, Surrey.

For financial problems other than those connected with social security, bank managers are extremely helpful. No matter how small the account, the bank should offer an advisory service. If the elder does not have an account and finds banks daunting, consider opening an account with the Trustee Savings Bank – the financial advice given by their managers is first-class. Banks can also give advice on income tax problems. Moreover, you should be aware of the fact that staff of the Inland Revenue are not just tax collectors; part of their job is to sort out worrying tax problems.

If the elder is unwilling to apply for help after advice has been given, refer to our discussion of this problem in the chapter on heating problems (see page 120).

Please note that in the following we have quoted the rates valid for November 1979. We have quoted specific figures throughout this chapter, although we realise that they will change, because this provides a frame of reference within which the rates current at any time can be more helpfully studied. Current amounts can be obtained from a Social Security Office. These are also given in *Your Rights*.

PENSIONS

Retirement Pension

Retirement Pension is taxable, and payable in an amount which depends on the amount of National Insurance contributions and present income from employment.

To qualify
To qualify, a person must:
a) have reached the age of 65 (for a man) or 60 (for a woman);

b) have declared his/her intention to retire on a specified date to the Department of Health and Social Security, which must have accepted that retirement has occurred;

c) have paid a sufficient amount in National Insurance contributions.

Amounts receivable

The basic rates at full pension are

Single Person: £23.30

Wife on Husband's contribution: £14.00

Married Couple: £37.30

(People who reach pension age after April 5, 1979 may qualify for an earnings-related pension under the Government's new pension scheme.)

These amounts are payable to those who simply paid the full necessary amounts of National Insurance contributions. They are varied by two principal factors:

a) Earned Income, and b) Contributions to National Insurance.

a) *Earned income*

The effect of earned income on basic pension received for a man aged 65–69 or a woman aged 60–64 is shown in the table below.

Weekly earned income (before tax)	*Effect*
less than £52	Pension unchanged
from £52 to £56	Pension reduced by half amount by which earnings exceed £45
more than £56	Pension further reduced by full amount by which earnings exceed £56

These restrictions end for men at 70 and for women at 65 and above these ages a person's pension is not reduced by earnings. From April 1979, neither additional (earnings-related) pension nor graduated pension will be affected in this way by earnings.

b) *Contributions to National Insurance*

The calculation of the applicable pension is simple for those cases where a person has contributed continuously since 1948 or earlier. People in this position get the full pension. In cases where contributions have been paid intermittently, the calculations are complicated and the pension paid is apt to be at a reduced rate. Another complicated area is the Earnings-Related Pension, which is based on earnings in employment from April 1978. The local Social Security Office will be able to assist with any queries on this point.

Married women

On the retirement of her husband, a wife is entitled to a pension on the basis of her husband's contributions, even if she has never contributed herself. If on the other hand, she has made contributions at other than the reduced rate for married women, she may qualify at age 60, for a pension on her own contributions. This independent pension will be awarded to her even if it is less than the standard pension on her husband's contributions. If it is less, the balance on the basis of her husband's contributions will be paid. The amount of the independent pension should be included on the Income Tax Return because a certain sum of a wife's earned income is free of tax and any pension due to her on her own behalf is treated for tax purposes as earned income.

THE NEW PENSION SCHEME OPERATIVE SINCE APRIL 6, 1978

The new pensions scheme includes cover for someone looking after another person at home.

Being unable to work regularly, so as to stay at home to look after someone, one need not lose out on basic national insurance contributions. From April 6, 1978 it is possible to get home responsibilities protection for basic pension.

This pension protection for a particular tax year is available to those who have, for at least thirty-five hours a week for the whole tax year, cared for someone who has received

Attendance or Constant Attendance Allowance throughout that tax year. It is also available to those who have received supplementary benefit so as to be able to care for an elderly or sick person at home. If, however, the old or sick person does not receive an Attendance Allowance, or the carer does not receive supplementary benefit then she *must* continue to pay Class III contributions (voluntary), but, if she is within five years of pension age she may already have enough contributions, for the standard rate of basic pension. The local Social Security Office will advise if one writes to them quoting one's National Insurance number.

When basic pension is being worked out, the number of years for which home responsibilities protection has been given will be taken away from the number of qualifying years of contributions needed for full pension. The full basic pension will be awarded if one has this reduced number of qualifying years, provided it is not less than twenty.

OCCUPATIONAL PENSION SCHEMES
There are three methods of determining pension benefits:

a) The final salary plan is probably the most satisfactory form of pension arrangement.

This scheme works on the assumption that earnings are at their height in the years immediately before retirement. A formula is used providing a pension with a fraction of a man's final salary for each year of employment. One-sixtieth of the final salary for each year's service is common, although one-eightieth is used for some schemes.

b) The money-purchase scheme invests each member's contribution through an insurance company. He will therefore be provided with a pension on his behalf strictly according to his contributions.

c) The average pay scheme provides a pension related to year-by-year pay. For those whose pay rises rapidly, this is a good scheme.

Pension on retirement
The maximum allowed by the Inland Revenue is two-thirds of final salary.

GRADUATED PENSION
Such a pension stems from graduated pension contributions made between April 1961 and April 1975. The sums involved are not large and the greatest amount anyone can get is about £3.65 per week, but most men and women will get less than a pound.

Leaflet GR20A gives further information on this.

FACTORS WHICH MAY OR MAY NOT AFFECT PENSION

Hospital
The amount of retirement pension is normally unaffected by a stay in hospital of up to eight weeks. After this period, however, the pension of a person with dependants is reduced by £4.66 and for a person without dependants, by £9.30.

After a year in hospital a person will normally have the pension reduced to £4.66 a week. But there are special rules applying to patients who have dependants. In such cases, it is best to contact the local office of the Department of Health and Social Security, or the Welfare Department at the hospital, where someone will explain the rules. Leaflet NI.9 gives further details, *How a Stay in Hospital Can Affect Your Social Security Benefit.*

Postponing retirement
Postponing retirement beyond 60 (for a woman) or 65 for a man, will result in an increase in the retirement pension. The pension is increased by one per cent (or one penny in the pound) for each seven week period from April 1979 for which pension is not drawn up to a limit of five years. The deferment for five years would result in an increase of about 37½ per cent (three-eighths) in the pension originally payable.

A married woman over age 60 who is deferring retirement at the same time as her husband, and whose pension is based wholly or partly on his contributions, can earn an increase of her pension at the same rate, i.e. one penny in the pound for each seven week period that she does not draw the pension. From April 6, 1979, this extra pension for a married woman will be based on the amount of pension she herself forgoes.

An increase is not earned for days during which some other National Insurance benefit is in payment.

Living abroad

In the case of trips of less than three months none of the pension orders by which a pension is paid will have expired and can be cashed upon return.

It is important when going abroad for periods exceeding three months to contact the local Social Security Office well in advance, so as to arrange payment to be made abroad.

The leaflet DHSS NI.38, obtainable from any Social Security Office, gives important information in respect of the applicability of increases in the pension rates.

Appeals

Following a claim, the amount payable is decided by an Insurance Officer at the local Social Security Office, which then notifies the claimant of the decision.

If the amount awarded (including nothing) is thought to be wrong, write, without delay, to the local office stating the reason for dissatisfaction. The office should look into the matter and let you know how the award could be challenged, if they are unable to alter the rate. They should also state whether or not there is a right to appeal to a Local Tribunal. There is a further right of appeal to a National Insurance Commissioner whose decision is final.

Over 80's pension

This is a non-contributory retirement pension and is essentially for persons aged 80 or more who do not have the basic retirement pension. There is also a smaller amount which is paid to make up a reduced retirement pension to the full value of the over 80's pension.

Married Women: £8.40

Single man or woman or married man: £14.00. These rates include the Age Addition of 25p a week payable to pensioners over 80.

TO QUALIFY – No contributions are necessary. However, the claimant has to have been living in the United Kingdom or the Common Market for ten out of twenty years between his or her sixtieth and eightieth birthday.

There are special arrangements which apply to women who were 87 or more, and men who were 92 or more on July 5, 1975 (and for any dependant). Check with the local Social Security Office about these.

TO CLAIM – Forms and leaflets NI.184 and NI.177A can be obtained from your local Social Security Office. Fill out the form, send it off and where possible, send birth certificate or passport with the form so that age can be verified. If neither of these is available, don't worry about it.

A couple should fill in one form. A dependent wife will get this pension only if she is 80 or more, or if she is less than 80 and her husband is 93 or more.

Widow's Benefit

These are taxable benefits paid to a widow which are based on her late husband's contributions to the National Insurance Scheme. There are a number of individual benefits:
a) Widow's Allowance; b) Widowed Mother's Allowance; c) Widow's Pension Related Addition.

a) Widow's Allowance

Widow's allowance is a resettlement benefit which is paid for the 26 weeks following the death of the husband. If a woman of 60 or over is widowed she can only get the allowance if her husband was not entitled to a retirement pension.

The weekly rate is £32.60 with increases of £6.30 for each qualifying child.

b) *Widowed Mother's Allowance*

Widowed mother's allowance is generally payable to a widow with a qualifying child when widow's allowance ends.

The weekly rate is £23.30 with increases of £7.10 per qualifying child.

The rate can be reduced where the husband only partially satisfied the contribution conditions.

The allowance can be paid, without increases for children, if the widow has a son or daughter residing with her who is under 19 but does not count as a child because he or she has left school.

c) *Widow's Pension*

Widow's pension is payable when:

- Widow's allowance ends and the widow does not qualify for widowed mother's allowance providing she was 40 or over when her husband died.
- widowed mother's allowance ends providing the widow is then 40 or over.

The weekly rate is £23.30 if the widow was 50 or over when her husband died or when she ceased to be entitled to widowed mother's allowance.

Reduced rates are payable for women who were widowed at ages between 40 and 50.

Age 40	£6.99	Age 45	£15.15
41	£8.62	46	£16.78
42	£10.25	47	£18.41
43	£11.88	48	£20.04
44	£13.51	49	£21.67

The rates can be further reduced where the husband only partially satisfied the contribution conditions.

Widow's benefit stops if the widow remarries or lives with a man as his wife.

RETIREMENT

A widow may elect not to claim retirement pension at 60. In this case, she can continue to draw her widow's pension until 65.

She can add the entitlement on her own contributions to this (if she reaches 60 after April 5, 1979) with the combined basic pensions restricted to the standard rate and the combined additional pensions restricted to the maximum that a single contributor could have earned from the start of the new scheme.

When she retires, her pension becomes a retirement pension (at least at the same amount as her widow's pension). When she retires she can then receive her own and half her husband's graduated pension. If she retires before age 65 but continues to work and earns more than £52 per week, she may lose some of her pension.

At age 65, the widow will receive the retirement pension even if she has not retired. Her (retirement) pension is then unaffected by her earnings.

To claim

At the time of registration of death, the Registrar of Deaths will issue a registration certificate. On the back of this certificate is a form which should be filled in and sent as soon as possible to the local Social Security Office.

In response a claim form will arrive. This too should be completed and returned without delay.

Appeals

See appeals in the section on Retirement Pension.

Further information

The leaflets NP.36, NP.32 and 32A, obtainable at any Social Security Office give further information.

OTHER BENEFITS

Supplementary Benefits

FACTORS AFFECTING THE AMOUNT

These are non-contributory benefits available to those whose incomes are considered inadequate to meet their 'requirements' as laid down by Parliament. Payments are equal to the amount by which their 'income' falls short of these 'requirements'. This is an amount which varies with circumstances. It should be noted that, on production of medical evidence of need for home care, a person may be eligible for a Supplementary Benefit Allowance, depending on financial circumstances.

To qualify

To qualify one must:

a) Be in Great Britain;

b) Be at least 16 years of age and have left school;

c) Not be in full time employment;

d) Have registered for work; if under pensionable age and medically fit to work;

e) Have an income which does not satisfy 'requirements'.

We now examine what is, for these purposes, meant by the terms 'income' and 'requirements'. We commence with the latter.

Requirements

A person's requirements are made up of the appropriate supplementary benefit scale rate plus an addition for rent or equivalent outgoings. Discretionary additions may also be made to meet special expenses.

Scale rates (weekly)

The scale rates are set out in the table below. The long term scale applies to those of pensionable age and to those, except the unemployed, who have received supplementary benefit continuously for two years or more.

RENT

a) Householder

Provided the amounts involved are not unreasonably high a householder:

i) Will have the full amount of rent and rates added, provided his/her dependents are the only people in the household and provided that this rent does not include such items as heating or lighting.

ii) Will, in the case where he/she owns and occupies the house have necessary outgoings treated as rent. These include payments of mortgage interest, rates in full, etc. There is an additional allowance of 99p a week towards insurance and repairs. Sums payable towards the principal owing on the house are not included.

b) Non-Householders

A claimant who lives in another's household but not as a wife/husband may add £1.70 in lieu of rent.

A claimant who boards, may within reason, add the amount of the board and lodging charge together with £6.85 per week (£5.95 short term i.e. less than two years) for personal expenses.

SPECIAL AMOUNTS

Special amounts are added whenever there are special needs. Thus, in some cases special

	Ordinary scale	Long-term scale	
		Claimant and wife (under 80)	Claimant or wife (over 80)
Married couple	£29.70	£37.65	additional 25p
Single householder	£18.30	£23.70	,,
Other sighted adult	£14.65	£18.95	,,

diets or domestic help is necessary. Again, there may be a special need to travel or to have a telephone or disability may impose heavy wear and tear on clothing or bedding. Some such cases are considered here, but not all, and it is important to realise that a special need will usually be considered and recognised as being just that.

a) Special Diets

An amount of £2.50 is added in recognition of the costs of a special diet for those who suffer from:

diabetes, peptic (including stomach or duodenal) ulcers, throat or larynx ulcers, ulcerated colitis, respiratory tuberculosis.

An amount of £1.05 is normally added for other medically imposed diets.

b) Special Laundry Needs

Laundry needs are recognised to be special in such cases as those of incontinence, illness, disability and old age or where there are no laundry facilities within the home.

c) Special Heating

Special amounts are added where extra expenditure is necessarily incurred in heating. This is considered to be the case when the accommodation is centrally heated. Note is also taken of cases where the claimant or elder has difficulty moving about, is seriously or chronically ill (e.g. chronic bronchitis) or where the accommodation is damp or hard to keep warm. Further information is given in Leaflet OC2 obtainable from Social Security Offices.

Income

Income for these purposes means the net amount received after deducting tax, national insurance and pension contributions, trade union subscriptions, fares to work, some other expenses occasioned by work, and, after deducting certain other allowances stated below.

a) Part-time Earnings

The first £4 per week of any part-time earnings are generally not counted.

b) Part-time Earnings for Unemployed

The first £2 per week earned by someone unemployed and required to register for work is not counted.

c) Head of a One-Parent Family

The first £6 per week is not counted.

d) Wife's Earnings

The first £4 per week is not counted.

e) Dependent Children's Earnings

These are wholly disregarded.

f) Occupational Pension or weekly payments for redundancy

The first £1 per week is not counted.

g) Disablement and War Widow's Pensions

The first £4 per week is not counted.

h) Other Income

Up to £4 per week of most other income is not counted. Some exceptions to this rule are: child benefit and most national insurance benefits and maintenance payments (voluntary or under Court Order). These are fully taken into account.

i) The Effect of Capital on this Calculation

The capital value of an owner-occupied house is ignored, so too is the first £1,200 of other capital. Each further £50 is considered to represent an income of 25p per week. Since this charge is representative of an annual rate of interest of approximately 26 per cent it is clearly advantageous to use such sums for the reduction of a mortgage and other purposes.

AMOUNT OF WEEKLY BENEFIT
This amount is calculated by subtracting the claimant's 'income' from the 'requirements' figure as determined by the claimant's particular circumstances.

EXCEPTIONAL NEEDS PAYMENTS
In addition to the weekly payments considered above, the Supplementary Benefits Commission makes lump-sum payments for certain exceptional needs.

To qualify
1) The need must be exceptional and necessary. That is to say, the payment is necessary to avoid hardship.
2) Claimants' savings, not including owner-occupied houses, must not exceed £300 unless they would be brought below £300 by the necessary purchase.
3) It is not essential to be in receipt of supplementary benefit to qualify. It is possible to obtain these payments with an income which is a little above the threshold for supplementary benefit, but they are not made to people who are fully employed.

Articles covered by the payments
Some of the things for which payment may be obtained are: footwear, bedding, furniture, other essential household equipment, fuel debts, rent arrears, removal expenses, hire purchase debts and travelling expenses while seeking work.

Other ways of raising a lump sum
In practice it is rare for those who are not supplementary pensioners to be granted an exceptional needs payment. If they require a lump sum, for example, to purchase an electric blanket, or pay an unexpected bill, it is possible to approach:

• Their former employer or the former employer of a deceased husband.

• The Army, Navy or Air Force unit in which they served.

These funds will also help the widows of ex-servicemen. The main national organisations are:

Forces Help Society, 118 Brampton Road, London, SW3 1UE.

British Limbless Ex-servicemen's Association, 185–7 High Road, Chadwell Heath, Essex.

Local War Pensioners Committee.

• Any national charity funded to help former members of certain trades and professions or their widows.

These are listed in the *Charities Digest*, published annually by the Family Welfare Association (501–505 Kingsland Road, London E8 4AU). A number of charities help elderly people who have no particular link with a trade or profession.

Friends of the Elderly and Gentlefolks Help, 42 Ebury Street, London SW1 0LZ, gives financial help to elderly people of all social classes and runs a number of residential homes.

Distressed Gentlefolks Aid Association, Vicarage Gate House, Vicarage Gate, London W8 4AQ, 01–229 9341, runs residential homes with nursing care; gives financial support, clothing, holidays in some cases.

Elderly Invalids Fund, 10 Fleet Street, London EC4Y 1BB, is able to advise on accommodation and other problems and may be able to provide financial help with residential fees.

Invalids At Home Trust, 23 Farm Avenue, London, NW2, 01–452 2074, may assist with money for equipment for invalids living at home.

Jewish Welfare Board, 315–7 Ballards Lane, London N12 8LP, gives both financial and practical help, for example with accommodation problems.

Guild of Aid for Gentlepeople, 10 St. Christopher's Place, London W1M 6HY, 01–935 0641, makes grants to gentlefolk who, by reason of age and disability are in financial difficulties.

Royal United Kingdom Beneficent Association (RUKBA) may grant annuities to people whose income falls below a certain minimum level.

Society of St. Vincent De Paul, 24 George Street, London W1H 5RP, may be able to offer help especially to Catholics.

• Local charities; the local Age Concern

office can supply the name and address of trustees.

These sources can also be tapped to help supplementary pensioners whose capital excludes them from obtaining an exceptional needs payment.

OTHER BENEFITS

The recipient of supplementary benefit, no matter how little, is automatically entitled to other benefits, such as free prescriptions, free dental treatment, spectacles and legal advice (subject to the capital limit). Others not in receipt of supplementary benefit may however qualify for help on grounds of low income. For further information see Leaflet M11 (free dental treatment, glasses, prescriptions, milk and vitamins) at the local Post Office or Social Security Office.

OTHER FACTORS AFFECTING THE AMOUNT

Hospital

On admission to hospital the rate of supplementary benefit hitherto paid to a patient without dependents will be reduced immediately. The requirements of the patient without dependents are normally taken as £4.66 for personal expenses, plus an allowance for outside commitments such as rent and other continuing expenditure on his home, but the outside commitments allowance will be reviewed after three months in hospital.

In case of admission of one partner of a married couple, there will be no reduction for the first eight weeks, except where the previous assessment included 'an exceptional circumstances addition' for the patient. After eight weeks, supplementary benefit will be reduced by £4.66 if the patient is one partner of a married couple. After two years in hospital separate assessments will be made for the person in hospital and the person remaining at home.

For further information, see Leaflet NI.9.

Appeals

Because many of the benefits available are determined only to the extent that they may be reasonable, it is difficult to establish what one should expect. For the same reason, it is important to appeal against an adverse decision on a claim or on a condition attaching to an award. Any person claiming or in receipt of supplementary benefit has a right of appeal to an independent tribunal.

Appeals Procedure – Further information may be obtained from social security leaflets SB.8 and SB.1. Recommended reading is the *Penguin Guide to Supplementary Benefits* by Tony Lynes and the *Supplementary Benefits Handbook* published by HMSO.

The Attendance Allowance

This is a non-contributory and non means-tested allowance which will often be available for your elder. It is tax free and available for those who are disabled physically or mentally and who need and have needed much looking after for at least the last six months. It may be spent as thought best.

ELIGIBILITY

To be eligible one must:

a) Have been a resident of the United Kingdom and present there for at least twenty-six weeks in the last twelve months. (If he or she was born abroad, or is not of British nationality, this period is longer).

b) Be so severely disabled physically or mentally that one requires by day frequent attention in connection with the normal bodily functions (at night the attention need only be repeated or prolonged) or continual supervision so as to avoid substantial danger to one self or others.

AMOUNTS OF ALLOWANCE

If the Attendance Allowance is necessary both day and by night the allowance is £18.60 or four-fifths of the basic pension in

1979. If attendance is held to be necessary only by day or only by night, the allowance is reduced to £12.40 per week in 1979 (three-fifths basic pension).

Variations in amounts

The only events which affect these payments are a stay in hospital under the National Health Scheme or in a local authority home or in other accommodation provided by arrangement with a local authority. It is then payable for four weeks at most.

Specifically, this allowance is not affected by national insurance, supplementary benefit, invalidity benefit, mobility allowance, any other benefit or by the recipient's personal income. But if supplementary benefit includes a special addition for attendance needs, it would be reduced when Attendance Allowance is awarded.

How to claim

Form DS.2 (which is attached to an explanatory leaflet NI.205) is available at your local Social Security Office.

The completed form should be sent to the nearest local Social Security Office. If it is felt that the form is inadequate to describe the situation oneself and one's elderly dependent are in, do not hesitate to add a covering letter. This letter should be firmly attached to the form and state the name and address of the old person.

Decision on claim

The medical decision is made by the Attendance Allowance Board which is independent of the Department of Health and Social Security. The non-medical decisions (e.g. concerning residence in Britain) are made by an insurance officer. Following the receipt of the application, arrangements are made for a doctor to come and report on the attendance needs and if necessary make a medical examination. If on the basis of the doctor's report the Board decides that the requirements stated above are met, it will issue a certificate specifying an allowance at either the lower or higher rate. If the remaining (non-medical) requirements are also satisfied, the insurance officer will authorise payment. The disabled or elderly person will be informed of the decision by post.

Reviews and appeals

Where it is thought that the situation really satisfies the medical conditions stated above and there is dissatisfaction with the decision of the Board, a review should be asked for.

To obtain a review, one should write to the Attendance Allowance Board not later than three months from the date of their decision. This letter should stress any factors which are felt to have been overlooked previously. The old person may then be visited by another doctor and when all the information has been reconsidered he/she should receive copies of all the reports seen by the Board together with a notice of their provisional opinion.

Disagreement with these reports and anything within them, or with the Board's opinion should be submitted in writing.

When the applicant's comments have been considered, a letter will be received stating the decision and the reasons for it. If this review is unsuccessful, there is a waiting period of a year before further application is permitted, unless there is a significant worsening in the condition of the old person. It is possible, however, to apply for leave to appeal to the National Insurance Commissioner (another independent authority) against the Board's review decision, *but only on a question of law* (e.g. if it is thought that the Board have not given the proper reasons or if they have not applied the medical conditions correctly in this particular case). The Commissioner cannot change the decision, only set it aside for fresh consideration by the Board.

Payment

Payment is by an order book and is usually combined with orders for any other state pension.

Invalid Care Allowance (ICA)

This is a non-contributory non-means tested but taxable benefit for people who cannot work because they have to care for a severely disabled relative. Payment is by means of a book containing orders cashable at a Post Office.

ELIGIBILITY

To be eligible a person must:
1) Be aged between 16 and 60 (65 for a man);
2) Be a resident of the United Kingdom;
3) Be spending at least thirty-five hours a week caring for a severely disabled relative (related by birth or marriage).

Note: For the purposes of this allowance, a person is classed as severely disabled if he/she receives
1) The Attendance Allowance (higher or lower rate) or
2) The Constant Attendance Allowance (normal maximum rate or above), paid with a war pension, industrial injury or disablement pension, workman's compensation or equivalent benefit.

INELIGIBILITY

A person is ineligible if:
1) She is a woman living with her husband or common law husband. This is so even if the severely disabled person is not her husband or common law husband and even if she has given up work to care for the disabled person;
2) He or she receives the same amount or more from some other basic benefit i.e. retirement pension, sickness or invalidity or unemployment benefit;
3) He or she earns more than about six-tenths of the Invalid Care Allowance.

AMOUNTS OF BENEFIT AND EFFECT ON EARNINGS

1) The basic invalid care allowance (ICA) is £14 per week;

2) A man receives an additional six-tenths of the basic ICA in respect of his wife or housekeeper;
3) The allowance is not allowed in the case of earnings greater than six-tenths of the basic allowance;
4) The allowance for a wife/housekeeper is not allowed if her earnings exceed about six-tenths of the basic allowance.

SUPPLEMENTARY BENEFIT

ICA is not means tested and so is available to those receiving supplementary benefit, but supplementary benefit is then reduced by the amount of the ICA. The only advantage is that ICA carries credit for national insurance contributions.

To claim

Further information is given on leaflet NI.212 (Invalid Care Allowance) which is obtainable at the local Social Security Office. A form attached to this leaflet should be completed and despatched in a free stamped addressed envelope to The Controller, Invalid Care Allowance Unit, Central Office, Norcross, Blackpool FY5 3TA.

Response to claim

A decision in writing will be received. If the decision is not satisfactory, it should be appealed. One's rights in this connection will be explained in the responding letter.

Mobility Allowance

This is a non means-tested taxable cash payment of £12 a week designed to increase the outdoor mobility of the severely disabled of working age. It may be spent as the recipient chooses.

To qualify

To qualify one must:
a) Be resident in the United Kingdom and have been so resident for at least twelve of the last eighteen months;
b) Be unable or virtually unable to walk and be likely to remain so for at least a year;

c) Be under 65 if a man and under 60 if a woman (changes in these restrictions are in the pipeline);

d) Be able to benefit from going out;

e) Not have an invalid trike or car supplied by the National Health Service nor have a private car allowance under the pre-1976 vehicle scheme. Such benefits may, however, be exchanged for the mobility allowance, see part B).

To claim
Get the leaflet NI.211 and the attached form from any Social Security Office. Read the leaflet and send the completed attached form to the address stated on that form.

Medical examination
To obtain this benefit it is necessary to prove the necessary physical disability, and normally this involves a medical examination. Such an examination may be waived if the individual receives the Attendance Allowance. If the medical is required, it may be expected that it would be held close to one's dwelling and if necessary, at one's home.

Appeals
1) If the application is refused on non-medical grounds an appeal may be made to a local tribunal. The decision of this tribunal may be challenged by appeal to a National Insurance Commissioner, whose decision is final.
2) If the application is refused on medical grounds, an appeal may be made to a medical board.
The decision of this Board may further be appealed to a medical appeal tribunal.

Payment
Payment is by order book, each order covers four weeks and may be cashed at the Post Office.

MOBILITY ALLOWANCE OPTION FOR PEOPLE IN THE OLD VEHICLE SCHEME

This is an option open to those who were helped under the Old Vehicle Scheme. These people may choose, without a medical examination and without an age limit, to take the Mobility Allowance in place of the old benefit.

To qualify
To qualify one must:
a) Now have a trike or car under the National Health Service or now have a private car allowance;
b) Not now have such trike or car but have had one or other of these on or after 1.1.76.
c) Satisfy the medical requirements of the Old Vehicle Scheme.

Financial merits
These vary with the financial circumstances of the recipient. It would seem advantageous for all except those who pay more than standard rates of tax to opt for the allowance. But each case must be decided individually.

To apply
The leaflet NI.225 and the attached form are obtainable from (in England and Wales) the Department of Health and Social Security Disablement Services Branch, 3A Government Buildings, Warbreck Hill Road, Blackpool, Lancs FY2 0UZ. The leaflet should be read and the completed attached form should be sent to the above address. In Scotland, leaflets and forms are available from the Scottish Home and Health Department, Room 205, St. Andrew's House, Edinburgh, EH1 3DE.

Industrial Disablement Benefit

This is an untaxed non-contributory benefit which takes the form of a lump sum payment or a pension. It is payable to those who, as a consequence of their work, have either suffered an accidental injury or have contracted a prescribed disease and as a result of this misfortune have suffered some permanent disability.

To qualify
1) It is normally necessary to show that the

disability is due to and happened while carrying out work. It is therefore important in the case of an injury that it has been recorded at the place of work and at the time of injury.

2) The injury must have occurred at least 26 weeks ago. These 26 weeks are covered by the Industrial Injuries Benefit.

Industrial Injuries Benefit

Payable for a maximum period of 26 weeks from the date of an 'industrial accident' (that is, an accident arising out of and in the course of employed earner's employment) or development of a prescribed industrial disease due to that employment for incapacity due to the accident or disease.

AMOUNTS PAYABLE

The extent of disablement is assessed as a percentage of up to 100 per cent. This assessment is made by a medical board. For assessments between 20 and 100 per cent a weekly pension is paid. The amount of the pension is the assessed percentage of £38.00.

For assessments between 1 and 19 per cent, a lump sum is normally paid. The smallest sum is £253 for the case of a one per cent assessment. This amount can be increased through the applicability of other allowances: a) Special Hardship, b) Constant Attendance, c) Hospital Treatment, d) Unemployability Supplement.

a) *Special Hardship Allowance*

This allowance is payable if the disablement is assessed at less than 100 per cent and the effects of the injury or disease have been such as to prevent the person from returning to his/her job and from doing work with a similar standard of earnings. As the conditions of entitlement to this allowance are so complicated, we would suggest that you contact your local Social Security Office and discuss it with the officers there. The maximum rate of the allowance is £15.20, subject to an overriding limitation that, where disablement benefit is paid as a pen-

sion, the allowance and the pension together cannot exceed £38.00.

NOTE: Complex considerations, including medical issues, may precede calculation of the rate of an award.

b) *Constant Attendance Allowance*

This allowance is payable if the disablement benefit is at the 100 per cent rate (£38.00 per week) and if the individual needs constant care and attention. The amount of this allowance depends entirely on the extent of the attendance needed, the normal maximum being £15.20, but it may be as high as £30.40 per week.

c) *Exceptionally Severe Disablement Allowance*

This is an extra allowance of £15.20 weekly payable where entitlement to constant attendance allowance at a rate higher than the normal maximum is likely to be permanent.

d) *Hospital Treatment Allowance*

If the person concerned is in hospital receiving treatment for an injury or disease for which the disablement benefit is less than the 100 per cent rate, this allowance raises the disablement benefit to the 100 per cent rate of £38.00 per week.

e) *Unemployability Supplement*

An allowance of £23.30 per week with additional amounts for dependents (see invalidity benefits) is receivable if a person has been rendered permanently unable to work by accident or disease.

This supplement is not payable at the same time as a special hardship allowance, unemployment benefit, sickness or invalidity benefit, retirement or widow's pension, or other unemployability allowance or supplement paid out of public funds.

To claim

There are a number of forms relating to these benefits available at Social Security Offices. That which is relevant depends on the nature of the disablement. Form BI.100A relates to injuries, BI.100 (Pn) to the cases of pneumo-coniosis or byssinosis and BI.100B to the other prescribed diseases. The form should be completed and returned to your local Social Security Office.

Medical examination

A medical examination is necessary to determine the degree of disablement involved. This will be held at home only if one is unable to travel. Out of pocket expenses for travel are recoverable. Following this assessment, the decision as to the amount payable is made by an insurance officer.

Appeals

Appeals against the decision made by the insurance officer should be made in writing to the local Social Security Office within twenty-one days of the date of notification of his decision.

Appeals against the decision of the medical board should be made within three months of the date of notification of the board's decision, unless the board has made a provisional assessment. In that case, one must wait for two years before appealing.

Further information

For further information see Leaflet NI.6 obtainable at any Social Security Office.

War Disablement Pension

Such pensions are untaxable and are available to those who have a disability due wholly or partially to service in the armed forces or as a result of a war injury.

Eligibility

Those eligible are people with a disability:
1) Resulting from military service in the First World War or since September 1939.
2) Resulting from service in the merchant navy in either war.
3) Resulting from injury due to enemy activity received as a civilian in the Second World War.

Amount

The amount payable varies with the degree of disability and in the case of service personnel on their military rank. For a private or equivalent rank, the pension for a disability assessed at 100 per cent is £38.00 per week. Lesser assessments are payable pro-rata.

Further information is available in leaflet MPL.151 (War Pensions and Allowances).

The War Pensions arm of the social security system has a well-organised welfare system with officers who are sensitive to the needs of war pensioners and their dependants. In addition, there are locally based War Pensions Committees, which are voluntary bodies recognised by the Department of Health and Social Security. These not only link pensioners and dependants with the war pension offices but with the appropriate regimental and service fund.

The address of the War Pensions Committee can be obtained from any Department of Health and Social Security Office, the British Legion or the Citizens Advice Bureau.

War Pensions can also be paid to the widow or other dependants of someone who qualified for a war pension when he was alive.

SUPPLEMENTING ONE'S INCOME

Before accepting what appears to be a fixed income, every person should investigate the various methods open to increasing that income, through maturity loans, annuities, savings accounts, Government Securities, National Savings Certificates, Premium Savings Bonds and Building Societies.

The question that rears up in your mind is undoubtedly, as a point of first entry, who is the best person to advise on the relative benefits of these options. The answer is that if you have a bank account, it would probably be the bank manager. Where a prospective investor doesn't have a bank account, the best yardstick they can use is probably to ask relatives or friends what they have done, and then to get all the relevant leaflets. And then, on the basis of what they have learned, to make their own decisions.

Maturity Loans (see page 160)

Mortgage Annuities

Persons with a reasonably high income but with little capital (except that which is tied up in their homes) can benefit from a mortgage annuity scheme. Under this scheme, an elderly owner-occupier can take out a mortgage loan against up to 75 per cent of the value of a house. The loan is used to purchase an annuity which will provide a fixed income for the rest of the borrower's life. With inflation, the value of the house should continue to increase, allowing further annuities to be purchased from time to time. On the death of the annuitant, the loan is repaid from the estate (generally from the proceeds of the sale of the house).

There are two categories of annuity – a single life annuity and a joint life and survivorship annuity. The latter of course will give full protection to a surviving spouse.

For more information contact the Mortgage Broker's Association, The Corporation of Mortgage and Finance Brokers, 34 Rose Street, Wokingham.

It should be noted that an annuity may affect supplementary pension rights and many annuities are not inflation proofed.

Annuities

An annuity is an annual income payable from some agreed date for so long as the beneficiary or the beneficiaries live.

An annuity may be purchased (normally from an insurance company) by regular small payments over a term of years or by a single payment. The latter type is of particular interest to us here.

The older one is when buying an annuity, the higher the annual income for a given payment, and for this reason the purchase of a so-called 'immediate annuity' is a particularly attractive form of investment upon retirement. There are considerable variations from time to time and from company to company in the terms offered, but usually the annual return on capital is significantly higher than any other form of investment.

An additional benefit accrues in that only part of the income is subject to tax; a fraction worked out by the insurance company is regarded as a return of capital and is thus free of tax. This fraction is determined by the age of the purchaser(s) but is normally more than half.

Annuities can be purchased on behalf of a single life or a couple, in which case the income lasts while either lives.

Annuities have one major disadvantage in that the capital involved is expended with the purchase and so cannot be willed to someone else.

Post Office Savings Bank – Ordinary Accounts

This is probably the most widely used form of saving. The principal characteristics are that one can deposit sums as small as 25p. Withdrawals up to £50 can be made at any time, but for larger sums special application has to be made on a form obtainable at any Post Office.

Interest on Post Office savings is paid at present at the rate of 5 per cent per annum and the first £70 of this interest is free of income tax (married couples £140).

Post Office Savings Bank – Investment Accounts

Anyone may open an Investment Account. The advantage of this account is that it pays a higher rate of interest. This rate fluctuates but at present is 12 per cent. Withdrawals can be made at one month's notice.

Bank Deposit Accounts

These accounts pay interest but at rates which vary from time to time. The bank accepts deposits at any time but requires seven days' notice of withdrawal. Interest received is taxable.

Building Societies

Building societies offer a good investment channel for those liable to tax at the standard rate. In that case, building societies offer a good return, as the interest is paid to an investor net of income tax. (The Building Society has already paid tax on it.) However, note that anyone who is not liable to tax at the standard rate cannot reclaim the tax already paid by the Building Society.

National Savings Certificates

National savings certificates provide an excellent method of saving. They are a Government security and the state is directly responsible for the repayment of capital in full, or in the case of an Index-linked certificate, for the payment of the new capital value and any bonus due.

The money invested in certificates may be withdrawn at any time together with any interest or index-linked increase or bonus that may be due.

Each certificate costs £10. They increase in value at a rate which increases with the time they have been held up to five years. Held for a period of five years, the effective rate of interest is 8.45 per cent compounded annually. This increase in value is not taxed.

For up to date information on NSC refer to Leaflet P.156W obtainable from most Post Offices and banks.

In the event of the death of the certificate holder, form SB.4 obtainable from most Post Offices will give instructions on what procedure has to be followed in claiming the certificates. Arrangements are in force through which, at the request of the executors of the deceased person, payment is accepted by the Commissioner of Inland Revenue before probate is granted, from the value of the Savings Certificates belonging to the deceased or any part thereof as may be necessary to meet payments claimed in respect of Capital Transfer Tax. Savings Certificates themselves are not accepted by the Commissioner of Inland Revenue in payment of death duties.

Where it is desired to take advantage of this facility, application should be made to the Director, Savings Certificate and SAYE Office, Durham DH99 1NS.

Index-Linked National Savings Certificates – Retirement Issue (Granny Bonds)

The purchase of this issue is restricted to those who have passed retirement age (65 men, 60 women) and to a maximum holding of £500 (50 × £10).

A special feature of these certificates is that they are linked to the Retail Price Index, which proofs them against inflation. If you encash them within one year of purchase, the purchase price only is refunded; if you encash them after one year and less than five years of purchase, you get your purchase price plus a sum equal to the inflation for the period. At five years they mature, and you then receive your purchase price, the inflation-linked increase, and a bonus of 4% of the purchase price.

Although the simple interest they pay on the purchase price is thus minimal, the extra inflation-linked gain is exempt from income tax, the investment surcharge and, most importantly, Capital Transfer Tax. With inflation as high as it is at present, these certificates provide an unusually large return.

Purchase

Retirement certificates may be purchased at a Post Office, a Trustee Savings Bank or through National Savings. The minimum purchase is of one £10 certificate. The maximum amount which any one person can hold is £500.

Premium Savings Bonds

These come in units of £1 but are sold in groups of five only. Bonds become eligible for inclusion in the weekly draw after they have been owned continuously for three clear calendar months after the month in which they were purchased. Each unit has the same chance of winning a prize in each weekly draw. The chance of winning with any one unit is very small, but on the other hand, prizes are as much as £100,000 and there is a new draw every week. Premium bonds can be purchased from any Post Office or bank. No more than £3,000 may be invested by any one person.

Any income arising from these bonds is free of income tax.

For further information, see the leaflet *Premium Savings Bonds* obtainable at any Post Office.

British Savings Bonds

These provide an excellent investment if your income is not high enough to attract tax.

Shares

Unless one has quite a substantial amount of capital, it is not wise to buy shares. If capital is invested, every care should be taken to buy blue chip shares. Again, a bank manager's view on whether the market cycle is favourably low or not is also likely to be worth having. Speculative investing is a gamble, that can end in financial disaster. Many people rely on dividends (see page 153) to boost their income.

Government Securities

These securities take the form of government promises to repay, normally at a specified future date, money borrowed in the past, and in the meantime to pay the owner interest at a specified rate.

Each security's nominal value is 100, which will be its actual value at that future date at which repayment will be made. Its present value is what it will sell for on the open market. This may diverge significantly from its nominal value. The degree of divergence depends on the change in the general level of interest rates which has occurred since the security was issued. As of 1978, interest rates are high. so most securities sell for less than £100. The current prices of each type of security, of which there are about eighty, are reported daily in the more serious newspapers.

The advantages of investment in these securities are that they pay higher rates of interest than are obtainable in most other ways and particularly when purchased through a bank or broker, can be converted into cash without delay. A potential disadvantage follows from the fact that their value is not strictly fixed, so that one can lose money if they are sold at some time when their value has declined, but by the same token, one may make money if their value has risen. It should be noted in this connection that capital gains or capital losses are exempt from tax if they are made more than twelve months after purchase.

Interest is paid without deduction of income tax and since it is taxable, it must be included in any return of income to the Inland Revenue.

Government Securities may be bought and sold either through a bank or through a broker on the one hand, or through a government agency on the other. The advantage of the first procedure is that it is faster, its disadvantage is that it is somewhat more expensive. Stock bought through private channels must be sold in the same way.

For further information, see the leaflet *Government Stock* obtainable at any Post Office or enquire at a bank or from a stockbroker.

National Giro

Giro is a low-cost current account banking service that keeps money safe and makes it easy to make payments when necessary, to draw cash when required and to save.

Bills can be paid by Giro. Arrangements can be made for regular payments to other Giro account holders – for mortgage repayments, rates, rents, TV rental, insurance, etc. Transfer can be set up to pay other Giro account holders; electricity, gas, telephone and many other household bills.

Personal loans can be arranged from Mercantile Credit Company Limited providing one's application is acceptable. Details of credit terms will be provided free of charge from the nearest Mercantile Credit branch (whose address can be found in the telephone book) by writing to them.

There are not any hidden extra charges under a Giro account. Details are clearly set out in the list called *National Giro Fees and Stationery Charges* issued by the Post Office.

To open an account, complete all the details on both sides of the tear-off application form and hand it with one pound in cash over a Post Office counter or send a one pound cheque or postal order to

Accounts Opening Section,
Freepost,
National Giro,
Bootle, Merseyside, GIR OAA.

For the busy carer, the Giro standing order system may save a lot of time.

A BUDGET

The notion of a budget may seem dull and uninteresting and, where there is little money available, rather pointless. Nevertheless, it is a fact that budgeting makes one more aware of getting 'value for money'. It should be noted that the initial attempt at a budget is not likely to give the best apportionment of resources, and one should therefore be ready to make changes in one's original plan.

The first step in designing a budget is to work out the total income available after tax. This is normally a simple matter of adding together all contributions available from whatever source. Typical sources are retirement pension and occupational pension, investment income, attendance and invalid care allowances and supplementary benefit.

Then comes the more difficult task of apportioning this money among the various categories of expenditure. These can be put into three broad groups:

a) Standing expenses; including rents, rates, insurance, hire purchase payments and house maintenance. Obviously, these do not vary, at least in the short term.
b) Fluctuating household expenses, including food, clothes, fuel and cleaning materials.
c) Extras, such as holidays, telephone, television licence, newspapers, entertainments and donations to charities.

The amounts available for the second and third groups are determined largely by the expenditure in the first, and it is fairly generally agreed that this standing expenditure should not exceed about one quarter of the total income. The design of a budget therefore involves assigning about three-quarters or so of the income amongst the items of groups b) and c). The manner of this distribution is obviously dependent on the income available. The smaller the income, the greater the fraction that will be spent on essentials, food clothing and fuel.[1]

A good diet is very important to good health, so that expenditure here should not be cut more than absolutely necessary. But it should be noted that very considerable savings can be made by careful buying (paying particular attention to the nutritional value for money expended. (See Diet, chapter 00) and by the avoidance of waste.

Once the expenditure on the items of group b) are worked out, it is largely a question of taste how the remainder of the income should be divided up amongst group c) items. But remember that the object of a budget is really to dispose your money so as to give your family maximum comfort and enjoyment.

[1] Remember that supplementary beneficiaries can sometimes obtain increased benefit for heating.

One buying technique which is a little complicated but which will help considerably with savings is to take advantage of the 'specials' offered by supermarkets, by buying up more of these than are required at the time. To do so while operating a budget, it is necessary to have a 'kitty' to make the purchase and then to set the articles to one side. Later, when such an item is used, its purchase price is taken out of that week's budget and repaid to the 'kitty'. The kitty then grows, and enables further buying and more saving. Every now and again, the 'kitty' can pay a dividend, to save for unexpected outgoings or to 'blow' on a treat or something special.

We are very aware of course that one person buying for herself alone will not be able to benefit from any bulk buying of perishable goods (or even of 'family-sized' purchases).

Careful buying is also very important in areas other than food. Clothing in particular is subject to very large reductions in price at sale times. The best thing is to take one's time over a particular purchase and to shop around looking for reductions. This can be a slow process, but as genuine 20–30 per cent reductions can be the end result, it is worth it.

TAXATION

We cannot cover everything one may need to know about taxes in this book. However, we have set out below some information about taxation which is particularly relevant to a person who is near retirement or who has retired.

If help is needed over tax and the matter seems simple, a bank manager should be able to help; failing this, go to the tax office. You will generally find tax officers most helpful.

There are three important taxes on income and possessions: Income Tax, Capital Gains Tax and Capital Transfer Tax (see section on legal pointers page 36).

Income Tax

This is a tax on income from earnings, pensions and investments, etc., received in each twelve-month period, from April 6 of one year till April 5 of the next. Tax is charged on taxable income which is income less certain allowances. These include (for the year 1980/81) the following *allowances:*

Single person's allowance of £1,165. All single persons get this allowance unless they qualify for age allowance. A single person includes a widow; a widower; a divorcee; a married man who is separated from his wife and so is not entitled to the married man's personal allowance; both parties of a marriage who have chosen to have the wife's earnings taxed separately.

This allowance is given automatically.

Married man's personal allowance of £1,815. A man gets this allowance for each tax year for which he is already married, on April 6. This is true even if he becomes a widower or separated at any time during the tax year. A separated man can continue to get this allowance if he maintains his wife wholly and voluntarily.

To obtain this allowance the wife's names must be inserted in the place provided in the income tax form.

Wife's earned income allowance – maximum £1,165. This allowance is available to a woman who was already married on April 6 and who has earned income of her own, provided these earnings are not taxed separately from those of her husband.

The amount of this allowance is the wife's earnings less any allowable expenses associated with her work up to a maximum of £1,165.

This allowance is given upon declaration of the wife's income.

Age allowance for married people – maximum £2,455. This allowance is available for a married man who is, or whose wife is, at least 64 on April 5 and whose 'total income' does not exceed £5,000 (179–80) This allowance is reduced by two thirds of the amount by which 'total income' exceeds £5,000 but does not fall below that of the ordinary married man. 'Total income' is gross income less outgoings.

Age allowance for single people – maximum £1,540. This allowance is available for single people who are at least 64 on April 5 whose 'total income' does not exceed £5,000 (1979–80). This allowance is reduced by two-thirds of the amount by which 'total income' exceeds £5,000 but does not fall below that of the ordinary single person.

Allowance for dependant relatives. This allowance can be claimed by someone who helps to maintain an infirm or elderly (at least 65) relative of his own or of his wife. Assisting a relative does not mean that he/she has to live with the claimant. The full allowance is given if the relative has no income apart from basic national insurance retirement pension. If the relative does have other income, the allowance is reduced by the amount of that other income. The allowance is also reduced where he/she does not live with the claimant, to the amount contributed if this amount is less than £75. This allowance is also available in respect of a man's mother or mother-in-law whether or not she be elderly or infirm, provided she is a widow, separated or divorced.

The maximum allowance is £145 for a single woman or one who gets married during the course of the tax year or for a married woman whose income is taxed separately from her husband's. A woman is regarded as being single if she has been married, but is now a widow, separated or divorced.

For all other claimants the maximum allowance is £100 and if two or more members of a family help to support the same relative, their allowances are in proportion to their contributions. These allowances are available in respect of each and every relative who is assisted.

Housekeeper allowance of £100. There are two bases on which this allowance (£100) can be claimed:

- As a widow or widower who has a woman living in the house and acting as a housekeeper. This woman may or may not be a relative, but if she is a relative the allowance is not available if someone else is claiming any allowance for her. Also, this allowance cannot be claimed by a widower for the tax year in which his wife died.
- As a single person who has a woman relative living in the home for the purpose of looking after his/her brother(s) or sister(s). These siblings must qualify for child allowance. The allowance is not available if the relative is one's mother and her (present) husband claims the personal allowance for a married man.

This allowance should not be elected by a widow or widower with dependent children. Rather, it is better for them to claim the additional personal allowance for children. If the relative qualifies, the dependent relative allowance may then be claimed as well.

National Insurance Retirement Pension is taxable. It is taken into account when calculating how much tax is to be paid on total income. Thus, basic NIRP by itself is not enough to bring income to the point where tax begins to be charged, therefore if someone has no income apart from this, he will not be asked to pay tax. But, he may have to pay some tax if, in addition to the basic retirement pension, he is receiving what is called a graduated pension or an increase in pension for working past retirement age.

- If at the time a person begins to draw a National Insurance Retirement Pension he goes on working, or if his former employer is already paying him a pension, his tax will be increased.
- Where a married woman has a pension, it will be liable to tax, and as with any other income it is added to her husband's in arriving at his total income, unless she files a separate return. This is not normally profitable.
- Where one is already paying tax, there will be tax to pay on earnings from a part-time

job. Such earnings may also affect the age allowance on tax.

- If an annuity is bought out of one's own capital, part of it is treated as repayment of capital, and so is not liable to be taxed. The remainder is treated as investment income which is liable to tax. The amount that is taxable depends mainly on an annuitant's age when the annuity is bought. The company from which the annuity is bought will normally deduct tax from the taxable part at the basic rate. Where one is not liable to pay as much tax as is deducted by the company from an annuity, the procedure is to write to the Inspector of Taxes and ask him to repay what has been overpaid.

It should be remembered that the whole of an annuity under a pension scheme is income which is liable to tax. It is taxable as earned income. Income tax is payable on income derived from renting all or part of a house or any other accommodation. (See also the implications of renting on capital gains liability page 153).

Interest on money invested in a building society is taxed at source at the standard rate and this tax cannot be reclaimed. One should be careful therefore not to have too much money in building societies.

Numerous categories of income are not liable to income tax and it is as well to know what the categories are:

Tax free income

Many people do not know about the tax free income that is available to them. The following list of tax free income is devised particularly to suit the situation of older people or those middle-aged people taking care of them:

- Grants for improving the home (see page 158).
- Grants for education (such as where a carer has returned to college to obtain more skills).
- Tax free pensions (for instance the Christmas bonus of £10 when it is available).

- Tax free social security benefits (for instance, Attendance Allowance and Disablement Pensions under the National Insurance Scheme).
- Rent and rate rebates (see page 157).
- Gifts from relatives.
- Monies from Save-as-You-Earn, National Savings Certificates, Premium bonds, Ulster Group Certificates.
- The final bonus from British Savings Bonds.
- The first £70 interest from an ordinary account with National Savings Banks or Trustee Savings Banks or Birmingham Municipal Bank Savings.
- Part of income from many annuities.
- Interest on a tax rebate.
- Income from a family income benefit life insurance policy.
- Only half a widow's pension is taxable.

Note that a registered blind person or where both old persons in a household are registered as blind, they receive a special scale rate if they are entitled to supplementary benefit.

Because income tax has been subject to so many changes during recent years we have not attempted to include any figures in this work. One should refer to the Tax Office for guidance. Our aim has been to provide basic information on the areas of payment and exemption only.

When writing to an Inspector of Taxes on any matter, quote the reference number from any previous correspondence you have had with him. When one goes to the Tax Office, it is advisable to take along one's tax papers. Tax Offices are usually open from 10 a.m. till 4 p.m. Monday to Friday.

Sometimes it is possible to ring a tax inspector and thereby save a journey. To locate his number look in the telephone directory under the heading 'Inland Revenue'.

Capital Gains Tax

What is this tax?
Tax on gains of a capital nature – if an asset

is got rid of, regardless of the means by which the asset was acquired. Any item that can be classified as being owned, counts as an asset – houses, shares, a horse, etc. An asset is disposed of not only if it is sold, but also if it is given away, exchanged or lost. A transfer of an asset between a husband and wife who aren't separated doesn't count as a disposal.

Among assets on which CGT is not generally levied are the following:

- One's own home. (However, if you have ever rented any part of your home you will become liable to capital gains tax on the rented part. This is a hazard that can come as an unpleasant surprise.)
- A second home which is occupied rent free by a dependent relative.
- A car.
- An animal.
- British Government stocks held for a year or more, or that were inherited.
- British money.
- National Savings Certificates, British Savings Bonds, Save-as-You-Earn.
- Any asset, provided the total value of all one's disposals of assets liable to capital gains tax adds up to £1,000 or less in the tax year.
- Personal belongings, furniture, antiques, jewellery (provided the value of each item at the time of disposal is £1,000 or less).
- Life insurance policies.
- Gifts of assets liable for capital gains tax which have been made during the tax year, provided their total market value is not more than £100.

The size of taxable capital gains can be reduced by setting off any allowable capital losses against them.

The gain is the amount one gets when disposing of the asset (or its market value at the time it is given away) less its initial cost and allowable expenditures.

Allowable expenditure includes:

- Any cost of obtaining or disposing of the asset (e.g. conveyancing, commission etc.).
- Capital expenditure which has added to the value of the asset.

If losses come to more than gains, the balance of the losses can be carried over and set against gains in future years.

Taxation of net capital gains

These are free of tax up to £1000 per year. Gains in excess of £1000 in any one year are taxed at a rate which varies according to the amount of the gain. The point to remember is that you are likely to pay less tax if you sell in smaller amounts, each year, rather than selling all your assets at one go. Seek the advice of an accountant before you sell any sizeable assets.

Dividends

The taxman has to be informed about income from investments. This covers dividends from companies, interest from bank accounts, etc.

Dividends from companies or distributions from unit trusts

Details about these sources of income can be obtained from tax vouchers. The amount of the dividend or the distribution, and the amount of the credit received from each company or unit trust must be entered.

Other dividends, interest, annuities, trust income already taxed

These include investment income taxed (usually at the basic rate) before being paid to the recipient. The gross (before tax) amount of taxable income from each source is entered.

Interest that is not taxed before it is received includes:

Interest received from National Savings Bank accounts (just £70 interest each year, tax free), High Street bank deposit accounts, Trustee Savings Bank accounts, British Government Stocks bought through the Post Office, or a Trustee Savings Bank, British Savings Bonds, War Loan, or Co-operative Society deposits.

Tax on Gain from a Life Insurance Policy

This is a quite complicated subject and the following should be read carefully.

Generally, the proceeds from life insurance policies are free from all tax. However, tax will have to be paid on any gain made on a policy taken out (or altered) since March 19, 1968 if:

- Tax is already paid and at higher rates or the investment income surcharge is paid and either
- The policy doesn't qualify for tax relief (for instance if it is a single premium property bond)
- Or the policy does qualify for tax relief, but it is cashed in or paid up in its first ten years (alternatively, within the first three quarters of its term, if that is shorter)

At the time the policy comes to an end, the gain is generally the amount received (plus any sums received at an earlier date which were not taxed at the time) minus the total of all premiums paid. In the case of a taxable gain arising because the person insured has died, the gain can be worked out by taking the cash-in value of the policy immediately before death, if it is less than the sum insured.

If there is a gain, it is added to investment income for the tax year in which the policy comes to an end. What has to be paid is any extra higher rate tax and investment income surcharge that is due. In the event that adding the gain to income means tax must be paid at a higher rate than otherwise would have been the case, the tax man should give you 'top-slicing relief', which means working out the average yearly gain by dividing the total gain by the number of complete years the policy was operative. Then add this average yearly gain to investment income for the tax year and work out the tax bill on the average yearly gain. To find out what the tax bill on the total gain will be, it is necessary to multiply the tax bill on the average yearly gain by the number of years over which the gain has been spread.

If part of the policy has been cashed in, and an allowance for cash is paid for each of the first twenty years of the policy, the allowance is one-twentieth of the total premium paid to date.

For each year after the first twenty, the allowance is one-twentieth of any premiums paid in the last twenty years (including the current year).

In the Event of Not Agreeing with the Taxman

Querying taxation does happen, and if statistics are any reliable guide, a quarter of those paying tax in fact receive rebates. It is necessary to know how to go about challenging the taxman and therefore we have set out a few basic directives.

Generally, problems arise because of the wrong PAYE code, or because someone suddenly realises that for years they haven't claimed a benefit to which they were in fact entitled, or because they receive a tax bill that they just don't agree with.

If it is necessary to change a PAYE code during the year, perhaps where there is entitlement to a new allowance or outgoing, the taxman should be informed as soon as possible so he can make a change in the code.

It is necessary to send back the last notice of coding and to state what change should be made.

Where an appeal is to be made against a notice of assessment the appeal must be made within thirty days of the date on it.

If a large tax bill has been received and the recipient can't afford to pay it all at once, then in some cases of hardship, permission may be granted for the amount due to be paid off in weekly or monthly instalments. Tax which isn't paid up when due has interest clocked up on it at a rate of nine per cent a year.

It is worth noting that if a mistake was made on a past tax return, or if a person fails to claim an outgoing or allowance to which she is entitled, she can claim back the tax overpaid in all or any of the last six complete tax years (and interest may also be paid back).

Where a tax rebate is long overdue, interest on the rebate (if it is for £25 or more) may be paid.

In the case that there is a difference of opinion with the taxman, appeal can be made to either the General Commissioner or the Special Commissioners. If the Commissioners make a decision on a question of fact, generally their decision is final.

Chapter 10
Housing Problems and Possibilities

The following material pertains to England and Wales only. The housing provisions and regulations are distinctly different in Scotland and Northern Ireland. If you need advice on this subject in either of these two countries we recommend that you contact the appropriate Environmental Health Department. This will be traceable through the Local Authority, listed in the phone book.

HOUSING ADVICE

Housing, like finance, is a complicated subject but there are a number of valuable sources of advice. The elder's health visitor (see page 21) will know about the financial benefits which are available to help with rent and rates (see page 166) and about local opportunities for rehousing. If a social worker (see page 14) is involved, she will also be able to give this advice, but is unlikely to become involved if the elder's only problem is housing. If the housing problem is caused or complicated by her disability, consult the domiciliary occupational therapist (see page 23). If there are structural problems such as the absence of an inside toilet or dampness, the environmental health officer is an invaluable source of advice (see page 26) and he will also be useful if the house is in poor repair. For example, if a floor is subsiding or rewiring is necessary.

If there is a Housing Aid Centre (see page 176) in the elder's town, its staff can be consulted on all these matters and on the thorny legal problems which we consider in this chapter. If there is not, the local Age Concern office (see page 14) or Citizens Advice Bureau (see page 14) are alternative advice centres. *Where to Live After Retirement* published by the Consumers Association is a most helpful book, to complement the information in this chapter and that on hypothermia and heating problems.

HOUSING RELATED FINANCIAL BENEFITS

If an old person's income disqualifies him for supplementary pension he has the alternative of claiming a rent rebate/allowance and/or a rates rebate instead. (See supplementary benefits section page 136.)

It is not possible to claim both supplementary pension and a local authority rate and rent rebate or rent allowance. It is necessary to choose between them and the choice is not always simple. The people who are able to give expert advice on this matter are supplementary pension officers at the Social Security Office. For this reason, it is advisable if there is any doubt as to which benefit would be the more advantageous, to apply in the first instance for supplementary pension.

Remember that there are many special supplements (laundry, heating, special diets, etc. see page 138) to the basic supplementary benefit. None of these is available if the rebate option is chosen.

Rebates and allowances are greater for a tenant or his spouse if he is registered with the Social Services Department as disabled or blind. The disabled elderly person can apply for an exemption from a rate increase on the value of an adaptation, alteration or additional accommodation that has been provided because of this disability.

Rent Rebates and Allowances

Except for those who receive supplementary benefit, most tenants who find themselves in difficulty paying their rent will receive aid from their local council. In the case of council and New Town tenants, the rent is simply reduced whilst tenants in private accommodation, furnished or unfurnished, are paid an allowance.

Factors which Determine the Aid

Three main factors are taken into account in determining the degree of aid given: gross income, rent, and number of persons living in the house. But there are many other relevant factors and anyone who feels that they might possibly qualify should contact the local council. This is particularly true of the disabled who rent furnished accommodation.

The way in which the amount of rebate/allowance varies with weekly rent and 'weekly income' is illustrated in the table below. This table applies to a married couple.

Rent		£4	£6	£8	£10
Weekly	£30	£4	£5.96	£7.16	£8.36
Income	£35	£3.51	£4.71	£5.91	£7.11
	£45	£1.72	£2.66	£3.86	£5.06
	£55	£0	£0.96	£2.16	£3.36
	£65	£0	£0	£0.46	£1.66

This is clearly a complicated matter and is further complicated by the fact that the 'weekly income' involved in the table may be less than one's actual income. Thus, weekly income does not include, among other things:
a) The first £5 of a wife's earnings;
b) The Attendance Allowance;
c) The Mobility Allowance;
d) The first £4 of a war or industrial disablement pension;

e) The first £4 of a war widow's pension.

Rate Rebates

Anyone who pays rates can apply for a rebate. But the amount of rebate granted depends on the applicant's income, the amount of the rates and the size of the family. The rebate covers only the general rate; water and sewage rates and special water rate are specifically excluded. These rebates are applicable to tenants who pay rent to a landlord and who may therefore not be aware that their payments include rates. A tenant who does not know what his rates are and doesn't wish to ask the landlord can find out from the local council.

To claim rent and rate rebates

These claims have to be made separately. The necessary forms can be obtained from the local council offices. If there is any query or problem about filling in the form, the clerk will generally help. A rate rebate is applied for at the Treasurer's Department and a rent rebate or allowance at the Housing Department. If it is not possible to go in person, a letter should be sent to the appropriate council offices stating that a rent rebate and a rate rebate (or whatever) is being claimed and asking for the forms to be posted.

If granted, the rebate will be backdated, as it is called, to the date of this letter. Where the rebate is awarded to an owner occupier or council tenant, the rates or rent will just be reduced. In the case of a private tenant, the allowance or rebate will be sent regularly – generally by Giro. No one else need know anything about the payment.

If an aged person is disabled, the amount of his rebate/allowance and/or rate rebate will be affected – the needs allowance will be higher and more income will be disregarded when the calculations are being made.

For more information on rent rebates or allowances, see the leaflets *There's Money Off Rent* (for use in England and Wales) and *Rent Rebates – Read All About It* (for use in Scotland).

Appeals

In the case either where a rebate seems unsatisfactory or has been refused, it is possible to appeal. At the time that the local authority writes informing one of how much rebate has been awarded they will also explain how to appeal against such award. There is one month in which an appeal must be made. In the event that the appeal is unsuccessful, advice on how to further contest the decision can be obtained from the neighbourhood law centre (the address can be found in the phone book).

FOR THOSE WHO CAN STILL COPE

At retirement or on increased infirmity, many persons assess their accommodation in the light of whether or not it has the potential to meet their future needs. Two factors which will influence any decision they make are their financial resources and what alternative housing is available.

Owner Occupiers

Owner occupiers will have the option of either adapting their house, changing their pattern of living, selling up and buying a smaller place or moving to sheltered accommodation.

Those who rent accommodation can consider what adaptations can be made to that accommodation or they can investigate the availability of other housing which will better suit their increasing needs.

Uprooting should never be undertaken lightly. All the advantages and disadvantages of a move should be thought over, and as far as is humanly possible, sentiment should not affect this decision.

How to Stay Put

One method of improving his ability to stay on will be by adapting his home.

Renovation grants

Where the owner occupier decides to adapt his home, he may apply for a house renovation grant. There are three different types of grant available: intermediate grants, improvement grants and repairs grants.

The procedures for application for any of the above grants – Contact should be made with one of the improvement grant officers in the City Engineer's Department, or one of the housing officers in the Chief Environmental Health Officer's Department. He will arrange for an officer to visit to discuss the works for which a grant is being sought.

Then an estimate and a plan have to be prepared, after which an application can be submitted.

After the Council has received a formal application, they will inform the applicant relatively quickly whether or not any information is lacking or if a grant is not available.

If the council decides to make the grant, it will have the premises inspected to determine the 'eligible expense' of the grant aided work.

After that the home owner will have to satisfy the city solicitor as to his legal title to the property.

The conditions attaching to house renovation grants are general and specific – those applying to all grants and those relevant to each particular grant.

The general conditions are:

- The dwelling must not have been built before October 2, 1962.
- The applicant must be a freeholder or have a lease with at least five years to run.
- For five years the dwelling must be used in the manner described in the applicant's certificate.
- Application for the grant must be made, normally, before the work is undertaken.
  The application must include:

- A plan showing the dwelling before and after improvement;

- An estimate of cost of the proposed work;

- A certificate of future occupation in duplicate;

- A completed application in duplicate.

Intermediate grants

These are available as of right, to help meet the cost of installing standard amenities for the first time and to carry out certain works of repair and replacement. Standard amenities here mean hot and cold water supply at a fixed bath and shower, normally in a bathroom, wash hand basin, sink and water closet.

Specific Conditions – In addition to the general conditions:

- To qualify, the property concerned must have a future life of fifteen years after the work is finished.
- After improvements, all the standard amenities will be available for the exclusive use of the occupants.
- The dwelling will be in a good state of repair having regard to its age, location and character.
- The property will be fit for human occupation.

Intermediate grants are available to adapt houses to the special needs of registered disabled persons.

Improvement grants

These are grants made by the Council to improve and repair older houses to a high standard, or to convert larger dwellings into flats.

Specific Conditions – In addition to the general conditions:

- Generally an improvement grant cannot be given if the property is to be owner-occupied and the rateable value exceeds £225 or if the dwelling is to be converted into flats and the owner is to occupy one of the flats, if the existing rateable value exceeds £350.
- To qualify, the property must have a minimum life of thirty years.
- All standard amenities, must be in a good

state of repair after the proposed works are completed.

- The maximum cost limit is £5000 for which the grant may be aided.
- Not more than 50 per cent of the total eligible expense for improvements and repairs can be attributed to repair work.

Where the owner cannot pay the balance, he should look at a maturity loan (see page 160) to 'top up' the grant.

Repairs grants

Minor repairs such as replacing a window pane or tap washer are best done by finding a volunteer (see page 11), if you cannot do the job yourself. Major repairs, such as reroofing, rewiring, need large sums of money. Some elders can claim repairs grants. These are obtainable in General Improvement Areas for repairs and replacements where the Council is satisfied that the applicant cannot carry out the work without undue hardship. Persons awarded this grant may include applicants entitled to supplementary pension or a rate rebate. Those who do not live in General Improvement Areas can apply for a maturity loan to cover the cost of major repairs.

Other general points relating to grants

Generally, if it becomes apparent during progress of the improvement or repair that further unforeseen work is essential, an additional amount of grant can be approved subject to the limitations of the maximum grant and improvement/repair proportions.

The grant will normally be paid to the applicant on completion of all works of improvement and repair to the satisfaction of the city council's officers. Under no circumstances should the householder initiate work in the expectation that this will strengthen his case.

In appropriate cases, it can be arranged for interim payments to be made during the progress of the work. In the case of interim payments, the applicant will have to undertake to complete all the work within one year from the date of the grant approval.

The council may, at their discretion, dispense with some of the grant conditions, where, due to special circumstances, they cannot be met, so even though it may not appear as if the elder can be helped under the conditions listed above, ask if discretionary powers can be used. Grants can even be claimed for heating apparatus, although it may be difficult to persuade the council to agree to such a claim.

Maturity loans

The local authority has discretion to grant loans. The housing authority housing advice centre staff will be able to advise on application procedure. The benefit of the maturity loan is that the capital need not be paid back during the lifetime of the borrower, but will be rendered when the property is sold on the death of the home owner. If the interests of the surviving spouse are to be protected, it is advisable for the property to be in joint names so that the loan will continue with the survivor. Of course, the interest is paid until the owner's death. The interest rate is the same as on an option mortgage and supplementary pensioners can ask for their benefits to be increased to cover the interest payments. Beneficiaries' interests under a will will be prejudiced under a maturity loan.

Adaptation

The onset of disability can make a house which was previously suitable, unsatisfactory or impossible for the elder to live in. For example, an old person living happily in a house with an upstairs toilet and bathroom may become severely handicapped if she is no longer able to climb the stairs as the result of a stroke. The domiciliary occupational therapist (see page 23) may be able to suggest adaptations to the house to overcome the design feature which is causing the handicap, with financial assistance from the Social Services Department.

The sort of adaptations which can remove handicap are:

- The replacement of front door steps with a ramp which can be negotiated in a wheelchair.
- The installation of a stairlift.
- The installation of a downstairs toilet and bathroom, even if there is one upstairs.
- Conversion of a bathroom to a shower room.

Taking in a tenant

Another way of improving his ability to stay on will be to take in a tenant into part of his house. Any owner-occupier who thinks about this option should:

- Be fully aware of the landlord's obligations (such as providing a rent book if the tenant pays weekly).
- Look at the financial complications that can arise. The tenant can appeal to the rent tribunal if he thinks the rent is too high. If they agree, the rent will be classified as 'registered' and cannot be raised for three years unless improvements have been made during that period.
- Be prepared for differences in life style.
- Be aware that he may let for a periodic or fixed term.
- Be aware of the CGT liability that may arise, see page 153.
- Generally, although there are financial advantages of taking a tenant into the house, every person should appreciate that the tenant now seems to have the law on his side. His presence may turn out to be very distressing, and the landlord may be put to endless trouble in trying to get him out.

Repairs – The landlord should have a specific agreement with the tenant about who will be responsible for repairs and maintenance.

In the event the landlord wants the tenant to leave – Although it is generally prudent to consult a solicitor about the tedious procedure that is involved, a knowledge of the essentials would be helpful.

The procedure varies according to the category of tenancy.

Periodic or fixed term – If the rooms are let on a periodic basis – by the month, quarter or year, then notice to quit in writing must be given – the length of the notice required relates to the letting period, with a minimum of four weeks. NOTE that the wording of the notice to quit is important. For guidance, consult the leaflet *Notice to Quit* which is available from Housing Aid Centres and Citizens Advice Bureaux.

In the event of a fixed period tenancy, a landlord is not required to serve a notice to quit if the period has expired. If the tenant won't leave when the tenancy has come to an end he will come under the statutory protection of the Rents Acts for as long as he uses the place as his home. When a tenant refuses to vacate after the fixed period of the notice to quit has expired, the landlord can go to the County Court for an order for possession.

However, the landlord should be forewarned not to try to evict a tenant physically – tenant eviction is a matter for the Court.

The Owner Occupier Who Decides to Move to Other Accommodation

Sentiment can play a very influential role in one's decision of whether to stay put or to move. Despite the unsuitability of their existing home in meeting their needs, many people won't move because of their sentimental attachments. Others move to be near relatives or old friends on the basis that they will give them support when they need it; however, often circumstances change and a move can prove a disappointment. Therefore, before the final decision to sell up and move is made, all the disadvantages should be considered, as well as the advantages. Some of the disadvantages of course, will centre about having to change doctors, not having neighbours who will generally help out if one becomes ill and with whom one has been acquainted over a long period, disposing of cumbersome furniture and having to buy more compact units, and the overall difficulty of adapting to a new environment.

The advantages could include financial savings on overall maintenance, lower fuel bills, no stairs to manage, more modern amenities, a smaller garden, a more interesting area (perhaps a seaside resort) and/or being closer to one's family. Housing should be sought which is near public transport, or (despite our earlier remarks) old and dear friends, has neighbours close by, is preferably within short walking distance of the church and shops, and which is in a borough with good domiciliary services.

Where an old person already owns his own home he will want to sell it before moving out, whether or not he actually intends to buy another home. It may be possible to get a bridging loan to cover the period between purchase of one place and sale of another. There are various methods of bringing the availability of the house to the notice of prospective buyers. He may list it with an estate agent or advertise it in the local paper or some other paper. Where he does not want to buy another home, he may try to sell it to the local authority in return for rehousing, or sell it to a housing association for flat conversion, with an agreement that he will be allocated one of the converted flats.

He could investigate the possibility of selling to the local authority in return for rehousing
The procedure here is to write to the director of the local housing authority enquiring whether or not they would be interested in such a proposition. As many details of the property as are available should be given. The better the state of repair of the property the greater the chance of the local authority coming to some arrangement. However, financial restraints may mean that it is unable to buy.

Or he could negotiate with a housing association
Some housing associations will buy an old person's home and convert it into two or three flatlets, and then allocate one flatlet to the owner. One of the most immediate problems under such an arrangement is that

two moves will be involved; one finding alternative accommodation while the conversion is taking place and the other on completion of the conversion.

Other old persons may decide to buy a smaller house (or a flat)

The information given below will also be pertinent to the person who buys a house or flat for the first time. One may decide to buy either the leasehold or freehold.

Where it is not possible to buy a freehold, a decision to buy the leasehold has its advantages

To all intents and purposes, people living in leasehold property under long term leases at ground rents can be categorised as owner occupiers.

At the end of a long residential lease, the landlord as a rule is not entitled to recover possession. The Landlord and Tenant Act 1954 provides that the leaseholder will be able to remain in possession as a tenant subject to the protection of the Rent Acts. It is not required of the tenant to take any steps to secure this protection. When the landlord decides to try to recover possession under one of the limited grounds open to him, he must serve various notices in prescribed forms which inform the tenant of his rights and what action he should take. The Department of the Environment issues a pamphlet about *Houses Held on Ground Lease*.

Certain conditions being complied with, leaseholders with a lease for at least twenty-one years who have lived in the house for at least five of the previous ten years are entitled to purchase the freehold.

Procedure on Buying a Flat or House

The procedure involved in buying a flat or a house is to contact an estate agent and to ask what properties they have on their lists which basically fit one's requirements. Before dealing with an estate agent, it is advisable to make sure he is a member of the Chartered Auctioneer and Estate Agents Institute. His

commission will be paid by the seller when the transaction has been completed.

After the right property has been found, the next step is to make an offer 'subject to contract' through a solicitor. The lending body will require a satisfactory report from their surveyor before advancing any money. But the prospective buyer should not be tempted to do without his own surveyor just because the lending body have sent theirs around. One's own surveyor will be looking for different things and may save one from a disastrous purchase. Additionally, the surveyor may stiffen the lawyer's bargaining position if he points out hidden faults, thus earning his fee many times over.

General Information for Owner Occupiers Wanting to Move

Home Relocation Ltd is a network of estate agents throughout the country. Its function is to assist persons wanting to buy property in an area of the country away from which they are currently living. Initial enquiries free. Further information can be obtained from:

Home Relocation Limited,
21 Soho Square,
London W1V 6AX.

Raising Money to Buy a Flat or House

As a general rule it is impossible to borrow the whole amount of money needed to buy a flat or house. The purchaser usually has to make a capital contribution which will be the difference between the mortgage financing available and the price of the house or flat.

A solicitor or recognised estate agent will be able to advise on different types of mortgage and where and how to apply.

The amount which will have to be paid each month under a mortgage agreement will depend on:

a) The amount of the mortgage;
b) The length of the mortgage;
c) The method of repayment.

Money for buying a house can be borrowed from a bank, a building society, the local authority, a trust fund or an insurance company.

The ways of raising money which can be considered are:

A repayment mortgage

This type has the advantage of repayment being spread over many years (the normal term is twenty-five years) and of income tax relief being given on the payments. (The mortgagor knows exactly what is required of him both financially and when.) The disadvantage is that tax relief gets less on a repayment mortgage as time goes on.

An option mortgage

It is possible to apply for such a mortgage from a building society. An example of how it works is for a purchaser to borrow £5000 for twenty years. He will not repay the loan by instalments. The loan is left outstanding throughout the twenty year period. At the time the loan is made the purchaser also takes out an endowment insurance (a type of life policy) for £5000 over twenty years and assigns the policy to the building society. When the policy matures, the money from it will be used to pay back the mortgage. As in the case of the repayment mortgage, regular monthly payments have to be made and the payments consist of interest on the mortgage and premiums on the endowment insurance; both payments will remain constant throughout the term and qualify for tax relief.

Insurance company loans

Insurance companies seldom lend less than £3500 and some start at a higher figure. The rate of interest on the loan is usually fixed throughout the whole period of the loan.

Local authority mortgages

These mortgages are often at fixed rates of interest which have the advantage that the borrower knows exactly how much to allow for mortgage repayments throughout the period of the mortgage. The advantage of getting a local authority mortgage is that the local authority will often agree to lend on houses less favoured by building societies. They may lend up to 100 per cent. The snag is that the rate of interest is often higher than that of building societies.

Private loans

Private mortgages out of trust funds within the family or through a solicitor are often given for an indefinite period. When the lender wants his money back, he gives the borrower notice; the length of the notice is fixed in the mortgage. The advantage of this type of loan is that it may sometimes be acquired at a lower rate of interest.

The Solicitor's Role

Once a source of financing has been found, the solicitor can proceed with a contract. It is his job to find out about town planning changes, rights of way, building by-laws, restrictive covenants, etc. He will check on the title and search the Land Register to determine whether or not there are any outstanding death duties, undisclosed mortgages or other 'encumbrances' on the property.

In the intervening period between exchange and completion, the purchaser will be regarded in law as the owner of the property and must therefore make immediate arrangements to insure the property.

It is the purchaser's solicitor's responsibility to prepare the draft of the conveyance and to send it to the vendor's solicitor for approval and/or amendment.

A period of around four weeks will generally pass between the signing of the contract and the completion of the sale, when the conveyance will be executed and the balance of the purchase money paid.

The legal fees payable on the purchase of a house depend on the price of the house.

After the purchase has been completed, arrangements will have to be made for the move. A move can either seem relatively effortless or it can be a virtual nightmare. How it turns out will depend on how much effort has been put into planning and carrying it off.

Preparing to Move

If a moving company is to be involved in the move, three or four written estimates should be obtained. Firm representatives will come and inspect the house contents so they can give an approximate estimate. Most movers cover packing, loading, transport, unloading and unpacking.

Read the mover's contract carefully. Particularly the liability for damage to one's property. House contents should be insured to cover the time they are in transit.

What to do when the move is imminent – Just before the move there are definite tasks that an old person should see are done:

- Arranging for gas and/or electricity meters to be read and the supply disconnected on the day of the move.
- Rearranging for gas and/or electricity to be laid on in the new house.
- Notifying the Post Office to close the telephone account.
- Arranging for a telephone to be installed at the new address.
- Informing the local authority Treasurer's Department of cessation of liability for rates.
- Filling in the form (P9440) from the Post Office for re-direction of mail.
- Taking new plugs or adaptors if the electric sockets at the new address are different.
- Stopping home help, home nurse or meals on wheel services if these have been used.
- Cancelling newspaper and milk deliveries.
- Informing the bank manager so that the bank account can be transferred to a branch near the new home.

TENANTS (PEOPLE WHO LIVE IN RENTED ACCOMMODATION)

A knowledge of whether or not one is a protected or unprotected tenant, who is responsible for repairs, the laws about security of tenure, the procedure to follow if a notice to quit is served, and the surviving family's rights on the death of the person named in the tenancy agreement or rent book can help an aged person or her carer to feel more secure. We have stated the main facts concerning private tenancies, including housing associations and local council tenancies.

The Private Landlord and Tenant

The Rent Act 1977, which consolidates previous legislation, looks to security of tenure and the level of rent of a private tenant, whether the accommodation is furnished or unfurnished. However, there is no protection under the Rent Acts for private tenants where the rent includes payment for board and service and that amount paid forms a substantial fraction of the rent.

How secure is one's tenancy?
Security of tenure depends on the category of tenancy, which is mainly determined by whether or not the landlord lives in the same premises as the tenant.

The 1977 Act, for clarity, divides private tenancies into 'Protected Tenancies' and 'Statutory Tenancies'. Both can be either 'regulated' or 'controlled', although most will be regulated. This means that they are subject to the Fair Rent Provisions.

Both Protected and Statutory Tenancies require a valid notice to quit to be issued, and both require a Possession Order granted by the County Court before the tenant can be dispossessed (evicted). A notice to quit should contain a schedule informing the tenant of his rights. Any tenant receiving a notice to quit is advised to consult the local Housing Aid Centre, Law Centre, Citizens Advice Bureau, all of which will provide free advice, or a solicitor, who will usually make a charge for advice given.

For a tenancy to qualify for protection, there must be an existing contract or lease, the property must be let as a separate dwelling, and the rent paid must be over two-thirds of the rateable value of the dwelling (except in the case of a controlled tenancy).

Some tenancies are specifically excluded from protection, and these include local authority, Housing Corporation and registered housing associations (including co-operatives) although legislation is expected during 1979 to extend security of tenure to these categories. (Tenancies of the Crown and those to students by colleges, holiday lettings and lettings of licensed premises are also excluded from protection, although these are of less relevance to the elderly.)

In the case of these unprotected tenancies, the landlord just needs to show that a valid notice to quit was issued in order to obtain a Possession Order from the County Court. Where the landlord is resident, the tenancy will be subject to rent tribunal protection, and this will apply to both furnished and unfurnished tenancies. The Rent Tribunal may extend the notice to quit.

The landlord is non-resident – (protected tenancy) – Where the landlord does not live in the same dwelling as the tenant, the tenancy is usually known as a protected tenancy, and except where the rateable value of the part occupied by the tenant exceeds certain limits – since 1973, £750 (£1500 in London) the tenant's rights are protected under the Rent Acts and the landlord must get a Possession Order from the County Court before he can dispossess a tenant. If an issued notice to quit has expired, the landlord must still get an order from the County Court. The legal aid scheme applies to such cases brought in the County Court.

The tenant is so protected that even in the case where there are substantial rent arrears, the Court can give an extension of time to enable the tenant to find alternative accommodation before he leaves.

If the landlord is resident – (unprotected tenancy) – Where the tenant rents part of the landlord's own home, he is not a protected tenant unless the accommodation is rented unfurnished and he has been living there since before August 14, 1974, sharing neither kitchen nor bathroom nor WC with the landlord. Neither does the protection apply to a person who has been living in furnished accommodation in the same house as the landlord since before August 14, 1974, unless he can prove that the furnishings provided by the landlord are so scanty as not to really count as coming within the definition of being furnished, so that he can actually come within the unfurnished tenant category under the 1974 Act.

An unprotected tenant cannot be evicted unless the landlord obtains a County Court order after serving notice to quit (see above).

Any application to the rent tribunal for security of tenure must be accompanied by a request for the rent to be fixed (unless of course this has already occurred). The rent tribunal will give a decision at the hearing whether or not the notice to quit is to be suspended, and if so, for what period the tenant may stay on. It should be noted that the maximum is six months. However, before the period expires, fresh applications can be made to the tribunal for a further extension. In the case that the tribunal decides not to extend, the tenant must leave within seven days.

The Difference between a Controlled and a Regulated Tenancy

A controlled tenancy

An existing tenancy contracted before July 6, 1957, is a controlled tenancy, providing it was never converted to a regulated tenancy, if the rateable value on March 31, 1972, was under £35. Rents for controlled tenancies were pegged under the 1957 Rent Act and are liable to be increased if the landlord improves the property or has carried out repairs since April 6, 1973, or if the rates have increased if it is the landlord who pays the rates.

A dwelling has to have all the basic amenities and be in good repair, and a qualification certificate to that effect has to have been issued by the local authority, before a landlord can convert to a regulated tenancy.

A regulated tenancy

If a tenancy is regulated it is subject to the regulations of the Fair Rent system. The conditions which have to be fulfilled before a tenancy can be treated as regulated are that the dwelling is privately owned, that the rateable value of the tenant's part is less than £750 (in London £1500) that the annual rent is at least two-thirds of the rateable value and that the landlord does not live in the same dwelling, or if he does, that the tenancy is an unfurnished one which was first granted to the tenant before August 14, 1974.

Either the landlord or the tenant or both jointly can go to the rent officer to have the rent registered or to ask for a fair rent to be determined. If a fair rent is requested, an application form has to be filled in, giving complete details of the tenancy – the accommodation and services provided, and putting forward a figure for an alternative rent.

The procedure is then for the rent officer to inspect the property and to talk to both the landlord and the tenant before deciding what is a fair rent.

A fair rent is based on the condition of the property and if any services are provided by the landlord, these are included.

When a rent has been registered it stays operative for three years, unless circumstances change, such as the landlord improving the property or the property deteriorating.

If either the landlord or the tenant disagrees with the rent officer's decision, he can appeal to a rent assessment committee. The chairman of the committee is generally a lawyer and the other members are usually a surveyor or valuer and a lay person. The

parties can be represented, but rent assessment hearings do not qualify for legal aid. The committee will hear the case and fix a rent.

Allowances and Responsibilities

A rent allowance

If an aged person is the tenant of a private landlord or of a housing association and her income, rent and family dependency qualify her, she is eligible for an allowance towards the rent. A leaflet, *There's Money Off Rent* can be obtained from a Citizens Advice Bureau, the Housing Department of the local authority and from housing advice centres.

A rate rebate

She may also qualify for a rate rebate and should check with the Treasurer's Department of her local authority and the leaflet *How to Pay Less Rates*.

Adaptations (see page 160)

Improvements or intermediate grants

Tenants should never feel that they have to 'make do' with the existing facilities in any dwelling they rent. They can require the landlord to put in adequate facilities. He can apply for a grant (see page 158) from the local authority to cover the costs.

Where a lease has at least five years to run, a lessor may apply for a renovation grant.

The leaflets referred to above are available at the Citizens Advice Bureau, Housing Aid Centre and council offices.

Repairs

Where a tenant has a written lease, the repair covenant will state the extent of the tenant's liability, although the wording of a covenant may not be conclusive, as interpretation may be varied by other provisions in the lease – particularly the length of the term. In cases of major repairs it is often worthwhile consulting a local Housing Aid Centre, Law Centre or Citizens Advice Bureau.

Although a private tenant's rights to repairs does depend on the terms of the lease, the tenant can ask, additionally, his local authority to serve an appropriate notice to get certain repairs and/or improvements carried out (under Section 9 1957 Housing Act and the 1974 Housing Act).

In long leases, the tenant often covenants to do all the repairs; in short leases the landlord usually assumes liability for external and structural repairs of common parts (stairs, hall, etc.) Generally, the landlord is not liable on his covenant to repair unless he knows of the need to repair. (It is advisable for a tenant to notify him in writing as soon as the repair becomes necessary.) Often a strongly worded letter will get a landlord to set about carrying out necessary repairs.

Where a tenant does not have a written contract he must keep the premises 'in a tenant-like manner', and may have to pay damages to the landlord if he allows the premises to fall into disrepair or destroys all or part of the premises.

In the case of furnished tenancies, the premises must be fit for human habitation, or be so at the commencement of the tenancy.

After improvements have been carried out, the landlord can apply for increase of the rent.

Where a Tenant Dies

The spouse, or a member of the deceased tenant's family, who has been living in the household for at least the preceding six months, is entitled to take over the tenancy. In fact, unless there have already been two transfers since the tenant's death, a statutory tenancy, as of right, can be transferred. This will protect a middle-aged son or daughter who has been caring for an aged parent and who has been living in the house for at least six months.

(If the original tenant was 'protected', it will become a 'statutory' tenancy on the death of the original tenant.)

COUNCIL TENANTS (PERSONS WHO LIVE IN ACCOMMODATION OWNED BY A LOCAL AUTHORITY)

(See also Local Authority Sheltered Housing Tenants)

Rent allowances
Rent allowances can be claimed by eligible local authority tenants. The actual procedures that follow a rent allowance being granted is for the council to reduce the rent. If the rent is collected at the door, the rent collector or housing officer as he is now called, will advise on rent rebates, otherwise the council tenant should apply to the housing department of the local authority. (For further information, see *There's Money Off Rent*.)

Rate rebates
Rate rebates are available for council tenants. Applications should be made to the Treasurer's Department of the local authority. The housing officer will also advise on rate rebates when he comes to collect the rent (where it is collected).

(For further information, see *How to Pay Less Rates*.)

Repairs
One big advantage of being a council tenant is that repairs are done by the council, without charge to the tenant.

The housing officer will make notes on any repairs or improvements necessary, otherwise requests for repairs should be made in writing to the district housing office, but minor repairs are the tenant's responsibility. Some old people invoke the aid of voluntary groups to do minor repairs, such as interior decorating. This lessens the drain on their financial resources. If they are in receipt of a supplementary pension, they are entitled to apply for an exceptional needs payment (ENP) for any essential work.

Adaptations

Applications for adaptations to enable a disabled person to live at home should be made to the housing department of the local authority or the domiciliary occupational therapist.

Tenancy on the Death of the Tenant

A surviving husband or wife will take over the tenancy. A single daughter or son who has been living with and caring for a parent in a council house will usually be required to move to smaller accommodation. To protect herself she should require the parent to approach the housing department director to ask for a joint tenancy so that at the parent's death the daughter (usually middle-aged) may stay on in the house as council tenant.

Among other possibilities for those who want to move from an owner-occupied or rented home are: accommodation in an almshouse, a granny annexe, a mobile home, residential hotel accommodation, or foster care.

Almshouses

Some persons who want to move may find that accommodation in an almshouse is the answer.

Almshouses are charitably endowed houses which provide residential accommodation for persons whose financial circumstances warrant their being accepted as residents. There are about 2000 almshouses with some 22,000 dwellings spread over the country.

There is an extensive on-going programme of building and improvement of sub-standard dwellings. Residents are not now generally referred to as 'almsperson' or 'almswoman' but as 'occupant' or 'resident'.

Each almshouse has its own criteria about who is eligible to live there. Generally the emphasis is on people who were born in or who have lived within the area of the almshouse, or who have worked in a particular industry or trade.

Applying to live in an almshouse

An application to live in an almshouse should be made to the Trustees of the almshouses.

Source of information

Information on eligibility for residency can be obtained from the General Secretary of the National Association of Almshouses, at Billingham Lodge, Wokingham, Berkshire RG11 5RJ.

Granny Annexes

The concept of granny annexes is not new. They are usually a bungalow by the side of the house or a flat in the house of an adult married child – a very sensible solution to housing elderly parents close to their children. Properly used, they achieve a greater sense of security for the older person and relieve anxiety on the part of the younger generation. Any increased infirmity is noticed as soon as it occurs. For the elderly person, family ties are important. Old people often want the independence and peace of their own place, and yet at the same time like to know that their family is at hand. 'My own little place' means 'I am still me. I still have my own identity and I am not a burden'. For the family it is a satisfactory arrangement. The children can go to gran's or grandpa's and build up that special relationship, which is not always possible in a multigeneration household.

If a granny annexe is to be a success, each party must set up a definite pattern of independent behaviour from the outset. A granny annexe becomes a farce if it is regarded as serving no other function than the place gran or grandpa goes to sleep. To encourage a give and take independence the younger generation can do the old person's shopping, have him to tea, dinner on Sundays, etc. but let him baby-sit for her, or shop for her if he goes out. One elderly gentleman we know says of his annexe – 'It's fantastic, the daughter's there if I need her. She slips in for a cuppa some evenings or I know I can go in there if I get that "what can I do with myself?" feeling'.

Before building such an extension it is necessary to check whether planning permission with the local authority is required. The 'compact home' as it can well be called, comprises somewhere to do some cooking, one's own bathroom and WC and a bed-sitting room.

Mobile Homes

Some families solve the caring problem (the planning department having no objection), by bringing their aged relative to live in a mobile home in the grounds of the younger generation's family home. The merits of this arrangement are essentially the same as those of a 'granny annexe' (see above).

Residential Hotels

This type of accommodation reduces housekeeping to a minimum. It usually comprises a bedroom. Guests eat in the communal dining room.

Any old person moving to residential hotel accommodation should obtain a written assurance from the manager that the room is not only for the winter months. In south coast resorts the aged are sometimes asked to leave to make way for summer visitors who pay higher charges.

The long term problem with residential hotel accommodation is that if the old person becomes infirm she could tend to be isolated and would miss out on the domiciliary services. Relatives should make periodic checks to ensure that their elder is able to cope.

Mrs Gould's Residential Advisory Centre for the Elderly (GRACE), Leigh Corner, Leigh High Road, Cobham, Surrey KT11 2HW, has detailed information on hotels and guest houses in twenty-four counties in Southern England All places have been visited by their staff. The information is free.

Before making such a move an old person should consider the changes that may have to be made in her living pattern – she may have to adapt to new places and faces. She would be apt to find it difficult to feel comfortable at a new lunch club, and new acquaintances won't know about her background.

Foster Care

One solution for persons who can no longer cope is to enter into foster care. This can be a happy development for those who are lonely as it can mean that after a lapse of years they are again part of a family.

This kind of scheme exists in only a few places in the United Kingdom. The principle behind it is to find persons or families who are prepared to take older people into their homes on a paying-guest basis.

Schemes vary. They can be run by Social Service Departments, (usually with local authority grants) or by voluntary organisations. The local Social Services Department can advise on whether or not such a scheme exists in the area. Payment for such an arrangement is generally negotiated between the parties themselves. If the boarder cannot pay the charge, he can apply to the Department of Health and Social Security for a supplementary pension.

FOR THOSE WHO CAN NO LONGER COPE ALONE

Sheltered housing, residential care or a nursing home are the alternatives available to the many old people who can no longer cope alone and whose families cannot or will not care for them.

SHELTERED HOUSING

This category of housing should always be investigated as a possibility. One may apply for sheltered housing either to the Local Authority or to a housing association.

Sheltered housing does not suit all aged persons; some people are unable to adapt to such a setting. Therefore, before making any definite decision, it would be wise to go and see over a scheme and to talk to some of the occupants.

The advantage of sheltered housing is that it definitely enables independence to be retained for longer. Tenants have their own living unit with their own front door and furniture.

The accommodation generally comprises a one-room bedsitter flat for a single person and a bungalow with one bedroom and sitting room for couples. Furniture is supplied by the tenants. All units have a small kitchen area. In some older developments, the bathroom and lavatory are shared among two or four flats. The modern units, however, are generally self-contained.

Pet lovers should make certain that the particular housing association which controls the unit they like will allow pets. Some landlords impose certain restrictions and limitations. Regrettably, some old people learn all too late that their dear pet cannot live with them, and, of course, this realisation causes them great distress.

A common room, a residents' visitors' room for overnight stays, and laundry facilities are general features in the majority of schemes. But of course, the main benefit is the presence of the warden.

The warden

The best kind of warden in a sheltered housing group is the unobstrusive co-ordinator who, without interfering, keeps an eye on all the old people under his or her care. Often the warden is a married woman – her husband may assist with certain jobs in the group of homes on a part-time basis. In a large group she may have a full-time deputy who works among several such groups 'filling-in' for holidays and monthly leave-days and unavoidable absences. It is important that the relatives of an aged person living in such a group should not off-load their responsibilities on to the Warden –

remember that he or she may have the responsibility for up to forty elderly persons of varying degrees of activity and independence. The warden should not be regarded as a kind of personal maid of all work for one particular old person!

The main duties of the Warden are by their very nature flexible and hard to pinpoint. They include:

- Keeping an eye on all the residents, as unobtrusively as possible.
- Supervising the general maintenance of the houses – reporting structural defects and general repairs to the appropriate department or authority and seeing that they are put right.
- Some wardens may do a little of the communal cleaning, but usually will have help with this aspect of things.
- Responsibility for administrative and clerical work connected with the running of the group. Often he or she will help also with form-filling problems a member of the group may have.
- He or she will often collect pensions and other benefits, or prescriptions when the recipient is unwell or the weather is very cold.
- If somebody is ill, the warden can arrange temporary domiciliary help – if an old person falls ill, check with the warden about this – sometimes the local authority providing such assistance will expect payment for this service.
- Where the tenants of a sheltered housing group wish it, the warden may arrange communal activities, and will see to the provision of a TV, cards, dominoes, etc. Again, if the old people in a group wish to join, for example, in local voluntary fund-raising efforts for one body or another, the warden can help to arrange materials and facilities for making things for bring and buy sales, etc.

It is important that the warden has a good working relationship with the doctors and welfare workers attending old people under her care. Relatives can help here by ensuring that their elder's doctor is known to the warden, and as much of her background medical and personal history as is felt necessary, so that she knows something about each resident and what to be on the look-out for.

Usually the warden will liaise with any official visitors for the old person (i.e. local social security officers, etc.) so that if she has any follow-up queries, she can ask the warden for help or clarification.

Obviously the warden cannot be an expert on all facilities and benefits available, but she will know where to find such information and who to contact for information and advice.

Where an old person has been in hospital and is about to be discharged, neither GP, hospital nor relatives should regard the warden as a resident nurse. But she can be an invaluable liaising link between all parties in the arranging of suitable nursing care.

Perhaps one of the most important roles the warden plays is in reassuring an old person that she is in good hands in case of emergency. Many old people are perfectly able to look after themselves and be quite independent, but nonetheless, fear the time when they might need help and not be able to get it quickly. The warden gives an aged resident this confidence.

Local Authority Sheltered Housing

Local authorities generally require residential qualifications, and moves to a different local authority are difficult, but people wishing to rent council accommodation in another area should write to the housing manager in the area concerned.

Local councils allocate housing according to need as determined by them on a priority basis. Owner occupiers will find it very hard to be allocated a council tenancy.

Some authorities have separate lists or different criteria for people over a certain age, generally pensionable age. In some cases, a residence qualification is waived if an elderly applicant's relatives live in the area.

Procedure to get on the list

The first step in getting one's name on the council housing list is to obtain a form from the local authority's housing department. Questions that are included on the form relate to the applicant's housing and its amenities; whether or not it is rented or owned, and often, information on income and current outgoings. An applicant is generally asked to state preference for a particular type of dwelling and for the area he would prefer to live in.

(A housing officer will help an applicant to fill in the form, where she is dubious about how she should answer a particular section.)

An aged person whose needs are very urgent because of inadequate or unsuitable housing, or illness, should attach a separate letter with the application forms specifying her particular problems. Additionally, she should send along a letter from her doctor confirming the condition of her health and special needs. The next step is for a housing department officer to visit the applicant so as to evaluate the applicant's present accommodation.

Once accepted on the waiting list, the applicant will be sent a registration card. Generally, no further contact will be made until the council has accommodation to offer.

Rent and Rate Rebates – (See as for Council tenants page 167.)

Housing Associations

Housing associations also provide dwellings to rent. Tenants are generally selected according to their housing needs and the association's criteria, quite irrespective of where they happen to be living at the time.

When an association is a charitable trust, the terms of its trust determine the category of people it can accept.

Many associations specialise in housing for the disabled.

Housing associations are either 'registered' or 'unregistered'. A tenant of an 'unregistered' housing association will become a protected tenant with the same rights as a private tenant (see page 165). The tenant of a housing trust or a 'registered' housing association will not be protected (see page 165).

Procedure for applying

The procedure for applying for housing association accommodation to rent is to write for a brochure which will contain information about who is in fact eligible to apply and whether there is a waiting list or vacancies.

A list of associations providing sheltered housing can be obtained from the National Federation of Housing Associations, 32 Southampton Street, The Strand, London, WC2, but it is often easier to ask the local Age Concern Office (see page 14) which housing associations have dwellings, or are planning to build sheltered housing, in the area in which the elder wishes to live. The major national housing associations, which have sheltered housing in all parts of the country, are:

Abbeyfield Society 35a High Street, Potters Bar, Herts.

Anchor Housing Association 15 Magdalen Street, Oxford.

Hanover Housing Association 168 High Street, Egham, Surrey TW20 9HX, 01-389 5451; Fiske Court, 5 Hanover Road, London, SW19, 01-542 3455.

Jephson Housing Association 5–7 Dames Place, Leamington Spa.

Royal British Legion Housing Association 35 Jackson Court, Hazlemere, High Wycombe, Bucks HP15 7TX.

World Property Housing Trust 34 High Holborn, London, WC1, 01–405 6783.

Further sources of information from Housing Advice Centres, the Local Authority Housing Department and the National Federation of Housing Associations (32 Southampton Street, The Strand, London, WC2) will have information on schemes offering sheltered housing. Where the need is urgent, the social worker should be asked to help to locate appropriate housing.

When applying for such housing, as much information as possible about one's needs, present housing, failing health and other relevant circumstances should be supplied. Many physically and mentally infirm aged are actually in dire need of sheltered housing with warden support, yet they may not be classified as belonging to a housing priority need group. Their present accommodation will be seen as adequate in terms of conditions and facilities. Therefore, an applicant should not hesitate to explain her real needs when applying to an association.

Local authorities have the right to nominate applicants from their housing list for vacancies in a housing association's sheltered housing scheme. However, housing associations are not bound to accept their nominations.

The rent that the housing association charges is determined by the rent officer as a fair rent. Rents are therefore subject to review every three years. When a new rent is set, for tenants already in occupancy, there is a maximum rate at which the increase can be put into effect (at present a rise each year of 75p a week).

Rent and rate rebates

Tenants of housing associations' sheltered housing, their financial circumstances permitting, are entitled to claim rent rebates and rate rebates, if eligible.

Eviction

A tenant can be evicted for failing to do what his tenancy requires. He must be given four week's notice to quit in writing. He cannot be evicted without a Court Order.

OLD PEOPLE'S HOMES (RESIDENTIAL, COMMUNAL OR REST)

The term old people's home is interchangeable with residential homes, communal homes and rest homes. Old people's homes are not equipped for nursing, and so will not generally admit a resident who is incapable of leading a fairly independent life. Such homes are establishments '... the sole or main purpose of which is ... the provision of accommodation ... for the aged'. They do not have to be in the charge of a qualified nurse, and neither do there have to be qualified nurses on the staff. Many homes, however, are in the charge of qualified nursing staff.

The degree of care given varies, but most homes will take people who need help with washing and dressing, those on a simple diet or those who need to use a walking frame to get about. Those with relatives in wheelchairs or who are incontinent or confused may find great difficulty in finding places for them.

It is important when choosing a home to bear in mind the distance from shops, Post Office, the church, public transport, entertainment, a pub and whether or not the other residents are likely to include people of their own interests and standards. Having some personal effects about helps to keep an old person closer to his past and enquiries should be made about whether this is possible in the particular home chosen.

Homes that take both sexes tend to provide a more natural atmosphere. Most people find difficulty in adjusting to life in an institutionalised setting when only their own sex is present. Where a couple are aged and sooner or later both are going to require admission to an old person's home, every care should be taken to see that a home is chosen which will take couples.

It is rather presumptuous of a relative to choose a home without the aged person seeing it and agreeing that he feels he would be happy in it. Many old people have a Dickensian image of old people's homes –

they think of them as places in which they would be robbed of their independence completely.

Relatives should make every effort to point out the positive aspects; a room with one's own personal effects, a community room where one can mingle with peers, a garden, close proximity to shops, church, public transport, and security from the fear of falling ill and not being found. Again, an old people's home will enable an aged person to retain his independence from his family, while on the other hand, if there are strong family bonds, these will not be severed merely because he is living in a home.

For a while after admission an old person may find it hard to settle in – adapting to any style of living which is more regimented than the one we are accustomed to takes time. However, residents do come and go as they please. Hours to get up and go to bed are often flexible, only meal times are normally fixed.

Recently additional emphasis has been given to occupational therapy, handicrafts and entertainment generally. Church services are held periodically in the home for those who are unable to get out easily.

Every resident has the right (within reason) to choose to remain registered with their own doctor or to change to the doctor for the home.

Relatives should be reminded that no-one can be moved against his will, except in exceptional circumstances (such as in the case of extreme self-neglect where living conditions are endangering health) into a home.

Homes are run privately, by voluntary organisations and by local authorities. We shall consider the special characteristics of each category in turn.

Privately Run Old People's Homes

Admission
Individual homes control their own admissions and the choice of a private old people's home is governed by the applicant's financial circumstances and actual physical condition.

For instance, where there is any suggestion of mental illness, however slight, it will be difficult to find a private old people's home which will take the aged person.

Charges
The charges in privately run old people's homes cover a wide range – up to £80 and over a week. These charges and what they cover should be fully investigated before an old person goes into a home. Thus in some homes heating and laundry services are added to the weekly rate. In some others these are included.

One of the awful problems that can arise for people in privately run homes is that they may have to move if their savings run out.

Local authorities are empowered to help towards the cost of an old person in a privately run home. Of course, a request for assistance should be made to the Social Services Department before the aged person is actually admitted.

Also, there are charitable bodies which will, where they consider it appropriate, give grants to elderly people towards private home fees.

Sources of information on privately run homes
Detailed information about privately run residential homes can be obtained from Mrs Gould's Residential Advisory Centre for the Elderly (GRACE, Leigh Corner, Leigh Hill Road, Cobham, Surrey, KT11 2HN). All places have been visited by GRACE staff and therefore their appraisal of accommodation to suit particular needs can be relied upon. The information is free. In enquiring about accommodation, the type of accommodation and area sought, medical condition of the applicant, how much one can pay and degree of urgency should be given.

Privately run old people's homes must register with the local authority in whose area they are situated; therefore the local authority will have a list.

The local authority has a duty to inspect all registered homes to ensure that the stan-

dards do not fall below what is called 'the specified level'.

Voluntary Organisation Homes
These homes are mostly small with less than forty residents. Many are run by religious organisations.

Admission
Application for admission will be indicated in the brochure.

Charges
Charges are fixed by each organisation and vary from home to home. Most homes will ask for details of financial circumstances, although it is unlikely one would be refused admission because of lack of funds. Sharing a room is generally cheaper. The average charge is £30 a week. Residents who are unable to meet the home's charge can apply to their local authority to be considered for a subsidy which will operate on the same basis as for residents in the local authority's homes.

Sources of information about homes
The Salvation Army, 110–112 Middlesex Street, London EC1 7HZ (men's services), 280 Mare Street, Hackney, London E8 1HE (for women's services), runs about forty Eventide Homes for persons of all denominations.

A booklet, called *Homes for Old People*, is issued by the Church Information Office, Church House Bookshop, Great Smith Street, London, SW1; it gives details of homes where older members of the Church of England can go. The Catholic Directory lists homes for Catholics. Jews can get information on homes from the Jewish Welfare Board, 74a Charlotte Street, London, W1, and Methodists can make enquiries through 1 Central Building, London, SW1. Old People's Welfare Organisations, housing associations and councils of social service run homes. Of course there are also homes for the blind, deaf or mentally frail, and details of these homes can be found in the Charities Digest.

The *Annual Charities Digest* is an excellent reference book. Public Libraries keep a copy.

The homes, as with privately run homes, have to be reported upon periodically by personnel from the local authority to ensure they comply with statutory requirements about premises suitability, staffing, etc.

Local Authority Old People's Homes

Admission
Applications for admission to a local authority residential home have to be made through the local authority Social Services Department in the area in which the old person generally resides.

Once this application has been made, a social worker will visit the applicant to discuss the need for residential care, to assess suitability and the degree of emergency. She will bring an application form to be completed with information about present and past circumstances and family, physical condition, for instance hearing and sight, how independent the applicant is, can she wash and dress herself, walk unaided upstairs, etc. Other questions will concern the business aspects of her life – whether or not a will has been made out, who her solicitor is, what insurance policies are held. Also required is a statement of financial circumstances, including information on occupational pension, retirement pension, social security benefits, savings interest on investments and whether or not she owns her home. The financial information is needed so that the local authority can assess how much to charge the applicant for residence.

There is a waiting list for most local authority residential homes. To enable a prospective resident to cope until there is a vacancy, the social worker may arrange for extra help – meals on wheels (on extra days if these are already provided some days), or a home help for more hours a week. Where an old person's circumstances slide downhill, she should contact the social worker in order to get her admission hastened.

Generally, once a place is offered it is expected that the offer will be accepted or rejected within a few days.

No old person should just be uprooted and 'dumped' in a local authority home. A relative or neighbour should go with her to reassure her. Some local authorities have an introductory letter welcoming new residents and explaining how the home is run.

Charges
Every local authority fixes a standard charge for its residential accommodation, which is based on the expenses of running the home. It is the maximum charge that has to be paid and varies from authority to authority. The amount a resident is asked to contribute towards her keep is based on an assessment of her financial resources.

Periodically the Government fixes how much of her retirement pension every resident of a local authority home is entitled to keep each week, to cover personal expenses. A minimum charge for local authority homes is also laid down and is the difference between the money allowed for personal use and the basic retirement pension. In the case that a resident doesn't have sufficient means to meet the minimum charge and still have the regulated spending sum, she is entitled to claim a supplementary pension. If she has more income than the basic retirement pension, or savings or capital assets of over £1250, she may have to pay more than the minimum charge.

Where there are assets that are not realisable (perhaps where a son or daughter is living in an elderly person's home), she may be asked to enter into an agreement with the local authority, that when such property is sold (whether in her lifetime or at her death), the local authority can claim a sum equal to the accumulated debt.

The weekly payment made covers board and lodging, laundry and other essential items such as soap and toilet tissue.

Sources of information
Contact the Local Authority Housing Department or the Social Worker.

NURSING HOMES

A nursing home can be said to be 'any premises used or intended to be used for the reception of, and providing nursing for persons suffering from any injury or infirmity'. It has to be under the charge of a resident of the home who is either a registered medical practitioner or a suitably qualified nurse. There must also be a proper proportion of qualified nurses employed in the care of patients.

All nursing homes in Great Britain are required to register with and be regulated by an Area Health Authority Board. Official supervision is generally the joint responsibility of a nurse and a doctor; the Area Nursing Officer for Local Authority Liaison and the Community Health Physician for Social Services. As a rule they pay at least one statutory visit a year and periodically visit informally.

It can be very difficult to find a home which will take an old person suffering from a progressive psychiatric disorder. Most nursing homes do have definite criteria on what category of patient they feel equipped to handle; for instance, some won't take those who are blind, others won't take those who can't dress themselves.

The majority of homes provide excellent care, are comfortably furnished, have central heating and are well kept, externally and internally. If an aged person is still mobile and mentally alert, every effort should be made to find a home that has a sitting room and a dining room, so that the old person will have a variety of surroundings.

Any relative helping to choose a home should go and visit as many as possible so as to try to assess the degree of care patients receive and, particularly, whether or not the atmosphere is happy. Asking old people how they feel about the care they receive is apt to

be a waste of time, as they may not be able to be completely truthful, fearing disfavour from the staff if they are critical.

Some homes are quite unsatisfactory, some staff can be impatient and treat their work as a 9 to 5 job. Adjustment to any type of institutionalised living can be difficult. It is essential that close family contact is retained if an aged person is to settle in happily.

Admission
Application for admission should generally be made to the home.

Charges
Fees are not much indication of the standard of a particular home, and can be anything from £100 a week upwards.

Sources of information on nursing homes
The Elderly Invalids Fund, 10 Fleet Street, London, EC4, can advise on the quality of many nursing homes, and the National Council for the Single Woman and Her Dependants, 29 Chilworth Mews, London, W2, keeps a list of short-stay nursing homes. The local authority will have a list of homes in its area. See also the reference to Mrs Gould's Advisory Centre for the Elderly (GRACE) on page 169.

FOR MORE INFORMATION ON HOUSING CONSULT:

HOUSING ADVICE CENTRES
The personnel at Housing Advice Centres provide advice, free of charge, on any housing problems relating either to private or council housing. The centres are run by voluntary groups or local authority housing departments. They are listed in the telephone directory under the name of the borough council in which they are, and the Citizens Advice Bureau has a list of them.

CITIZENS ADVICE BUREAUX
Addresses will be found in the telephone directory.

Local housing authority departments
Addresses will be found in the telephone directory, under the name of the local council.

The Department of the Environment
The DOE (in Scotland, The Scottish Development Department, SDD), is the government department responsible for housing policy in both the public and private sector. It issues explanatory leaflets which are free. The address is:

The Department of the Environment,
Building 3, Victoria Road,
South Ruislip, HA4 N2.

The leaflets can also be obtained from the Housing Advice Centres and CABs.

The National Federation of Housing Associations
This body is at 32 Southampton Street, The Strand, London, WC1, and can supply details of housing schemes throughout the country.

The social worker
The social worker at the local authority social services department can provide advice, and practical help to old persons about their housing situation.

Some Organisations with Residential Homes

The Abbeyfield Society,
35A High Street,
Potters Bar, Herts, EN6 5DL.

The British Red Cross Society,
9 Grosvenor Crescent,
London, SW1X 7EJ.

The Church Army Sunset and Anchorage Homes,
CSC House,
North Circular Road,
London, NW10 7UG.

The Civil Service Benevolent Fund,
Watermead House,

Sutton Court Road,
Sutton, Surrey, SM1 4TF.

Distressed Gentlefolk's Aid Association,
Vicarage Gate House,
Kensington,
London, W8 4AQ.

The Friends of the Elderly and Gentlefolk's Help,
42 Ebury Street,
London, SW1W 0LZ.

Jewish Welfare Board,
315–317 Ballards Lane,
London, N12 8LP.

Methodist Homes for the Aged,
1 Central Buildings,
London, SW1H 9NS.

Mutual Households Association,
Cornhill House,
41 Kingsway,
London, WC2B 6UB.

The Religious Society of Friends,
Friends House,
Euston Road,
London, NW1 2BJ.

The Royal British Legion,
Pall Mall,
London, SW1Y 5JY.

Royal United Kingdom Beneficent Assoc.,
6 Avonmore Road,
London, W14 8RL.

The Salvation Army Women's Social Service,
280 Mare Street,
Hackney, E8 1HE.

Men's Social Services,
110–12 Middlesex Street,
London, E1 7HZ.

The SOS Society,
14 Culford Gardens,
London, SW3 2SU.

Women's Royal Voluntary Service,
17 Old Park Lane,
London, W1Y 4AJ.

Chapter 11
Caring for an Aged, Infirm or Disabled Person

Looking after an aged, infirm or disabled person can be satisfying or it can be difficult. Generally there will be satisfaction in a relationship which has always been a happy one. A dear kind mother rarely becomes a demanding, possessive, aggressive old person, and alternatively, a gentle agreeable husband seldom develops unreasonable domineering characteristics through infirmity or disability in old age. Some personality changes can be attributed to illness; however, many manifestations of unpleasantness are simply exaggerated earlier behavioural traits.

Anyone who undertakes the care of an aged, infirm or disabled person should consciously take steps from the outset to preserve her own independence and individuality.

Every prospective carer should check on what primary health care team support is available, and what social services and voluntary help can be invoked to alleviate the caring burden. Then a proper perspective should be kept throughout the caring period, and the appropriate support system set in motion as soon as its need is indicated.

The primary health care team – occupational therapist, an auxiliary nurse, a health visitor (see pages 21–3) – will give guidance and shoulder a substantial part of the caring burden.

The social worker (page 14) can assess the situation and advise on action which will reduce the overall responsibility; she can arrange for equipment (page 86) to be borrowed, for attendance at day centres (page 55), for nursing home care (page 176) or for residential care (page 173) and her intervention should not be shunned, merely because she is younger than one would want or works according 'to the book'.

The GP can arrange for short term admission to a geriatric unit (page 95) or where constant nursing is required, for night relief. Before a carer actually becomes involved, the idea of night relief or short term admissions may be seen as out of the question, yet the constant demand on the carer's energies without respite, can lead to a breakdown in her health.

Voluntary services (page 11) can provide valuable help by way of relief sitters-in and persons to help with home maintenance. We do not live in an ideal society and none of us enjoys accepting help gratis, yet we must be realistic and, if voluntary help will relieve us, we have a duty to ourselves to accept it.

Self dignity is every person's right and a harmonious environment can exist only where it is not undermined by one or other party. The aged should be encouraged to cope for as long as they can, and those who assume responsibility for their care, should not become completely immersed in the role to the exclusion of the preservation of their own quality of life.

Prior to embarking on the discussion of any particular group, may we emphasise that the majority of aged people carry on alone to the end, or virtually to the end, because that is what they want.

We are going to examine how best to evaluate whether or not an aged person should be left to carry on. Also, the general challenges and some solutions to problems in the caring relationship, categorised into emotional, financial and practical, that can arise where the old person is cared for by a person or persons in the family, and then more specifically each group's particular problems.

Before an adult child undertakes the care of a parent, or parent-in-law, an objective evaluation of the parent's need should be made on the basis of the following:

- The parent's real state of health, as determined by her GP.
- Where her spouse has just died, whether or not she is a well-adjusted person, who, after a normal period of mourning, should be able to adjust adequately to coping alone.
- Whether or not there are responsible people in daily contact with her who will be alerted to any sudden changes – such as milkman or postman. The neighbours could be asked to watch for any change in the general pattern – the milk not being collected from the doorstep, mail being left in the letter box, clothes not being taken in from the line, etc.
- Whether or not she would be able to maintain her home practically and financially and cope with its structural problems, such as stairs or outdoor WC, bearing in mind that housing grants (page 158) for improvements and adaptations and financial allowances such as rent and rate rebates may be available (see page 156).
- The housing being made as hazard-free as possible – railings on the stairs wall, bath grip rails, non-slip mats, lighting over the stairs.
- The house should be checked to see that it is adequately heated in winter.
- The gas should be monitored for leaks and the electricity checked for faulty wiring.
- A telephone should be installed.
- Whether or not she will be objective and admit when she can no longer cope.

If the family decides, and more importantly, if the aged parent recognises and agrees that she can no longer cope, family intervention and the primary health care team – occupational therapist, district nurse, and the social services – home help, meals on wheels, may be able to provide adequate support for her to carry on alone for a while longer. However, sober thought should be given to the extra time and energy that the family will have to invest in giving support under these conditions. The constant wear and tear on their own health can produce serious family conflict situations and can cause their own health to break down. Many old people develop an exaggerated dependency at this time and become unreasonable and unpleasant if all their whims are not met.

In the event that increased help is needed, the available options are sheltered housing (see page 169), nursing homes (see page 176), residential care (page 173), or more extensive family support through the aged person's family assuming responsibility for her care.

Often an adult child's decision to bring a parent into her own home to care for her results from family or social pressure. The thought of what family, friends or neighbours will say if a parent is put into sheltered housing or residential care can be very influential, and in many cases such an arrived at decision will, regrettably, not be good for either the old person or the family.

However, in the event that an old person's family does decide to care for her, they should be aware of some of the more common problems that could arise.

THE EMOTIONAL ANGLE

At an emotional level the family must want to look after an aged person; a reluctant caring atmosphere can cause severe distress in the dependant, and resentment in the carer.

- Where she moves in with her family, she will have to make profound adjustments to her 'new' life-style. It will not be simple effectively to relinquish control over her own life after years of having been self-reliant. Her adjustment may prove difficult and she may manifest her adjustment difficulties in unco-operative, dominating behaviour.

- To encourage her to retain as much of her independence as is acceptable within the changed environment, she should keep up with her old contacts. Physical infirmity and the need for intensified caring ought not to condemn an aged person to being deprived of peer company.

- Many well-meaning families essentially coddle their aged parents – they put them in rocking chairs in the corner and wait on them hand and foot. Such attitudes can be destructive. Independence means doing as much as possible oneself. For instance, although an old person is very disabled from a stroke or arthritis, she should be encouraged to dress herself. There are gadgets available to assist; long handled shoe horns, gadgets to pull up zippers, etc.

No-one should be left to stare out of a window all day. The interest of ninety-nine per cent of people can be stimulated into some creative activity or some absorbing hobby. Dressmaking, knitting for the grandchildren, making lavender sachets, making coathanger covers, hand sewing Christmas gifts or gifts for all members of the family and friends; pressing flowers, weaving, painting, making sweets, growing African violets, collecting china, glass or for that matter, anything. Men often find carpentry all absorbing. On a less creative level, dominoes, bingo, cards, fishing, women's guild meetings, travelogues, can fill many hours, provide an opportunity to reminisce and give one a reason to make the effort to put on a tidy appearance and to get out and about. Many old people either stay in bed or just sit because life has ceased to be challenging. It is the responsibility of those around them to re-activate some old interest or to encourage them to develop new interests. Everyone should be encouraged to do as much as possible for herself, to keep up her hobbies (a mutual hobby between carer and the disabled person is a rewarding investment); and to participate in what is going on around her.

- If the dependent has to be left alone while the carer goes out or goes to work, she should be tolerant and not endeavour to dominate the carer's life while she is there. Many infirm or disabled people cannot accept their infirmity or disablement and they tend to use their family as a prop for their own psychological maladjustments. Of course, they may be apprehensive or even fearful of the future, yet their carer is entitled to retain her own sense of identity despite having agreed to shoulder the caring responsibility.

- The majority of carers do feel anxious when they have to leave a disabled or infirm person alone and their anxiety adds to the overall strain of the caring role.

- In any caring situation, there can be a reversal of previously accepted roles, and intensive interdependence can and does build up.

- If caring is to prove tolerable, the carer must have some respite, and it is critical for her to get away periodically for holidays.

- In an effort to alleviate part of the caring burden, other members of the family should be encouraged to share the responsibility and demands.

Particularly where the old person needs constant care:

- She will increasingly feel that she is a burden on the family or individual adult child.

- All essential help services should be invoked before the situation becomes critical.

- Short term admissions to a geriatric ward should give the person responsible for caring, whether it is one person caring alone or a family, some relief from the perpetual demands on their time and energy.

THE FINANCIAL ANGLE

At the financial level the whole impact of assuming the caring responsibility should be closely looked at; the effect on occupational pension, the likely assimilation of savings and the availability of financial benefits, both short and long term. Many persons blithely give up their jobs to take care of the infirm or disabled elderly in the misinformed belief that 'the government will pay them'. Nothing could be further from reality. There are two, shall we call them, main caring benefits; one is known as the Attendance Allowance, which an old person may claim if her disability fits a definite criterion (see page 140) and the Invalid Care Allowance which is payable to a carer (see page 142) who is under pensionable age and who has given up work to care for an old person who is in receipt of the Attendance Allowance.

- State Pensions of those not working because they are looking after someone at home may now be protected (see page 133).
- If an aged disabled person is not to feel she is an encumbrance, and the person responsible for her care is not to feel that their resources are being strained, some definite financial arrangement should be decided upon from the outset.
- In the case where a single person gives up work (and consequently jeopardises her chances of returning to employment in the future) then ideally, the disabled person should make some financial provision for that person under the terms of her will.

THE PRACTICAL ANGLE

At the practical level, every measure available should be taken to ensure as complete an adjustment to the new environment as possible. The aged person's immediate surroundings, the area which has been allocated to her as her own living area, should reflect her personality and taste. She should be encouraged to furnish her room with her own furniture, and this should be her domain. In an ideal arrangement, each party should be able to withdraw into some privacy if they wish.

Some families actively encourage privacy for their elder by providing her with a small, safe-to-use cooking unit on a table in her room; for instance, an electric toaster, frypan and kettle, so that she can make a quick snack or make herself or a friend a cup of tea without having to make use of the family kitchen.

- The old person should be encouraged actively to contribute to family life by accepting responsibility for certain chores (as far as her state of health permits). For example, if a woman, she could do the dusting, peel the vegetables, sort the laundry and make the puddings. It is very important that they be regarded as in her domain. The whole purpose of giving her a sense of responsibility will be lost if someone in the family either directs her *modus operandi* or perpetually criticises.

An elderly man, if well enough, could be responsible for part of the garden, for seeing that the newspapers are bundled up, etc.

Generally, a healthy fatigue follows some physical activity with responsibility behind it.

Caring should be systematised; duplication and overlap should be avoided and every effort made to conserve time and energy. A few examples should illustrate the wisdom behind the above statement:

- If a disabled person is to be bathed, bed cradles, etc. should be moved, linen made ready to change the bed; equipment used in bathing and a change of clothing should be at hand.
- Where a house has upstairs bedrooms, items to be taken up or down should be accumulated in a plastic hamper at the top and bottom of the stairs, and one trip made only when there is a manageable load.
- Setting a bed-bound person up for a couple of hours; drinks, food, books, radio, portable TV (with a remote control switch), a clock, an easily accessible lamp, etc. can give the aged ill person a definite sense of independence, and economise on the carer's effort and time.

- The main emphasis in the whole caring scene should be on the end product; the process is important only in that it affects the main product, and it is this which is the important factor. Financial resources will determine how many 'corners one can cut'. Drip dry clothes, carpets instead of linoleum, frozen pre-packaged foods, etc. all save labour.
- Some degree of loneliness can be offset by getting a dog, a cat or budgie into the home. No-one can feel all alone if a cat or dog is curled up on the end of the bed, or a budgie is chirping in a cage by the window.
- All supportive services should be invoked before they are urgently needed, to relieve the caring burden. It should be remembered at all times that there are two entities in every caring relationship – the infirm or disabled person and the carer. Each must, as far as possible, work at the relationship being a happy one.

In an effort to avoid duplication we have not repeated information which is common to the overall caring responsibility; readers are asked to refer back to the general section above in addition to the section pertinent to them.

DIFFICULTIES WITH WHICH THE CARER MAY HAVE TO COPE

The relationship that can develop between the aged infirm or disabled person and the carer can be complex. There are undoubtedly many caring situations in which mutual love and understanding blossom, and on the demise of the disabled person the carer feels that her devoted attention has been very worthwhile.

Disablement can produce personality changes, and it can make a once self-sufficient person almost completely emotionally as well as physically dependant on another. Some carers become so involved in the caring role that they subjugate their own needs in those of the aged person and somewhere in the fulfilment of that role they lose their own identity. Let us examine some of the 'teeth in the loving trap'.

Unpredictable display of affection and appreciation

Many infirm old persons tend to inundate generally uncommunicative, unhelpful family members with admiration and praise when they appear on the scene, and show little if any gratitude to someone who is always there, and who has assumed full responsibility for their care. This attitude can cause distress and even depression in an already over-strained carer. Probably knowing that such an attitude is universal will make it easier to tolerate.

Anger

It is not uncommon for someone who is caring for an old person to lose patience, to become angry at the limitations put upon their own lifestyle, at the constant demands on their time and energy. Before the critical period, as we shall call it, is reached, that is, when the carer suspects that control is being lost, a professional should be consulted.

Anti-social attitudes

There are some aged people who behave abominably either because they have always had a domineering, irrational approach to everyone and everything, or because they want to retain the last vestiges of power over others. Such behaviour can and does lead to unreasonable demands being made on carers. A person who has previously been easily dominated will almost certainly become more dominated. Quite often the old person will cleverly conceal the 'Dr. Jekyll' tendencies, and be very pleasant and agreeable when others are present. Alternatively there are some carers who are aggressive, overpowering individuals, whose behaviour towards an infirm or disabled person is most reprehensible.

Return to the child role

When an adult child undertakes the care of an old parent there is a propensity for the parent to treat the carer as a child again. This attitude can produce irritation and frustration in the carer and a general unco-operativeness in the parent.

Depression

The limitations that caring can place on a carer's life style can cause the carer to become depressed. This depression will often manifest itself in illness and overall fatigue. Just watching a loved person's health deteriorate can produce a depression.

Alcohol as an escape

A treadmill from which there doesn't seem to be an escape, tensions, constant demands on time and energy, being unable to unwind, a sense of being trapped, can all lead to carers using alcohol as an escape. Often what began as the only way to get away from it all for a brief period will tend to become an alcohol problem.

The aged themselves are not exempt from using alcohol as an escape from the impact of their disablement on their lives or their sense of feeling a burden on their family.

Emotional blackmail

Perhaps one of the most cruel and tantalising types of behaviour is emotional blackmail. The adult child continues to indentify with the parent: the parent is their vehicle for self recognition and self identification. Many parents use this filial tie as a tool – they dominate a carer's life by insisting that if they are left alone they could die. This blackmail puts a strain on the carer – despite her need to get away from the scene, she will be afraid to go in case the old person should die. She will be afraid of the guilt she recognises she will know if the parent does in fact have an accident or die, when she has been left. A dilemma often builds up; the carer's logic and urge for self preservation drawing her in one direction, and the fear of any resultant guilt drawing her in the other.

Exhaustion

The prime motivating force for many adult children to accept a full-time caring role is due to the exhaustion from simultaneously trying to do a full time job and cope with caring. The incessant 'on the way home from work visits' to check that everything is all right, or for the out-of-towner, the whole weekend taken in tripping to and fro and doing cleaning and shopping while there, can cause anyone's health to break down.

For those who have assumed the caring role there is, ironically enough, often a great reluctance to invoke the aid of the statutory or voluntary services until the carers own health begins to fail. Many carers actually deceive themselves into believing that only they can cope, even when they recognise that they are quite worn out. At that stage, outside intervention can prove virtually impossible and even be resented. Often we hear the anxious words that 'the home help won't do the corners as well as mother likes them done' or 'the volunteer may let father fall out of bed'. Worrying is normal but worry devoid of logic is serious, as all perspective can be lost.

Frustration

Caring can and does produce varying degrees of frustration. Those who have relinquished a life of their own, a career, marriage, retirement dreams, can become overwhelmed by general dissatisfaction and frustration with their actual life.

A guilt complex

Guilt can be all destructive. There are a number of causes of guilt in a carer; a deep seated wish to be relieved of the whole role; a hankering to go back to a career and to leave the old person to cope; for agreeing to a disabled person being admitted to residential care and for not having assumed the caring role.

Physical and mental strain

Caring can seriously affect either or both mental and physical health. The demands on one's emotions are often endless. There is seldom any prospect of the type or intensity of the demands changing – on the contrary, they will probably only intensify with time and the deterioration in the health of the old person.

Preservation of dignity
Regrettably, there are those carers who develop a maternal attitude towards the person for whose care they are responsible. Their behaviour robs the old person of their last vestige of dignity. One of the most demeaning situations any human being has to face is where she is spoken down to or spoken to in the third person such as 'how are little old we today?' Quite possibly, such behaviour is one only of thoughtlessness, yet it can lead to resignation or to distress.

Propensity to social isolation
Any old infirm or disabled person is very vulnerable to social isolation. Few aged people regard their families as representing 'social contacts', thus every effort should be made by those taking care of the disabled aged to bring others into the caring scene from the very outset of the disability. (See relief sitters-in, volunteers, etc. page 11).

Carers of the aged disabled are also very prone to such social isolation, which can affect their physical and mental health during the caring period, or on the demise of the dependant, or both. This can be particularly so for the single daughter. Many women forego the chance of marriage or any kind of relationship with a man because they feel that the elder's need for care represents the higher priority.

In truth, a carer who marries should still be able to give loving care to an elder. She will be less isolated and have her husband and later her children as support.

Undoubtedly there are old people who quite often tacitly discourage their single daughter (and sons) from outside relationships on the understandable, if however selfish, grounds that they will be deserted. Any continuous interference by a parent in any relationship should be interpreted as the parent looking out for herself. The adult child should decide to take the course that will bring her the most happiness, bearing in mind that her parent had a fulfilled life and that she won't have her parent forever.

One of the cardinal rules of caring is that the carer must regularly get away from the scene. The responsibility for preventing serious social isolation from overwhelming her life is therefore in her hands. She should invoke family, voluntary and statutory help to give her some respite from caring and a little time to herself.

Interdependency
A strong interdependency can build up between the carer and the aged dependant, unless steps are taken from the outset to preserve each other's independence. Each can get to the stage of being virtually totally reliant on the other. The infirm or disabled person will rely entirely on the carer. She will become jealously possessive and refuse outside intervention by family, friends, professionals or volunteers.

The carer will begin to feel that only she can cope. She may even begin to treat the aged person as 'her doll' – a useless, helpless being who has to be cared for twenty-four hours a day. It is amazing how many single women carers insist that they are actually involved in caring for twenty-four hours a day.

Loneliness
Loneliness, or the condition of feeling lonely, does not necessarily have to occur in a situation where one lives alone; it is possible to be lonely in a crowd. Those whose lives are restricted by the demands of the person for whom they are caring often become lonely through the virtual social isolation imposed on them by those demands. When the relative dies, they can be devastatingly lonely in that not only have they been socially isolated, but they believe they no longer have any real purpose to their lives. It is essential to keep in contact with people and not to become com-

pletely immersed in the care of the aged person.

Resentment

There are certainly some aged persons who deeply resent having to depend on anyone and they manifest this resentment in a contrary attitude to those who care for them.

Then there are those who have taken on responsibility for meeting an old person's caring needs, but who deeply resent the burdens that caring imposes on them. Their resentment can even be extended to other, untaxed members of the family.

In the final analysis, how well the carer copes with the challenges and problems of the caring role will depend upon her awareness of what to expect, her ability to make decisions and adhere to them , and her knowledge of what help is available and the measures she can implement to alleviate her burden.

Caring relationships and situations have been classified according to the familial relationship between the infirm or disabled person and the carer.

A married woman taking an aged parent (or other aged relative) to live with her family:

where the woman continues to work,
where she has to give up work.

A husband caring for his wife:

where he continues to work,
where either he has retired or he has to give up work.

A wife caring for her husband:

where she continues to work,
where she gives up work.

A single woman caring for an aged infirm parent (or other disabled relative) (most of this information equally applies to a single caring son, and some aspects will of course apply to all categories of career):

where she continues to work and care for her parent,
where she gives up work and stays at home,

where she stays at work and takes her parent to live with her,
where she wants to get off the work treadmill,
where she decides to give up her work and her own living accommodation and return home to care for her disabled parent.

THE SPECIFIC CHALLENGES AND SOME SOLUTIONS FOR A CARING MARRIED WOMAN

At one time few married women were economically active, or more simply, worked outside the home, and the ambit of their ultimate responsibilities often extended to the care of their infirm or disabled old parents or parents-in-law.

Today, however, society's structure has radically changed. The aged can no longer presume that when they reach the stage of needing help, that as a matter of course, they will have the option to move in with their married child. And before a married person takes an infirm or disabled parent or parent-in-law (or other aged relative) into her household, the first requirement should be that there is a stable marriage that does not have any extra demands on it, such as the needs of a handicapped child, or cramped living conditions.

Where many grandparents add a new and exciting dimension to life for grandchildren in some households, three generations together can produce serious conflicts in others.

Where a married woman has assumed the care of an aged parent and continues to work

Emotionally

● There may be a conflict of loyalty between her work and her caring responsibilities.
● Once she has returned from work, she may find that her loyalties are divided between

the old person who has been alone all day on the one side, and her husband and children on the other side. These added demands can lead to inner conflict, frustration and an increase in overall fatigue.

Financially
- If she continues to work she should be able to afford more help.

Practically
- The twofold demands made on her time and energy can provide a treadmill situation which seems never ending.
- A home help, if available, could alleviate part of her overall responsibilities. The disabled person's attendance at a Day Centre may relieve her of part of the burden and worry.

Where a married woman gives up her job

Emotionally
- She may feel frustrated that she can no longer pursue her career, or have the companionship that working brings.
- The aged parent may become completely dependent on her at an earlier stage than would otherwise have been the case.
- Her own family relationships may suffer from her being unable to invest adequate time and energy in them because of the parent's increasing demands.
- Her social life will virtually cease.

Financially
- The family's standard of living could be seriously reduced because she is no longer economically active.
- A married woman generally cannot claim the Invalid Care Allowance even though the person for whom she is caring receives the Attendance Allowance.
- Her State Pension may now be protected (see page 133).
- Her chances of returning to paid work will be affected.

Practically
- Because she is home all day, she will tend to accept that the whole caring load is her complete responsibility and she will tend to be dilatory about bringing in available supportive services.
- All appropriate caring equipment should be used.
- Short-term admissions to hospital should be used to give her a rest from caring full time.

Some married sons or daughters who have never quite severed the umbilical cord, and whose marriages are not very happy, tend to neglect their own families by accepting an intensive invigilating role over their infirm but quite capable and coping parent. What the adult child is doing of course, is making the parent's infirmity an excuse for not devoting their principal energies to their own home and family.

THE SPECIFIC CHALLENGES AND SOME SOLUTIONS FOR A CARING HUSBAND

Traditionally a wife accepts responsibility for the housekeeping and family home nursing; she identifies first with that role. If she becomes disabled, she will have either to delegate or completely relinquish the role, and this change in contribution pattern can have indirect repercussions on an already strained atmosphere.

Where a husband assumes the care of a disabled wife and continues to work

Emotionally
- He will probably have a conflict of loyalty to his work and her care.
- However disabled the wife is, she will generally be distressed or even resentful that her husband has to take over her role. This will be particularly so where she has not worked outside the home.
- The husband may feel resentful that his wife is disabled and that he therefore has to look after her.

- A wife's disablement can seriously affect their conjugal relationship; sexual expression can be the pivot on which happiness depends, and its frustration can cause discontent and misery. SPOD, 49 Victoria Street, London, SW1, 01–222 6007, will refer any enquirer to appropriate therapists and counsellors, who will advise on how to continue to enjoy sex if one is disabled.

We all have our own particular brand of conjugal responses, or more bluntly, making love, and for years we may have continued to engage in particular forms of love play and postures. Disability can seriously affect these 'methods' as we'll call them, and because we are too embarrassed or too distressed we may avoid discussing any problems with our partners. SPOD therapists and counsellors are trained to help in identifying problems and in finding alternate 'methods', so that as normal as possible a conjugal life can be carried on. It is important to remember that to trained professionals the human body is a unit which should function as well as possible, and they do not look upon your particular problem as a matter of curiosity; their objective is to help you strictly from a professional standpoint.

- His social life will virtually cease.

Financially
- He should be better able to afford help.
- He won't lose part of his occupational pension.
- He should be better able to afford holidays.

Holidays fulfil two important functions; they break routine and they present the opportunity to see new places and to meet new people, which give another dimension to life. Some people enjoy going off to a quiet retreat type of place, others like to return to a favourite place, others appreciate going as a member of a group. The essential point is that a holiday is a must! Caring is wearing on one's emotions and stamina, and in getting away, both the mind and the body can be built up again.

Although the disabled wife may remonstrate about being left with a relative, in a geriatric ward, or with someone else in the house substituting for the caring husband, in fact the change, if made, will generally pep up her spirits and give her a new perspective. A husband can make the change easier for her to accept by reassuring her that for both their sakes he needs a rest. If a relief carer is to take over, the more dominant of his wife's foibles can be explained and every care taken to ensure as far as possible that a personality clash doesn't occur.

For those who want to take a holiday in groups, one company offering older people good package tours is Saga. One should not feel lonely on one of their tours. The Saga offer includes:
- Return rail travel from one's local BR station to Gatwick or to London from where a coach is used for transport to Heathrow, if air travel is involved.
- Light refreshments served during travelling.
- All airport taxes paid.
- Transfer between the foreign airport and the hotel or apartment.
- Full board accommodation throughout the holiday (except for self catering holidays).
- In a foreign country, the services of an English speaking representative.
- Comprehensive insurance cover to protect against cancellation charges, medical costs, baggage and personal accident.

There is plenty of companionship and opportunity to meet and make new friends.

For more information, write to Saga Holidays, 119 Southgate Road, Folkestone, Kent. Tel: 0303–30321.

Practically
- A home help or meals on wheels or his wife's attendance at a Day Centre should relieve him of part of the overall caring burden.

Where he has retired or where he has given up work

Emotionally
- Unless he is a truly remarkable person, he will be disappointed that he couldn't fulfil his retirement plans. Or he will be very

disappointed that his retirement plans will be affected by his reduced income. Many men have a pyschological barrier to assuming what they regard as the 'wife's job', and their resentment can be manifested in an abrupt thoughtless attitude which can be very distressing, particularly where there had previously been a relatively happy relationship. The wife's disability will be more difficult for her to accept in such an atmosphere.

- Socially, he will tend to become isolated, and therefore he should arrange for regular sitters-in to come, so that he can get away from the scene. He shouldn't feel guilty about taking a holiday.

Financially
- He won't be able to afford so much help.
- If he had to give up his job, his state pension may be protected (see page 133).

Practically
- There shouldn't be so much pressure on his schedule and he should be able to better organise his time.
- He should bring in the appropriate support services before their need is critical.
- All appropriate caring equipment should be used. Equipment ranges from an elevated lavatory seat, to aids to help with dressing and eating, to equipment to assist a disabled person in walking. The more independence a person has, the happier she will be. It can be very demeaning for anyone to have to help with putting on underclothing, to be spoon fed or to be helped with drinking. There are gadgets to help with zippers, etc. and there are long handled eating tongs. A simple rubber bicycle handle cover pulled onto the end of a knife, fork or spoon handle will make the handle non-slip and easier to grip. A two handled drinking cup can preserve some dignity. A zimmer frame will give confidence to the person finding mobility difficult. Hoists can be a big morale booster and a tremendous help to a carer.

The district nurse will advise on what equipment is advisable in your dependant's particular case.

- He should continue to ask his wife's advice re housekeeping so that she will retain some definite sense of identity. For instance, before he goes shopping, he can consult her about restocking the larder. She'll relish going through her dried goods, canned goods, substitute foods, etc. list and advising him on what are the best buys for that particular time of year. If she suggests simmering up the turkey bones for soup when he was about to throw them out, he will make her happy if he agrees that turkey soup would save on their budget (which it would) and be very tasty. As Shakespeare said 'All the world's a stage ... each man in his time plays many parts'. It is important to remember at all times that disability is a burden to bear, but the presence of the burden should not rob the disabled person of her (or his) dignity and sense of usefulness.

THE SPECIFIC CHALLENGES AND SOME SOLUTIONS FOR A CARING WIFE

Where a wife has to take care of a disabled husband and continues to work

Emotionally
- She will have a conflict of loyalty to her work and his need for care.
- If traditionally he has been the decision-maker, she may feel anxious and frightened about attending to the business aspects of their lives.
- Because she has accepted that part of her role is family home nurse, she will be particularly distressed about leaving him while she is at work.
- If there has been a good relationship, he will feel anxiety about the extra load his disability is placing on her.
- She may have to cope with the menopause and their changed conjugal relationship

(see the specific challenges of a caring husband re conjugal problems.

- Disability occurring around retirement age can produce severe depression and although she may be able to cope with the physical demands made on her by his disability, his resultant depression may be 'the straw that breaks the camel's back'.
- Her social life will virtually cease.

Financially
- She should be better able to afford more help.
- She should be better able to afford holidays.

Practically
- A home help, meals on wheels, or the husband's attendance at a Day Centre, should relieve her of part of the caring burden.
- Her husband's periodic admission to a geriatric unit should help.

Where a wife has to give up her work

Emotionally
- She may resent having to give up work and having to live on a reduced income.
- Socially she will tend to become more isolated and therefore should arrange for relief sitters-in so that she can get away regularly. She should take a holiday.

Financially
- Her occupational pension will be affected.
- She won't be able to afford so much help.
- Her state pension may now be protected (see page 133).
- Her chances of returning to paid work will be affected.

Practically
- She should be better able to organise her schedule and have more time to relax.

- She should bring in the appropriate support services before their intervention is critical.
- All appropriate caring equipment should be used.
- She should consult her husband for directives on home maintenance, particularly for jobs she should be able to manage, as she will generally save money and help his ego this way. For instance, she should be able to paper a wall, paint a room, change a washer in a leaking tap, change a fuse, etc. under his guidance. Of course she should try to assess how long any particular job will take and whether or not it will be too strenuous for her; only she will know how much reserve energy she has.
- Overall a husband caring for a wife or a wife caring for a husband should be sensitive to the other's continuing need to feel an important part of the other's life.

THE SPECIFIC CHALLENGES AND SOLUTIONS FOR A SINGLE WOMAN CARING FOR AN INFIRM OR DISABLED PARENT (OR OTHER AGED INFIRM DISABLED RELATIVE)

(Most of this information can be applied to the single caring son's position.) This category of carer may find herself in one of the situations given below:

- Where she continues to work and care for her parent.
- Where she decides to leave work and stay at home to care for her aged parent.
- Where she decides to give up her job and her own living accommodation and return home to care for her disabled parent.
- Where she stays at work and takes her aged parent to live with her so that she can care for her.
- Where she wants to get off the 'work treadmill'.

Where a single woman decides to continue to work and care for her parent (where she lives in the parent's home)

Emotionally
- She will experience a conflict of loyalty with her work and her parent's need for care.
- She will be anxious about the parent while she is away.
- Generally, unlike a family situation, there won't be anyone else either on whom she can rely, because of her single situation and because, if there are siblings, they often 'don't want to know'.
- Her social life will virtually cease.
- The strain of being continuously in demand once she has returned from work, together with broken sleep, can be quite overwhelming and prove emotionally and physically exhausting.

Financially
- She should be able to afford more help.
- She should be able to take much needed holidays.

Practically
- A home help, meals on wheels, or her parent going to a Day Centre, should relieve part of her overall burden.
- Her parent's periodic admission to a short term geriatric unit should help.

Where a single woman decides to give up her work and stay at home to care for a disabled parent

Emotionally
- If there has been parental domination and possessiveness before, this will tend to become exaggerated.
- Some people wallow in being martyrs – and assume burdens to breaking point.
- She is likely to be frustrated and resentful if she cannot carry on with her career.
- She will become increasingly prone to social isolation.

- Increased vulnerability to an intensive interdependency pattern.
- Her social life will virtually cease.

Financially
- She could become financially dependent on her parent.
- She will have to run down her savings to £1249 before she can claim Supplementary Benefit (see page 136).
- If she is under pensionable age, and may qualify therefore for the Invalid Care Allowance, she will have to wait six months (if her parent is disabled enough to receive the Attendance Allowance) before she can claim the Invalid Care Allowance (see page 142).
- Her occupational pension will be reduced.
- State pension rights for those who have given up work for home caring may be protected by the Home Responsibilities Protection regulations which came into effect in April 1978 (see page 133).
- Her chances of returning to remunerative employment will be seriously jeopardised.

Practically
- The combination of the impact of the demands of caring – broken sleep being part of that impact – being continuously active and the responsibility for the housekeeping will be reduced.
- It is essential from the outset to deploy whatever supportive services are available and establish some definite relief periods, in an effort to preserve a sense of self identity and not to become exhausted.

For information on short term relief and Holiday Homes send for the respective National Council for the Single Woman brochures (see address NCSWD page 176).

Where she decides to give up her job and her own living accommodation and return home to care for disabled parent

Emotionally
- She will have to relinquish the self-effected way of life which she has created for herself.

- She will miss the stimulation and independence her work gave her and probably feel resentful.
- Where she has been having a relationship with a man or any other close friendship, these will be affected.
- Unless she is adamant about 'running her own life', she will incur the real risk of having what should be her decisions made for her by her parent.
- If she was previously dominated, the possessiveness will tend to increase.

Financially
See above.

Practically
- In an effort to preserve a sense of self identity and not to become exhausted, it is essential from the outset to deploy whatever supportive services are available and to establish some definite relief periods.

  For information on short-term relief and holiday schemes, send for the respective National Council for the Single Woman and Her Dependants brochures (see address page 176).

Where a single woman stays at work and takes her parent to live with her so that she can look after her

Emotionally
- Each party will have to make adjustment to the arrangement.
- The single woman's social life will be affected.
- She will be vulnerable to possessiveness and intensive interdependency and should take constructive steps to protect her independence.

Financially
- As she is still working, she should be able to afford more help.
- Her occupational pension will be protected.

Practically
- She will be able to stay at work longer.
- The demands on her overall energy will be increased.
- She must maintain some social life and take holidays.
- She should have some long-term plan on what she will do when or if her parent needs full-time care.

Where a single woman wants to get off the 'work treadmill'

There are single persons who make their parent's infirmity an excuse to society for getting off the work treadmill.

Emotionally
- The adult child may have been predisposed to trying to avoid unpleasant situations and, as their aged parent becomes increasingly infirm, they will try to escape the unpleasant situations (inability to make friends, not being promoted, feeling unattractive to the opposite sex).

Financially
- Unless the old person is really in need of care, the single person will not qualify for any financial benefits.
- Leaving work will reduce her occupational pension.
- Long-term she will damage her chances of returning to remunerative employment.

Practically
- As the caring burden increases, she will probably have more misgivings and end up feeling 'trapped'.

A CARING WIDOW (OR WIDOWER) OR DIVORCEE

Essentially, the single woman's challenges and solutions are common to this group. Perhaps a widow (more often found in the caring role than a widower) is in a more difficult position in some respects than a single person who has never married.

Emotionally

A widow will have established (under normal circumstances) another family unit, have developed a pattern of life around that unit and have had a status similar in society to that of her parent. Re-adapting to the parental 'nest' environment can therefore produce different frustrations and conflicts. Where a woman has been widowed or divorced at an early stage in the marriage, and her parent has been a tower of strength during the aftermath, she often feels a particularly strong sense of duty to repay all that help and understanding during the parent's infirm years.

Despite the problems many carers encounter, the majority are generally very happy that they cared for their old relative (or friend) and say 'I would do it all again'.

Chapter 12
What to do when Someone Dies

This chapter is specifically written for those who are suddenly confronted by the procedure involved in funeral arrangements, etc. As different religious beliefs affect methods and periods of mourning, we have deliberately taken a general approach to the overall topic. There are excellent books written on how to cope with bereavement and therefore we will not attempt to expound at length on that aspect of the subject.

Few people know what to do when someone dies. Death is not a generally discussed topic. However, as sooner or later the majority of us will have to accept responsibility at such a time, a basic knowledge of the main duties will be of inestimable help.

In this chapter we outline the various actions that are necessary immediately after the death, the authorities that have to be contacted and the usual burial procedure. Later we discuss possible bereavement reactions and offer some advice on refinding one's own identity in society.

In the event of an old person dying at home, it is necessary to call the doctor. He has the responsibility of issuing a Certificate of Death. If he has not seen the deceased for a period of longer than fourteen days the coroner has to be informed of the death (see page 32). If an old person had expressed a desire to be cremated, a second doctor's signature will also have to appear on the certificate. The doctor who is called will arrange the second signature.

Where the death has occurred in hospital, the doctor who was in charge at the time of the death will issue a Certificate of Death. And if cremation is to follow, that doctor will arrange for a second doctor to sign the certificate.

The next task is to inform family and friends – this can be very difficult as relatives of course will generally be shocked and upset. The public can be notified by insertion of an announcement in local or national press.

Once the death certificate has been issued, the undertaker may be contacted. At this stage the surviving relatives, particularly the person who has been doing the caring, will generally feel quite overwrought and unable to cope with the arrangements, yet the majority of mourners do cope at this time. They 'hold up' because they are acutely aware of not wanting to fail a loved one in this last earthly act on their behalf. They tend to build a defence mechanism around themselves and to go about the arrangements with a particular calmness.

Some relatives feel happier if the undertaker removes the deceased's body to his premises for it to await the funeral; others prefer it to be left in the house.

The law requires that the death is registered at the office of the Registrar of Births, Marriages and Deaths within whose boundaries the death has occurred. Those persons who do not live in a metropolitan area should note for future reference that some offices are only open on certain days of the week.

If you feel you cannot go to the Registrar's office, then a relative or friend can register a death for you.

Details of the death certificate are entered on the Register, and the Register has to be signed by the person registering the death with the Registrar's pen. The Registrar will want to know the deceased's age and occupation, and age of next of kin. It is essential to register the death within five days in England and Wales, and eight days in Scotland. Once this procedure has been duly completed, a copy of the entry and a disposal certificate, and one free copy of the Certificate of Registration of Death is given to the person registering it. It is advisable to ask for two extra copies, as they may be required for insurance claims purposes and when settling the estate. A small charge is made for extra copies.

Where there is to be an inquest the death cannot be registered.

Equipped with the Certificate of Disposal, it is possible to proceed with the burial arrangements or to apply for cremation. If cremation is to take place, then four more forms have to be filled in. Of course, there is good reason for the requirement of extra forms in the case of cremation, because it is a physical impossibility to exhume a body after cremation, and any later query about the death could not be investigated. Even though no suspicion attaches to your relative's dying, standard procedure nevertheless has to be followed in all cremations.

At this stage the majority of people employ a funeral director to arrange the funeral. He has to be told whether or not the family want the body embalmed, what type of shroud is desired, what type of coffin is needed, whether or not it is to be elaborately lined, how many mourning cars are to be provided and of course, the cemetery or crematorium that has been chosen. His fees can range from £250 to virtually several thousand pounds. If the deceased wanted her remains to be taken to her birthplace, located in another city or country, then the cost is likely to be very high and should be thoroughly investigated before any arrangements are finalised. A written quote of the funeral expenses should always be obtained, as anything more than what are called 'the respectable basics' will quickly add up. Relatives who cannot afford to provide a costly funeral should not feel guilty about it, and the last worry they should have is 'what others will think'.

The custom of wearing all black and being veiled is really only observed for state funerals nowadays. Therefore, the family should not fret over not being able to dress in full mourning clothes.

The question of whether or not grandchildren should attend a grandparent's, aunt's or uncle's funeral often arises. Probably the decision should be made on two grounds: how emotionally stable the child is, and her attachment to the old person. Children should never be told that 'Granny has gone away' because they may assume some guilt for the old person's absence. Perhaps unbeknown to the parent they may have been naughty when last with the old person, and they may feel that the naughtiness caused her to leave for good. It is customary in many families for the womenfolk not to go to the graveside but to make tea for friends and relatives after the funeral. In some cultures, such as the West Indian, a vigil is held on a particular night, and there is joyous singing and celebration for the soul of the deceased person.

At the time between the death and the funeral many people find great support in the presence of their vicar, priest, or rabbi, or in praying to Allah, Buddah or their gods. For those who are Christians, belief in eternal life tends to be all sustaining, as they believe they will be reunited with their loved one in life after death. Buddhists can look forward to reincarnation. The presence of close relatives and friends can temporarily shield a bereaved relative from awful loneliness, after perhaps twenty years of few other contacts than with the deceased.

The funeral procession can start either from the undertaker's premises or from the deceased person's or a relative's home. Alternatively, the body can be taken directly to the cemetery or crematorium, and the mourners can meet there.

If a church service is to precede the burial, the coffin is taken into the church by the bearers, and placed in front of the altar. Family or close friends consider it an honour to pay their last tributes by carrying the deceased's coffin. Some Anglican and Roman Catholic churches allow the coffin to be taken in to the church the previous evening and remain before the altar until after the service.

Where the service has been held at another place, or where no service has been held, the coffin is carried direct from the hearse to the grave. At the grave, the bearers remove the wreaths, and lower the coffin into the grave on webbing slings. Committal words are said, after which the mourners go back to their cars.

Some of the Committal words used at a Church of England burial are:

I am the resurrection and the life, saith the Lord: he that believeth in me, though he were dead, yet shall he live: and whosoever liveth and believeth in me shall never die (John 11.25–6). We brought nothing into this world, and it is certain we carry nothing out (1 Tim. 6.7). The Lord gave, and the Lord hath taken away, blessed be the name of the Lord (Job 1.2).

No-one should go to the funeral of a loved one alone, as the impact of the final act of interment can be very shattering.

In the case of cremation, the service takes place either at the church, with the Committal words said later at the crematorium, or the whole service is at the crematorium. At the stage that the committal words are said, the coffin passes out of sight, either by a curtain being drawn across it or by being moved mechanically through a door.

If the ashes are not left to be scattered, or placed in a niche in a wall at the crematorium, arrangements can be made for the undertaker to send them to a relative. Many relatives have a special rose tree planted at the crematorium in their deceased elder's memory, and the ashes are scattered over the rose garden.

Later, a headstone or other memorial in a churchyard or cemetery can be erected, subject to the restrictions imposed by the church or cemetery.

Of course, funerals do occur without any form of religious ceremony at all. But if a body is to be buried without a ceremony, forty-eight hours' notice is required to be given to the vicar of the relevant parish. Generally vicars will give permission over the telephone. Where no particular form of service has been stipulated, yet one is required, the Church of England service is usually the one that is held.

Denominational burial grounds insist that their own church service be followed.

The fees of the clergyman, gravedigger, chaplain and officials (where required, the organist, etc.) at the cemetery or crematorium are generally paid in advance. The normal procedure is for the undertaker to make the actual payments and put the charges on the total account he submits.

To help defray the cost of a funeral, the Death Grant should be applied for (see below).

THE DEATH GRANT

The full rate: £30
Reduced rate: £15

Although neither rate will cover the full cost of a funeral, it will help a little with the expenses. The grant is paid on the contributions of the deceased, or on those of the husband or wife.

Where the deceased was aged 87 (or 92 for a man) before July 5, 1975, no grant will be paid. If she was 77 (or 82 for a man) before July 5, 1975, only the reduced grant will be paid. The grant is paid to the widow, widower or whoever has paid for, or is going to pay for, the funeral.

To claim the death grant, call in at your local social security office (the address can be found in the phone book) with the death certificate (his/her marriage certificate, if your mother or father is the widow or widower claimant) and a written estimate of the funeral cost.

Where you can't afford a funeral, the local authority is obliged to arrange a simple one. If they arrange the funeral, they receive the death grant. Where you receive a supplementary pension you may get help with the funeral from your local social security office.

See leaflet NI.49 for more information,

obtainable from the local social security office.

BEREAVEMENT

Dying is an inescapable part of living; yet few of us discuss emotions and reactions to dying before we are actually confronted by the death of a loved one. Many old people in fact want to discuss dying and their religious beliefs. Even those who have not been actively religious during their earlier life feel a need to look forward to something after death.

Yet, in Western society we treat the subject as taboo; it is as if we are afraid to talk about it from fear that the ritual and ceremony of it will involve us in death itself.

The death of a close relative closes a chapter in our own lives. In some degree all of us see ourselves as an extension of our parents, and when they die, we lose a certain sense of immortality. For many married people their relationship is seen as inextricable, and the death of a partner can leave the other with feelings ranging from desolation to anger at being left.

The realisation of the physical finality of death, the fact that we won't be able to talk to the deceased again, to tell her that we didn't mean to be thoughtless or selfish, or to feel an all enveloping security from her presence, can cause a surviving relative to feel like a rudderless ship in a sea of despair. Grief is normal, and we must all go through it before we can hope to restructure our lives, yet some of us fall into greater gulfs of sorrow than do others.

It must be remembered that everyone needs to go through some period of grief after a relative has died. If grieving is denied or tranquillised too much, there is a risk that the person left will not be able to re-integrate into society at a happy and adjusted level.

At first, an all-pervading numbness is common. Having to deal with the funeral arrangements at this time can save us from ourselves, and therefore it is unwise to let someone else take over.

After the funeral, insurance and probate matters have to be attended to, and the deceased's clothes and belongings have to be sorted out, and either distributed or disposed of. It is normal to be very distressed at such time, clutching at the last living physical evidence, such as demurring from tossing out a tooth brush or slippers. Then suddenly it will seem that all the formalities have been taken care of, and the terrible abyss that is left will be more evident. During this stage, many bereaved people call to or talk to the deceased. Others imagine they see her. What is happening, of course, is a subconscious effort to reject the death. It is not uncommon for panic to set in at this time, and it often happens that the bereaved feels she is losing her sanity. It is important for her to recognise that grieving in all its dimensions is normal, and that others have felt exactly as she feels.

Gradually the overwhelming distress and aimlessness lessens and the bereaved sometimes blames herself for the deceased dying, despite any medical evidence to the contrary. She will be quite apt to feel that she didn't do enough, that she should have called another specialist in, or if the deceased died while she was away, that she had neglected her. During this period, guilt feelings can produce serious degrees of depression, even to suicidal level. If depression continues, or if it deepens, it is absolutely imperative that the bereaved see a doctor. Perhaps nothing stronger than a mild tranquilliser will be necessary to help her. Each of us has our own pace of adjusting to a normal life, but years of grieving probably indicate that medical treatment is very much needed.

The 'final stage' as we shall call it, doesn't come overnight; it comes only when the bereaved is able to make a determined effort to assert her own individuality and to re-establish her own identity. Some people make easier recoveries than others, some have relapses, yet generally 'time does heal', and, although fond memories remain, the pain of grief vanishes.

During bereavement, the surviving relatives, and more particularly the person who has been responsible for the deceased's care, are often confronted with making decisions which will affect their whole future; their housing, their finances, whether or not to return to work, and how to get back into a normal life.

ARRANGEMENTS FOR THE FUTURE

Housing

A widow (or widower) will generally have to decide whether to stay where she is, to move to smaller accommodation, or to live with one of the family. The essential factors in this decision will be her ability to adjust to coping alone, her state of health, her finances and, of course, the options available to her. In the case of rented accommodation, a widow's (or widower's) tenancy is generally protected under statute, therefore there is no real pressure on her to move.

In the case of a single person, however, the question of housing on the demise of a parent for whom she had been caring can be a serious issue. The parent owner-occupier could have obviated this problem by providing for the carer to have a life tenancy under the terms of her will. It can be argued that, where a single woman has always lived at home, at an economical level, she should be able to buy a place of her own. However, few single women start to save for that provision before they are in their mid-thirties, primarily because the majority of them expect to marry. Then those who have saved are apt to have used their savings up, either in caring for their parent because they did not qualify for supplementary benefit, or to provide 'extras' during the caring process – or more simply, to meet large unexpected or essential bills.

Where an aged parent is a private tenant, the tenancy may be transferred twice after his death, to family members.

If the deceased and the single person had lived in a council house, the single person's tenancy will not be protected on the death of the parent unless there had been a joint tenancy. Due to the acute shortage of housing stock, the majority of local authorities require the single person to move to smaller accommodation. Therefore, every effort should be made to become a joint tenant with a parent as soon as the caring responsibility is assumed.

Moving should not be undertaken without serious thought (see page 161). Many persons move before they have given themselves a chance to adapt to living alone, and they regret the move deeply. The psychological upheaval can be more traumatic than the physical upheaval.

Finances

Where there have previously been incomes from two sources coming into the house, the death of one of the contributors can cause profound problems for the surviving person.

Let us suppose that it is the wife who has died, and that during her lifetime both she and her husband had received the old age pension, and additionally, that she received the Attendance Allowance. On her death, the husband would have to meet all expenses out of his pension.

Again, suppose that a mother was being cared for by a single daughter and that, while she was alive, the mother had had income from a pension, dividends, an annuity, had owned the house and, additionally, was in receipt of the Attendance Allowance. Her daughter had received the Invalid Care Allowance and some supplementary benefit. On the death of the parent, the overall financial commitments will basically be identical except for outlay for her parent's food, yet one source of income will no longer be extant. Her living standard will accordingly be reduced.

Conscientious budgeting (see page 149) may have to be implemented by many people; others may have to move to smaller accommodation. One hedge against such a predi-

197

cament is to take out an insurance policy while relatively young; another is to have a paying skill such as dressmaking or typing, if one cannot follow one's vocation. There is always a demand for cottage industry workers, typing, book-keeping, for electrical repair work, house maintenance, etc.

Whether or not to return to work

Of course, the most positive action that can be taken to augment one's income is to return to work. Skills may need 'brushing up', extra courses may have to be taken, or it may be necessary to completely retrain for another career. The Equal Opportunities Commission, Overseas House, Quay Street, Manchester M3 3HN, have published a booklet *Fresh Start*, which contains information for women on getting back into the job market.

Where it is at all possible, everyone under pensionable age should work. Financial security is the main result of being employed, but the spinoffs of social contact and re-establishing a purpose to life are equally relevant.

Getting back to a normal life

The death of a husband, wife, parent or sibling can be a shattering experience. Some persons tend to retreat into themselves, others feel exhausted, and others are uninterested in everything about them. It is important to realise that any one of us can feel unable to cope at this time.

CRUSE will be of inestimable help to a widow or widower who needs reassurance and guidance. Address: 6 Lion Gate Gardens, Richmond, Surrey.

The National Council for the Single Woman and Her Dependants (see page 176) will be able to help a single person who has lost a parent.

Social integration is never easy. Sometimes many abortive efforts will be made before one actually takes the step that breaks a long period of social isolation. Going back to work, and finding others with similar interests, are both ways of making new social contacts.

A remarkable observation on human beings is, 'that despite themselves and their predicaments, they do keep on keeping on', to quote Dame Flora Robson, DBE.

INDEX

Notes

Notes

136

Useful Telephone Numbers

GP_____

_____

Health Visitor_____

_____

District Nurse_____

_____

Social Services Department_____

_____

Age Concern Local Office_____

_____

Citizens Advice Bureau_____

_____

Dentist_____

_____

Optician_____

_____

Ambulance (*In Emergency Only* Dial 999)

Others_____

_____

_____

_____

_____